Why We Call It Rebirthing

Rebirthing is a simple self-improvement technique of immense practical value. It causes profound relaxation, refocusing and renewal of the human spirit, mind and body. Easy to learn, it is also intensely pleasurable. Its results are permanent.

So why is it called Rebirthing? Two reasons . . .

First, the technique causes one's natural sense of pleasure and relaxation to expand and encompass all past experience. This usually results in full recall of one's own birth.

Second, the technique always gives a person an experience of starting life anew with clearer purpose, greater compassion and pervasive joy.

Rebirthing is an astounding adventure, a journey deep into your own heart and yet out into the world as well. You will discover on this journey that you have the ability to give yourself the kind of life you have always wanted. More important, you will discover your role in transforming the Earth into a place of abiding peace, prosperity and cooperation.

Dedication

I, Jim Leonard, dedicate this book to my parents, Al and Anna Lee Leonard, and to my angel wife, Anne Jill Leonard, who have given me love, support, and wisdom, as proof to me that life is infinitely good.

AND

I, Phil Laut, dedicate this book to my parents, Betty and Phil Laut, who are among the most successful parents I know and who gave me a great start in life.

REBIRTHING
The Science of Enjoying All of Your Life

by
Jim Leonard
and
Phil Laut

TRINITY PUBLICATIONS

French Edition
Rebirthing - The Science of Enjoying All of Your Life is available
in French under the title "Le Rebirth."
Published by: LES EDITIONS MCL
C.P. 402 Succ. H
Montreal H3G 221
Canada

ISBN 0-9610132-0-6
Library of Congress Card Catalogue No. 83-70721
Integration Symbol on Cover and Title Page
Copyright © 1983 by Anne Jill Leonard
First Printing July 1983
Second Printing October 1983
Third Printing February 1984
Fourth Printing June 1985

The integration symbol on the cover and title page was created and
drawn by Anne Jill Leonard. She also did the rest of the graphics
for this book, with the exception of E. G. Boring's figure on page 6.

TRINITY PUBLICATIONS
1636 North Curson Avenue
Hollywood, California 90046 USA
213-876-6226

Acknowledgments

We gratefully acknowledge the following people for their manifold contributions to our lives and to this book:

Jean Gilpin, who supported us with love, encouragement, coffee and sandwiches during the writing of this book.

Leonard Orr, the founder of Rebirthing and an inspirational teacher.

Al and Anna Lee Leonard, Jim's parents, for providing Jim a supportive space in their home where he was able to do some of the writing away from his usual distractions.

Anne Jill Leonard, Jim's wife, for supporting Jim materially and otherwise during the writing of this book, for doing the graphics and assisting with the editing.

Sondra Ray and Fred Lehrman, for their timely assistance and advice.

Sal Rachele, for suggesting some of the affirmations.

Ida van Raam and Joanne Hahn, for acquainting us with International Forgiveness Week.

Otto Altorfer, for his helpful editorial advice, the inspirational example he provides by the way he lives his life, and his friendship and support.

Marz Attar, for helping Jim to explore some fine points of the philosophy presented in this book.

Herakhan Baba, for his presence in the World.

Sue and Don Weatherley, Jim's in-laws, for their friendship, their wise counsel and supportive criticism of Jim's ideas.

Jack Szumel, for his enlightenment, his friendship, and his contagious enthusiasm—Jim's first trainer.

Elana Lynse, Phil's first Rebirther.

Theano Storm, Jim's first Rebirther.

Gayle Carlton and Jane English for their contributions regarding Caesarian birth.

Lucy Liggett and Stan Sherr, for their editorial advice.

Ned Berke for suggesting a graphics presentation.

Alan Moore for suggesting one of the fourth element techniques.

Kali Victoire for proofreading and editorial assistance.

All of our teachers, students and friends in the Worldwide Rebirthing community.

Table of Contents

PART III
HOW TO CREATE YOUR REALITY

PART IV
YOUR PAST AND YOU

PART V
IMMORTALIST PHILOSOPHY

PART VI
YOUR FUTURE AND YOU

APPENDICES

Introduction
Why Read a Book on
Self-improvement?

Self-improvement is the greatest hobby in the world. It is also the oldest human activity, for it was self-improvement that made us human in the first place.

The object of all self-improvement practices is to increase the practitioner's happiness, power and well-being—to expand the things that work for you, not to find out what is wrong with you. In this book we emphasize solutions.

Self-improvement is the goal of all religions, all philosophies, all therapies. It is the goal of sports, yoga and holistic health techniques. It is the goal of education. It is also the goal of medicine, science and technology. The evolution of self-improvement has always paralleled the evolution of human consciousness.

We are living in an age increasingly dominated by high technology—this must be balanced by high-technology self-improvement methods as well. Reading this book will acquaint you with the latest developments in the self-improvement field.

We, the authors of this book, are grateful for this opportunity to share these developments with you and we welcome you to make them your own.

The techniques described in this book are simple, direct, extremely effective and fun. You can easily learn to apply them yourself with total autonomy. They require a minimum of time and yet create maximum results. You can even learn to apply many of them while you are engaging in other activities—a boon for modern, busy people.

Besides Rebirthing, which is the main technique described in this book, we also present detailed instructions for many other self-improvement techniques. You can begin using almost all of them immediately to your great benefit and satisfaction.

Improving anything is only possible when you have a thorough knowledge of what you are improving. This book will teach you how to know yourself more thoroughly than you ever have before.

No one would want to explore the darkest recesses of the soul without bringing along a light. Rebirthing allows self-improvement to occur at the deepest levels of your being because it facilitates you in operating within a context of lightness.

Rebirthing is just as much physical as it is mental; indeed, it restores the natural linkage between the mind and the body. You could say that it utilizes the body to get in touch with the mind, and you could also say, with equal validity, that it uses the mind to get in touch with the body. It causes transformation by causing one's innate joy and well-being to encompass and permeate one's totality. The mind becomes happier and the body becomes healthier. It enhances a person's effectiveness by bringing the entirety of one's being into alignment with one's purpose. It is a surrendering to one's self and it is an act of great love.

Rebirthing was first developed in the early 1970's by Leonard Orr, a modern pioneer in self-improvement. Because it causes rapid evolution for the people who practice it, it is natural that the technique itself has also evolved rapidly. The Rebirthing section of this book is a very thorough treatment of the most modern methods.

It is accurate to state that if you learn to Rebirth yourself there will not be a single aspect of your life that will be untouched by it. We are aware that this statement may well arouse your skepticism. Unless you try Rebirthing, you will not believe how well it works. Demanding proof that it will work for you before you try it is like standing in front of a cold fireplace and telling it, "If you give me heat, I'll give you wood."

"Well, then," you may ask, "can a book teach me how to work on myself so deeply?" The answer is that this book will prepare you very thoroughly for Rebirthing and you will still require a personal teacher to guide you through your first few Rebirthing experiences. This is not because the technique is complicated or dangerous; it is simple and completely safe. During Rebirthing a person experiences physical sensations and mental images that are so unique that they could be frightening without having someone there who has experienced similar things and has learned to enjoy them and feel safe with them. Rebirthing only works efficiently when it is pleasant. The role of the Rebirther is to ensure that your experience will be as pleasant as possible. The services of professional Rebirthers are not expensive and after a number of guided sessions you will be able to do it on your own. In this book, we give you complete information on how to locate and choose a Rebirther for yourself. To do so is to give yourself one of the greatest gifts possible.

WHAT REBIRTHING ISN'T

Rebirthing isn't therapy, religion, psychology, medicine, hypnosis, or anything to join, and is not a substitute for any of these things.

WHAT REBIRTHING IS

Rebirthing is a modern, holistic, self-help method which has been used successfully by millions of people throughout the world. It utilizes a precisely defined, wondrous breathing technique to give one a profoundly positive and detailed awareness of one's own mind, body, and emotions. It enables the mind and body to restructure themselves gently, in a way that greatly increases the individual's happiness, effectiveness and good health. Fundamentally, Rebirthing is about surrendering to what is so in one's experience, and beyond that, it is about gratitude for the miracle of existence.

WHAT REBIRTHERS AREN'T

Most Rebirthers are neither physicians nor psychotherapists, although some are. If you think you might be physically or mentally ill, seek proper professional care from a licensed health professional.

If you are under the care of a physician or psychotherapist, and you wish to be Rebirthed, then by all means acquaint your doctor or therapist with what the technique is, first, and put your doctor or therapist in touch with your chosen Rebirther, second. Under those circumstances, we only recommend Rebirthing for you to the extent that you, your doctor or therapist, and a competent, professional Rebirther all agree that it is a good idea for you to do it.

In the authors' combined twelve years of experience with

Rebirthing, it has never once been observed that Rebirthing in any way proved detrimental to anyone's treatment by a doctor or therapist; it has, indeed, proved to be a great aid in psychological and physical healing. However, physicians and therapists were producing excellent results with their patients and clients long before the advent of Rebirthing, and, if you are physically or mentally ill, we consider it important that you include your doctor or therapist in any decision you make regarding Rebirthing.

WHAT REBIRTHERS ARE

Rebirthers are experienced and trained professionals who have a great enough sense of safety, integrity and compassion to guide people through Rebirthing sessions with consistently good results.

In this book we describe in detail how people become professional Rebirthers.

WHO CAN BENEFIT FROM REBIRTHING

Rebirthing is extremely beneficial for anyone who can breathe without mechanical assistance (breathing is an integral part of the technique) and who is willing to take full responsibility for producing the results (it is a *self*-improvement technique).

REBIRTHING SUPPORTS YOUR AUTONOMY
AND YOUR TAKING RESPONSIBILITY

You cannot expect to get any kind of good results in life without first taking full responsibility for producing them. This is especially true of Rebirthing, because it is the nature of the Rebirthing process that *you* produce 100% of whatever results you get from doing it; Rebirthers can only teach you and guide you. Expecting your Rebirther to produce a result for you is like taking golf lessons and then expecting the golf professional to hit all your shots for you. Rebirthing itself is a tool that you can use to produce results for yourself. Expecting Rebirthing itself to produce results for you is like buying an ax and expecting the ax to chop your wood for you. Once you learn to Rebirth yourself you can produce the results for yourself whenever and wherever you choose; you do not become dependent on anyone, and you do not become dependent on the technique, either.

HOW OLD ARE THESE METHODS?

Nothing in this book is new. The truth has always been available to all who have chosen to seek it. We have had extensive experience Rebirthing Christians, Jews, Buddhists, Yogis and Hindus, among others, and have been told that our teachings are in alignment with the teachings of all those ancient traditions. Perhaps our presentation is new, perhaps some of our techniques are new—we at least had the *experience* of inventing some of them. Since we do not know everything, we have no actual way of knowing who some of our predecessors may have been. The material in this book is so fundamental to humanness that it seems unlikely to us that we are the first to discover it, or that it could have been first discovered *recently* by anyone.

HOW TO USE THIS BOOK

We have written this book in a careful, logical, orderly way. The information in each section prepares the reader for the information that comes next. We do not assume that the reader has had any previous experience with self-improvement. Anyone who starts this book at the beginning and reads it sequentially through to the end should be able to grasp even the most highly advanced material that we cover.

Almost all of the processes and techniques that we describe in this book are things that you can start using immediately. We recommend that you do so.

Nothing in this book should ever be substituted for common sense. We emphasize here, and throughout this book, that what we are presenting is useful *models* and that reality does not completely fit *any* model, all of the time. For example, if you broke your leg, even though Rebirthing might ease the discomfort and increase the flow of healing energy to your leg, common sense dictates that you should go to a doctor and get your leg set in a cast; we certainly would recommend doing so immediately.

Immediately following the main text of this book is a glossary of terms that may be unfamiliar to you or that may be standard words that we use in somewhat non-standard ways.

The best possible way to use this book is to read it through once, take several Rebirthing sessions from a good, professional Rebirther, and then read it through again.

PART I

THE TRUTH ABOUT
BEING HUMAN

CHAPTER I

How to Free Your Mind

When you look at an object, you can only see one side of it at a time; that is the nature of vision. In exactly the same way, when you think about something, you can only think about it in one context at a time; that is the nature of thought. Context determines what your mind thinks just as surely as viewing-angle determines what your eye sees.

For example, a person who is literate only in Chinese could look at this page and see exactly the same patterns of ink on paper that you do. The reason you can read these words and the Chinese reader cannot is that you have a context available to you that enables you to attach meaning to these patterns of ink on paper, and the Chinese reader does not have that context available.

"Content" means the "thing itself" and *"context"* means the way you interact with it.

Understanding how change of context changes human experience is fundamental to understanding human life in a practical way. Before we can teach you any methods for improving your life, it is first necessary to establish a basis of contexts in which you understand our models of how the mind works and how life experiences come into being. That is the purpose of this part of our book.

THE MIND IS REDUCTIVE

The mind is incapable of knowing what anything is and is also incapable of grasping fully that it cannot know. All the mind can

3

do is create models and then insist that reality fits those models, which reality never fully does.

To describe anything completely would require an infinite number of statements. Since it is highly inconvenient for the mind to create an infinite number of statements, it must decide which aspect of a thing is important and then use that aspect as a symbol of the whole. The choice of which aspect to use in this way determines to a large extent how effectively the mind will create happiness and power for the individual.

For example, suppose that the content of your experience is that you have exactly $1,000 in the bank. Both your feelings about the money and what you do with it will be determined by whether your mind calls it "plenty of money" or "being almost broke". Both of these contexts are equally "valid" and equally "true" and the mind has absolute choice.

As another example of content, consider the observable relative motion of the Earth and the sun. We can hold this phenomenon in the context of the sun rising in the east and setting in the west, or we can hold it in the context that the sun is not actually moving but only appears to be doing so because of the Earth's rotation. Both frames of reference are absolutely valid and you choose one or the other of them depending on what you are doing. If you were lost in the woods you would choose the former so that you could get directions. If you were calculating celestial mechanics you *could* choose either, but you would probably choose the latter in order to make the mathematics simpler.

Whenever a person experiences difficulty in accomplishing something, it is because the person is holding the situation in an inappropriate context. When the mind is stuck in a particular context, it may appear that limitations are built into the situation. Limitation is actually a function of context and the appropriate change of context makes what had appeared to be limitations become something else.

Imagine a car contemplating its difficulties in going up a steep hill in 4th gear. The car may think, "My difficulty is obviously caused by the relationship between my weight, my power, and the steepness of the hill. Since I am obviously not powerful enough to go up the hill and since the exertion is starting to hurt, I might as well just stall out." And within its 4th-gear context, the car is right!

One way of stating the purpose of this book is that it is to teach you how to shift your own gears.

Human beings watched the flight of birds for thousands of years and longed to fly, too. They made various attempts and met with little success. Birds still flew the same when the Wright Brothers watched them, but the Wright Brothers had different contexts in which to hold the observable phenomena. Their shift to the proper context was the advent of a new era.

THERE IS NO UNIVERSALLY APPROPRIATE CONTEXT

There is no context that a person would wisely choose to be stuck in all of the time; the ability to shift contexts freely is highly desirable. We are not advocates of "positive thinking"; we are advocates of appropriate thinking. "Positive thinking" is not appropriate all of the time and being too rigidly attached to it can be limiting or even dangerous. Two examples:

Who would not agree that it is better to be knowledgeable than ignorant? We have met people who held the "positive thought" that they knew everything about something—irrefutable logic for someone who wants to be "positive," but it stops them from learning anything new. Positive or not, well-acknowledged ignorance is the most useful learning aid there is.

We have also met some people who took positive thinking seminars and went into business with such "positive thoughts" as "I can achieve anything," "I think BIG" and "The Universe is providing me with the results I have chosen." They then invested money in an enterprise they couldn't handle and lost it. Positive thinking is wonderful and it certainly has its place, but it makes a poor substitute for common sense and diligent action. In business, at least, we suggest that enthusiastic and appropriate realism is more appropriate than blind positivism.

Every model has its limitations and any model that is clung to rigidly is sure to become a trap.

THE MIND IS A LIBRARY OF CONTEXTS

In order to interact with the world around us we must sort the data we receive through our senses and then classify everything according to type and function. We perform this astoundingly complex task with astounding speed and take it astoundingly for granted. To make this possible we carry around with us a high-speed, "computerized" library of contexts known as "the mind". The interaction between mind and experience that determines which context the experience will be held in is known as a "thought".

Your mind organizes its contexts and classifies its contents according to the instructions of the head librarian, which is known as "you". Since you are the head librarian, you can reorganize your mind or reclassify your experiences in any way you see fit and at any time you choose.

LIBRARY SCIENCE 101

One of the best ways to change contexts is to hold a thought that can only be true in the context you are switching to. For example, if you were thinking in terms of the sun being stationary and its rising and setting being an illusion, you could change contexts easily by thinking either, "The sun rises in the east and sets in the west," or "The place on which I am standing is stationary."

As a further example, consider the following optical illusion:

FIGURE 1: CHANGE OF CONTEXT CAUSES CHANGE OF EXPERIENCE.

The artist of this drawing, whose name was E. G. Boring, called this his "Wife or Mother-In-Law" figure. In one context it is a young woman looking away and to the left. In the other context it is an old woman in profile. To illustrate how changing contexts works, consider that if you are seeing the young woman you can look at her chin and think, "This is the tip of the old woman's nose," and you will shift to seeing the old woman. Or if you are seeing the old woman and you look at her eye you can think, "This is the young woman's ear," and shift to seeing the young woman.

This is the principle by which the technique of affirmation, which is described in detail in Part III of this book, operates. The oft-heard expression, "Your thoughts create your reality" is really a shorthand way of describing this process.

Notice that if a person had some kind of an investment in seeing only *either* a young woman *or* an old woman in this drawing, then that person might be tempted to say that there is no valid way to change contexts. Such a person might experience *being* incapable of seeing both faces.

Mastering the ability to change contexts will free your mind.

To test your understanding of this principle, please solve the following puzzle before going on to the next page:

FIGURE 2: TEST YOUR ABILITY TO
SOLVE PROBLEMS BY CHANGING
CONTEXTS.

Instructions: Connect all the dots using four or less straight lines, without lifting your marking implement or going back over any line you have already made.

How to solve the problem:

STEP 1: Try the obvious:

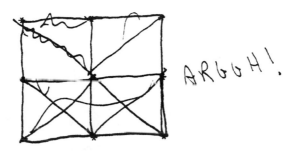

FIGURE 3: OBVIOUSLY NOT THE
SOLUTION.

STEP 2: Consider the thought, "This is impossible."

STEP 3: Notice that the thought, "This is impossible," is true in the context in which it is impossible. Further notice that the thought, "I will find a way to do this," is true only in the context in which it is possible to do it. With utmost decisiveness hold the thought, "I will solve this problem."

STEP 4: Notice that the context in which you previously tried to solve the problem is not compatible with the context you are now holding. In other words, notice that it is impossible to do it the way you tried to do it before.

STEP 5: See if the rules of the problem actually limited you to the exact method you were using before.

STEP 6: Notice that the rules do not say that you are limited, in your line drawing, to any particular boundaries, although you had assumed so before.

STEP 7: See if this new context is compatible with the thought, "I will solve this problem."

STEP 8: Solve the problem thus:

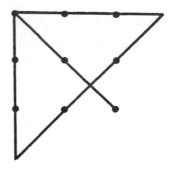

FIGURE 4: ONE OF INFINITELY
MANY CORRECT SOLUTIONS.

ALTERNATIVE SOLUTION #1:

The rules do not specify the size of the marking instrument. If you used a pen with a large enough tip (or a paint brush) you could connect all nine dots with just one stroke.

ALTERNATIVE SOLUTION #2:

You could take a pair of scissors and cut the figure into three strips with three dots each, then tape the ends of the strips together to form one long strip and connect them all with one stroke of a pen.

ALTERNATIVE SOLUTION #3:

Find another way to solve the problem entirely on your own. There are an infinite number of solutions.

A good question to ask about this method of changing contexts is: "During the period between the time I start thinking the new thought and when I discover the context in which it is true, do I have to hold the thought on faith alone?"

Glad you asked! The answer is no; not if you hold the process itself in a context in which faith is not necessary.

ALL STATEMENTS ARE EQUALLY TRUE

The statement, "All statements are equally true" is true because truth is a function of context. Everything is the way it actually is, but "truth" is how the mind will think about it. Do not mistake truth for the thing itself.

"The sun goes around the Earth" is true within the context of the actual experience of anyone who is on the Earth. However, we can also choose a context in which the seemingly preposterous statement, "The Earth is rotating about an imaginary axis which runs through its north and south poles" is true.

The statement, "The moon is made out of green cheese" is true in the context of many cartoons, both animated and otherwise. At least theoretically, it is also true in a limitless number of other contexts, as is any other statement anybody can make up.

While "The moon is made out of green cheese" may be a silly example, it is extreme enough to be useful. The purpose of thinking about truth in this way is that it allows you to think about truth in more than one way. When you are using your mind to accomplish something, it is not enough to have "the truth," you must put the truth into a frame of reference that is useful to you in accomplishing that particular purpose.

We recommend practicing this kind of thinking until you master it. Amaze your friends! Take the most preposterous statements they can make up for you and then prove that those statements are actually true by identifying contexts in which they are true. If your friends are clever enough to give you statements with built-in contexts, then put the entire statement, limiting contexts and all, into a broader context in which it is true. Doing this will not only convince you and your friends that you have an agile mind, but will also increase your ability to solve any kind of problem.

Please note that the kind of proof we describe above is a method of switching or establishing context; scientific proof is about discovering, demonstrating, or describing phenomena, thus *content,* once a context has been established.

Lying about something means lying about the content. The truth remains the truth no matter what context it is put into but a change of context may require that the truth be stated in very different words.

Hold the thought "All statements are equally true" until it is firmly rooted in the cells of your brain. This thought can speed up the results of your affirmation process ten-fold. It also can prevent a lot of arguments. For instance, if you usually think about things in a certain way and you go to hear someone speak who has a different tradition of thought, there are two things you can do: you can find fault with everything the speaker says or you can shift to a context in which everything the speaker is saying is true, in which case you might learn something. A terrific way to disagree with someone is to say, "What you are saying is obviously true and the opposite is obviously just as true."

When you are ready, go on to practical applications. For instance, if you are tired of feeling unloved you can hold the thought "Everybody loves me infinitely" and then prove it in five or six ways. After you do so, you will have contexts in which you feel loved all the time that will be available to you whenever you choose them. It is a certainty that most people will find you more lovable if you interpret their natural behavior as them loving you.

CHAPTER 2

Time

There are two contexts in which we all hold time. They are both absolutely essential to the functioning of the mind and they are, of course, equally valid.

To the first context, we give the name "momentary time". In momentary time, only the present moment exists at all. We experience this context in the sense that we can only *touch* the present moment.

The second context we call "linear time". Linear time is the context in which the past actually happened and the future actually will.

In momentary time, right now is the original "moment of creation," the only moment possible. Our so-called "memories" of the past, our speculations about the future, and the apparent "flow" of time are all sort-of illusions, "created" in this moment exactly as they are.

In linear time, creation is a result of a long process of cause and effect going back to some theoretical origin: the Big Bang or Genesis or however a person chooses to think about it.

Motion, in linear time, is the change of position of something during an interval of time.

In momentary time, motion is an inherent quality that has nothing to do with "change" of position. If we have apparent memory of something being in a different position at an "earlier" time, that apparent memory is just part of what we exist with in this moment, and that is all.

14

In linear time we have freedom and in momentary time we have direct experience.

You have no freedom in momentary time because whatever exists is already here and is all that *can* exist, including your desires for things to be different. A way to explain this momentary-time phenomenon in terms of linear time is to say that by the time you have changed something you are in a different moment.

There is no *direct* experience in linear time because in linear time the present moment is void. By the time we receive data through any of our senses, the occurrence that originated the data has already become part of the past.

Happiness exists within the realm of momentary time. You are happy to the extent that you are happy with what you've got right now.

Power exists within the realm of linear time. By "power" we mean "the ability to create the result that you intend".

Some people are relatively powerful, but not happy. Other people are relatively happy, but not powerful. Obviously, we would all like to be both happy and powerful.

We are happy and powerful to the extent that we hold our experiences in contexts that facilitate our being happy and powerful.

CHAPTER 3

The Origin of All Negativity

By "negativity" we mean "habitual use of contexts that are inappropriate to optimizing one's own happiness and power".

The origin of all negativity is "making something wrong".

To understand what we mean by "making something wrong" consider that in any given moment you are experiencing exactly whatever you are experiencing. You can be grateful for that experience. Or you can compare what actually exists to an imaginary standard, such as "what I wish were there," or "what ought to be there," or "what used to be there," etc., and decide that what actually exists falls short of what you can imagine. The former option is called "celebrating it". The latter option is called "making it wrong".

Whenever you make something wrong, you experience an unpleasant emotional feeling in your body that lasts for as long as you are contemplating whatever it is that you are making wrong. Verify this for yourself. Next time you complain about something, notice how you feel.

People have a strong drive to feel good as well as a strong drive to be right, so what they do is insist that what they are making wrong really is wrong and then they withdraw awareness from it in an effort to feel good. This withdrawal of awareness is known as "suppression".

When you suppress, nothing changes but your degree of aware-ness. What you are making wrong is still the same and you are still making it wrong. The unpleasant feeling is still in your body but you have chosen to become unaware of it.

Following make-wrong and suppression, the thing you've made wrong becomes something to hide from or run from. The unpleas-ant feeling gets stored in the body as chronic tension or some other physical problem (more about this later). What happens in your mind is this:

A new mechanism is created in your unconscious mind (by which we mean the part of your mind that you choose to be unaware of) which continuously evaluates your moment-to-moment experience and compares it to the imaginary standard. Thus, once you have made something wrong and suppressed it, you continue to make something wrong, in the same way, in every moment.

Throughout this book, we shall be diagramming this type of mechanism in the following way, in order to make it easier to think about:

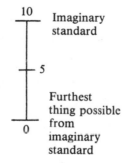

FIGURE 5: DUALITY MECHANISM.

The unconscious mind continuously compares every experience to imaginary standards and gives every experience a "rating" that we can think of as being between zero and ten, with ten being the best and zero being the worst.

One way that you can be aware of many of your own make-wrong duality mechanisms is to notice which thoughts and situations tend to put you into a less-than-happy mood. Duality mechanisms are the origin of all bad moods. However, you will not be able to notice all of your duality mechanisms by paying attention to your moods. The oldest, most deeply suppressed mechanisms influence your general attitudes about life, rather than your transitory moods, and to become aware of these you will need a profound process, such as Rebirthing.

THE ORIGIN OF UNWANTED BEHAVIORS AND EXPERIENCES

Whenever you make something wrong, you create a desire for it to get better and your mind starts thinking up plans for how to make it get better. At the moment of suppression, the best plan your mind has come up with so far becomes an important part of the new mechanism. Subsequently, if your actual experience in some moment is evaluated by your unconscious mind as being too far down the scale, then that plan, which is now known as the "compulsive adaptation," is put into action automatically by the unconscious mind. In these diagrams we use an arrow to indicate the compulsive adaptation.

The whole mechanism, in its most fundamental form, is diagrammed like this:

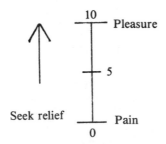

FIGURE 6: MOST BASIC MAKE-WRONG DUALITY MECHANISM WITH COMPULSIVE ADAPTATION.

Whenever you find yourself doing things compulsively or creating situations unintentionally, the origin lies in one of these mechanisms.

As long as consciousness is withheld, the mechanism will remain. It simply isn't possible to change one's mind about something without knowing what one is changing one's mind about.

To help you understand how this works in actual practice, we'll give you two examples, in story form. The first example is made-up. The second example is a real one uncovered in Jim Leonard's work with a client.

EXAMPLE 1:

When Joe graduates from high school his dad gives him a car as a graduation present. Joe has been expecting a car and has been hoping for a late-model sports car. What his dad actually gives him is an old station wagon.

One option that Joe has is to be grateful for the car and notice the humor in expecting a sports car and receiving an old station wagon. For the sake of illustration, however, let's say that he makes the car wrong and decides that his dad gave him the old station wagon because his dad was a cheapskate: making the gift wrong is the same as making the giver wrong. To suppress his unpleasant feelings, Joe goes over to a friend's house and watches television. Having concluded that he didn't get what he wanted because less than enough money was spent, what ended up in Joe's unconscious mind is "The way to get what I want in life is to spend more money," which we diagram like this:

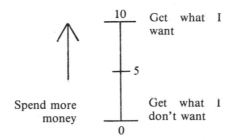

FIGURE 7: JOE'S DECISION ABOUT WHAT IT TAKES TO GET WHAT HE WANTS.

And Joe lives happily beyond his means ever after!

We also wish to point out how Joe's unconscious mind may have set up the whole situation in the first place. Suppose that earlier in Joe's life, when he was a sophomore, his girlfriend jilted him and he decided that she didn't like him because he had too big of an ego. He suppressed it and ended up with a mechanism that will do what it can, throughout his life, to humble him. Setting up an expectation for a sports car and getting a station wagon was an ingenious way for his unconscious mind to accomplish this result.

Go right ahead and laugh at poor Joe and his silly mechanisms! Your life, too, is made of stuff like this.

EXAMPLE 2:

Six-year-old Steve is playing in his room when his mother comes in and hassles him about his room being messy. If Steve made nothing wrong he would just have compassion for his mother in her time of travail and know that he had nothing to do with it. In that case no negativity would be created.

What Steve actually decided, however, was that since his mother wasn't smiling at him he obviously wasn't lovable. He started crying and his mother backed off her attack a little. He noticed this (sharp little devil, he!) and went into a full-on, helpless crying jag. His mother, feeling guilty and wanting him to shut up, gave him a hug and comforted him. What Steve got in his unconscious mind was this: "The more I act helpless the more people think I'm lovable," which is diagrammed thus:

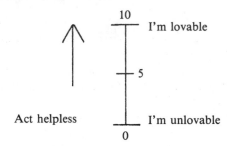

FIGURE 8: HOW STEVE THINKS HE CAN MAKE HIMSELF MORE LOVABLE

By the time Jim got Steve for a client, Steve was forty-two years old. Steve had noticed, over the years, that he had a tendency to feel and act quite helpless when confronted with certain situations. Jim and Steve did a State-Your-Complaint process (described in detail in a later chapter), discovered the mechanism, and, using the process, Steve eliminated his problem at its source.

Note that at the time the mechanism was created, the compulsive adaptation probably actually worked the way it was supposed to: when Steve would act helpless his mother would come closer to fitting his mental images of what loving him should be like. However, most people would not think that a 42-year-old man who is acting helpless is more lovable than one who is acting capable.

It very often happens that a compulsive adaptation, although intending to raise things up the scale, actually pushes things further down the scale. Thus, once the compulsion gets triggered, an endless loop begins and continues until something stops it.

It is important to note, though, that *all* parts of you are at least *trying* to produce a good result for you.

Experientially, these compulsive adaptations are known as "urges," as in "an urge to drink a martini," "an urge to eat something sweet," "an urge to go home from work early," etc. Most people have one or more urges that seem to never go away. For instance, some people have a near-continuous urge to prove that they are superior to everybody else, some people have a near-continuous urge to drink alcohol, and some people have a near-continuous urge to not be alone; at your local tavern you could probably find somebody who has all three of these examples operating almost all the time. Most of your urges come up only in certain circumstances, however, such as an urge to smoke a cigarette when you talk on the phone, or an urge to eat bacon and eggs for breakfast when you are leaving on a long car trip.

As you can easily imagine, urges are often for things that do not really further a person's happiness, good health or prosperity. This is not surprising when you consider that urges arise from make-wrong duality mechanisms.

Most people have one urge or another operating in each moment. Many people think that the purpose of their lives is to satisfy their urges: as soon as they finish satisfying one urge, another will come up to take its place, and off they'll go to satisfy that one. Choosing to satisfy your urges is the same thing exactly as choosing to be controlled by your unconscious make-wrong duality mechanisms. To the extent that you let your urges control your actions, you will experience yourself as being either fundamentally purposeless, or as having purpose but being ineffective. The sense of futility that comes from letting one's urges control one's life is known as "ennui." Ennui is not the possession of a chosen few; all of us have it to one extent or another. You do not need to make yourself wrong for your ennui, but telling the truth about it is a wise idea. The opposite of ennui is to decide consciously what you are going to make your life be about (your purpose) and then to set goals, make plans and use enough discipline to fulfill that purpose. Several sections of this book contain detailed information on how to deal with urges in a life-supporting, non-suppressive way that allows you to stay pleasurably on-purpose.

People have an astounding propensity for making things wrong and almost everybody has hundreds of these unconscious duality mechanisms. The mechanisms develop minds and personalities of their own and they have conferences with each other and form alliances and make wars on one another and so on, each trying to fulfill its particular responsibilities. Listen to your thoughts and you will hear the loudest portions of their clamor.

Naturally, your conscious mind wants to think it's in control. So whenever you find yourself in some situation that your conscious mind thinks it didn't create, you have a headstart on making that wrong, too. In this way, the mechanisms tend to reproduce themselves, and layer upon layer of suppressed negativity tends to build up.

THE UNCONSCIOUS MIND

Throughout this book, we use the term "unconscious mind" to mean "the part of your mind that you choose to remain unconscious of in an effort to avoid sadness about the past, frustration about the present, and fear about the future." It is filled with make-wrong contexts which contain made-wrong experiences, each of which is attached to an unpleasant emotion which is stored in the body.

Also contained in your unconscious mind is a vast array of information and wisdom. Your "five senses" receive a great deal more information in every moment than your conscious mind ever notices, but your *unconscious* mind receives, classifies and stores *all* the information that ever comes in through your senses. A skillful hypnotist can help you recall obscure things like the color of tie your father was wearing on a particular day in your childhood, whether or not your conscious mind ever noticed his tie that day. In addition, there may be parts of your unconscious mind that have immense practical wisdom regarding your proper course of action to achieve your goals. An example of how these parts become suppressed is that if you made your parents wrong you probably suppressed whatever wisdom tends to remind you of what you made wrong about them.

Suppression results in fragmentation of the mind into many parts. Sometimes these parts control your actions directly, without the conscious mind having any idea of what's going on; other times the unconscious mind exerts strong influence over the conscious mind's thinking process, and influences your actions in that way. The conscious mind is only a very small part of the overall mind.

Rebirthing is a very straightforward way to make your conscious mind aware of what is in the unconscious mind, and to align the unconscious parts to your consciously chosen intentions.

THE NATURE OF SUPPRESSION

We have shown why suppression occurs (it's the only way to be "right" about making something wrong and feel good at the same time) and we have explored the results suppression produces in the mind (unconscious negativity and compulsion). We now want to give you some models of *how* suppression occurs and what results it produces in the physical body.

Every thought in the mind has a corresponding feeling in the body. You may be able to verify this for yourself. If you are able to *feel* your thoughts on a fairly consistent basis then you are well on the way to eliminating your patterns of suppression. Rebirthing greatly facilitates the ability to feel thoughts and there will be much more about this later in the book.

The thought and the feeling are actually the same thing, merely perceived in two different ways simultaneously, in much the same way that a bagpipe player can be perceived with both the eyes and the ears simultaneously.

Anything with which you have any interaction has at least one thought in your mind that corresponds to it. The most basic interaction you can have with anything is identifying "what it is." In order to do that you have to have a thought.

A thought that puts anything into a make-wrong context automatically puts the feeling corresponding to "what it is" into a make-wrong context also. This is just another way of saying that you get an unpleasant feeling whenever you contemplate something you're making wrong.

When you are experiencing any kind of emotion or feeling, you can "tune in" to exactly what it feels like and you can notice exactly where you are feeling it in your body. It actually has a location and pattern. This is what we mean by the term "pattern of energy" which we use extensively throughout this book. Notice, however, that while there are only a few "emotions" that are given names (anger, fear, jealousy, etc.), there are perhaps thousands of nameless, yet important, patterns of energy that we all experience routinely.

One good model for describing suppression deals with the relationship between the physical body and the "spirit body." The "spirit body," in this model, is the "body" you have in dreams. It includes your mind, your sense of identity or self, and all your conscious awareness. During dreaming you do not experience your physical body because during dreaming your spirit body is not *in* your physical body. When you are awake you experience your physical body to the extent that your spirit body is in contact with it. Suppression, in these terms, is the long-term withdrawal of the spirit body from areas of the physical body where something is happening that the person has chosen not to experience. Some people have much more awareness of their bodies and their feelings than other people.

Within this model, your spirit body is what gives life and organization to a bunch of molecules and keeps them working together in the neat form we call "your physical body." The withdrawal of the spirit body from the physical body, because of suppression, results in the blockage of vital organizing energy to that part of the physical body. The molecules become less well organized, a condition known as "aging" or "sickness." The areas of blocked energy inevitably affect other parts of the body in ways that a person could easily make wrong. This would then lead to more suppression, more blocked energy, etc.

All we are really saying here is that you will have more energy if you celebrate being alive than you will if you make a lot of your life wrong and try to hide from it.

Suppressing an emotion inevitably leads to more of that emotion. Emotions have natural cycles that lead to their resolution. Suppression prevents these cycles from completing themselves and results in a build-up of that emotion in the mind and body. This build-up will seek an outlet, a situation to over-react to, to relieve the pressure it creates.

The mechanics of this process are interesting. I offer one good example. People often use cigarettes to suppress frustration. The cigarette smoke puts a coating on the lungs that actually makes it a little bit frustrating just to take each breath! Habitual smokers smoke to suppress the frustration their cigarette habit causes! (We must share that we once saw a fellow in a bar wearing a button that said, "I drink to forget that I'm alcoholic.")

Thus, suppression, once begun, usually results in the build-up of layer upon layer of suppression and the more-or-less steady withdrawal of the spirit body from the physical body. Death is caused by suppressing the spirit body all the way out of the physical body.

Almost everyone begins suppressing at birth. If you don't remember your birth then it's because of the suppression that you began at that time.

In Parts II through VI of this book we shall explain, in detail, how to use Rebirthing and related techniques to break this fatal chain of events.

How do people suppress things? There are many ways. Mind-altering drugs are a popular way and serve as an excellent illustration. Recreational drugs, prescription drugs, and the anesthesia given by hospitals and dentists are all excellent ways to cause suppression. Not everybody gets the same results, but, generally, alcohol suppresses fear, nicotine suppresses anger and frustration, marijuana suppresses sadness, and caffeine suppresses the long-lasting, energy-sapping results of other forms of suppression. If you use any of these substances habitually, try stopping abruptly for two weeks if you want to find out whether you have been using it to suppress. If you are honest with yourself, just *thinking* about stopping for two weeks may be enough to tell you the answer.

To get an idea of how this works, consider that anger causes dilation of the blood vessels, making a person turn red in the face. Nicotine causes the blood vessels to contract, thus suppressing a normal physiological feeling of anger. An observant person can see the suppressed anger and frustration in the body language of many habitual cigarette smokers.

Similarly, fear causes contraction of the blood vessels, making a person go pale; alcohol dilates them. Whiskey is sometimes called "a shot of courage." People say and do all kinds of things when they are drinking that they would be afraid to say or do if they weren't. That's because alcohol blocks a person's ability to *feel* fear.

People who are very suppressed may feel a need for constant doses of caffeine just to function, because maintenance of their structures of suppression uses up so much of their energy. Suppression means diverting part of your energy to the purpose of holding back other parts of your energy, so you won't feel them. This is very energy-consuming. A little caffeine (or a lot) can make the difference that allows the person to keep all that suppression going and keep functioning, too. Of course, there are many other stimulants used in the same way. Some people are addicted to daily hard exercise, or other things, to achieve the same end.

LSD and other psychedelics work basically as "super-stimulants" in this context. The only reason LSD allows people to experience otherwise unconscious parts of themselves is that it temporarily "suppresses the suppression." A way to verify this is to consider the physical and mental condition of most people who have taken large doses of LSD frequently over long periods of time. Anything that promotes deterioration of the mind or body is suppressive.

In general, one can suppress almost anything with a stimulant and stimulants are among the most suppressive and widely used of all suppressive drugs.

We are not writing a pharmacopoeia, but the foregoing is to give you an idea of how chemical suppression works.

Other popular suppressive techniques include: habitual distraction (watching TV for instance), telling lies, either to oneself or others, dismissing emotionally charged matters as "unimportant", procrastination, etc. Loneliness is a popular thing to suppress, and overeating, sex (including masturbation), watching TV, and reading are all excellent ways to suppress it.

Just about any activity *can* be used to suppress. The activities mentioned above are not necessarily always used for suppression. Even if you try your best not to suppress, you are a human being and there are going to be times when you make things wrong and suppress anyway. Making yourself wrong for that, or making supression itself wrong, will not help.

CHAPTER 4

The Ecstasy Principle

We want to point out something very important: make-wrong, suppression, compulsion, and negativity are all phenomena of the mind and body. *You* are *not* your mind or your body!

You can tell that you are not your mind or your body because you are *experiencing* your mind and body. *You* are pure *Experiencer*. Anything that is part of your experience *cannot* be you, just as anything the eye sees cannot be your eye. (When the eye looks in a mirror it sees a reflection in a mirror, not itself.)

This concept of the Experiencer will be referred to throughout the rest of this book, so we present some important facts about it here.

Recall our discussion of momentary time and linear time. The Experiencer *only* has momentary time experience. In other words, even if your mind is remembering the past or thinking about the future, the Experiencer only has *present moment* experience of the mind doing that.

This means that the Experiencer is incapable of making comparisons. In order to make a comparison you have to "switch back and forth" between the two things being compared. The mind can do this but the Experiencer cannot.

The Experiencer, therefore, is incapable of making anything wrong.

The Experiencer experiences everything as being perfect. What people usually mean by "perfect" is "10 on a scale of 10," but that's not how we're using it. What we mean here is the absence of a scale, the experience that every experience is unique and therefore cannot be compared to anything else.

All phenomena are in the realm of "entertainment" for the Experiencer, the real you. Your mind and body are reading these words and contemplating their meaning. The Experiencer has no interaction with anything other than just experiencing it.

The Experiencer can be thought of as the space in which all manifestation occurs.

The Experiencer is always in a state of *Ecstasy* regardless of what the mind or the body might be going through. By "Ecstasy" we do not mean an emotion. The word "ecstasy" comes from ancient Greek *ek stasis,* one translation of which is "standing apart." The Experiencer is standing apart from anything that it is experiencing. At this level, there is no judgment of good or bad, right or wrong, pleasant or unpleasant, etc. There is also no time. There *is* the experience of the mind creating these things, and the Experiencer experiences that experience ecstatically!

The Ecstasy Principle is this: Everyone is always in a state of Ecstasy whether they like it or not.

A corollary of the Ecstasy Principle is that, regardless of anything that exists in your reality, either you are enjoying it, or you are enjoying not enjoying it, or you are enjoying not enjoying not enjoying it. That's as far as one ever needs to go to get to the truth about happiness.

Face it! It's miraculous that anything exists at all! To be here experiencing anything at all is a miracle of infinite magnitude! This is the realm of the Experiencer.

You could say that the Experiencer is infinitely ecstatic because it is infinitely stupid. It's so stupid that it doesn't know that there's anything wrong!

Sometimes people think that they need things to be a certain way if they are to be happy; they don't. For instance, notice that although a man might think that a Mercedes Benz is what he needs to be happy, if the Mercedes were there but not the man's existence there would be no happiness, but if the man's existence were there and no Mercedes, there could well be happiness. Existence is all anybody needs in order to be happy.

It makes no difference to the Experiencer whether you are making passionate love or are getting hacked to bits by a madman—the Experiencer is just blissfully aware of the miracle of it all. Of course the mind and body *do* care about what happens to them, a *lot,* and it is to the mind and body that this book is addressed.

EVERY EXPERIENCE IS BOTH
PLEASURABLE AND BENEFICIAL

Anything you ever experience is enjoyed by at least two parts of you. The Experiencer enjoys it because the Experiencer doesn't know any better. The part of you that created the experience, or drew you into the experience, probably worked long and hard to set it up in order to give you some kind of supposed benefit, so it feels successful and enjoys it. It is up to you whether your conscious mind enjoys it and you always have the option of enjoying anything.

Every experience is also beneficial in at least two ways. First, you at least learn something from anything that ever happens. You can block that learning out of your conscious mind if you want to, but you nonetheless added to your storehouse of information about the world. Second, every experience is beneficial because it is what comes before whatever comes next. If you are grateful for anything you've got now, then you might as well be grateful for everything that ever happened in the past, too. If any minute detail had been different, everything now would be different, too. (Contemplate for a moment the incredible series of "co-incidences" that led up to the particular sperm cell uniting with the particular egg cell to form your body!)

No matter how many ways you can think of that you receive benefit and pleasure from anything, you can always think of at least one more way, which is why we say that you receive *infinite* benefit and *infinite* pleasure from everything.

Please note that you even receive infinite benefit and infinite pleasure from your negativity and everything it creates. Making your negativity wrong only leads to more negativity Making any result of your negativity wrong is the same thing as making your negativity wrong. You have the ability to include absolutely anything in your celebration of your existence and doing so eliminates negativity at its source.

CHAPTER 5

The Truth about
Being Human

There is nothing suppressed in a person but suppressed bliss. Make-wrong and suppression occur when a person falsely denies the bliss that is present in an experience. When that person reactivates the suppressed material and finally admits that it *is* blissful, *then* the supposed problem disappears.

The only thing that is in the way of anyone's happiness is resistence to the overwhelming bliss of acknowledging how good of a deal life is. Birth trauma is astronomically less important than bliss trauma.

The truth about being human is that it is an infinitely good deal! Not only are we in a state of ecstasy regardless of the content of our experience, but we also get to choose what that content will be.

Which means we get to play games! We get to make up the rules and set the goals and play games!

Part VI of this book is about deciding which games you want to play and then playing those games to *win*.

CHAPTER 6

Integration — The Key to Happiness and Power

Integration means becoming aware of something that you've made wrong and suppressed, and then ceasing to make it wrong. Integration is the result that Rebirthing creates. Integration is the transformation from suppression to celebration. The purpose of this book is to teach you, in detail, how to cause integration.

[*Personal note from Jim Leonard:*
Before we go on, I want to give you a little bit of history. Rebirthing was invented before its result had been discovered. In the "old days" of Rebirthing, we could see that the process produced results, even if we had no basis for describing the result in a logical way. We called the result "release" and we mainly had a lot of superstitions about how to cause it. Rebirthing, even back then, produced results of a depth and breadth that most people had never experienced before in their lives, and yet the process was often meandering, inefficient, and needlessly painful. I spent years delving into the exact nature of the "release" and working out the theoretical and practical basis for causing it efficiently. I did this largely because I got tired of making my living by putting people through an agonizing process to achieve a blissful result. Agony to achieve bliss never did make much sense to me, and my mind rests

more comfortably now that I know that the process is blissful as well as the result!]

Rebirthing is an *enormously* direct and efficient way to cause integration as you shall see. It is no exaggeration at all to say that, if you do it well, you can use Rebirthing to cause each successive layer of suppressed negativity to integrate *within a few seconds.* When it is done efficiently, it is *very pleasurable.*

The reason we don't call the result of Rebirthing "release" anymore, now that we understand exactly what it is, is because the word "release" implies the letting go of something bad. Thinking that something bad needed to be got rid of is what caused suppression to occur in the first place. The truth is that there never was anything bad. You took something that was perfectly wonderful and decided that it was bad. The only way to stop getting a bad result from that bad decision is to "integrate" what you had made wrong into your overall sense of gratitude and well-being. It may seem that we are making too big a deal of a simple word, but the word shapes the attitude. The difference between integrating something and trying to "release" it is the difference between getting a pleasurable, efficient result from your Rebirthing and needlessly perpetuating your struggle.

Our purpose now is to give you the theoretical basis that will allow you to understand the nature of integration. This will greatly facilitate your ability to cause integration when you learn about the "how-to's" in Part II.

In order to integrate something that had previously been made wrong and suppressed, it is not necessary to "go back" to the original episode where it was made wrong. It is not necessary to remember anything about it. Sometimes memory of the event will spontaneously surface when integration occurs. More often it will not. The presence or absence of this kind of memory is irrelevant to producing the result.

In order to integrate, it is necessary to become aware of what one is integrating. This awareness is known as "activation" and it can be awareness at either the level of the mind or at the level of the body.

Once a suppressed make-wrong duality has been activated, all that is necessary to integrate it is to stop making it wrong. It is actually much easier not to make something wrong than it is to make it wrong. Gratitude and celebration are natural, because it is fundamentally enjoyable just to exist at all. You don't have to do anything to enjoy something; you have to do something *not* to enjoy it! For this reason there are many ways to integrate something once it has been activated.

We want to point something out here to make sure there is no misunderstanding. When we talk about "not making anything wrong," we are not talking about moral decisions or any other kind of decision about what anyone will choose to do in the near or distant future. Rebirthing and integration are about momentary time. Choice does not exist in momentary time. In momentary time you are experiencing whatever you are experiencing, and you are either celebrating it or you are making it wrong but it is there, just the way it is, whether you like it or not. In linear time you do have choice about what you will do in the future. Distinctions between "right and wrong," "effective and ineffective," "wise and unwise," are of utmost importance in deciding what to do. Our potentials for discipline and morality are two of our greatest blessings.

Although Rebirthing is about momentary-time experience, it has a profound impact on our linear-time abilities. It effectively eliminates compulsive attitudes and actions that would otherwise get in the way of our effectiveness.

Integration, fundamentally, means telling the truth about what you are experiencing. It occurs when you surrender to your experience being the way that it actually is. You know that you have integrated something when you notice that you no longer resist it. Either it has disappeared altogether or else it is still there and you enjoy it. In any case it ceases to be an issue and your mind is freed to deal with more important things.

Integration does not necessarily eliminate preferences, although it might. It does give you conscious choice about your preferences. Preferring that something change in some particular way in the future does not necessarily mean that you are making it wrong the way it is. If you have one million dollars and you prefer to have two million dollars, that does not mean that you are making your one million dollars wrong. You can celebrate your million dollars, celebrate your choice to prefer having two million dollars, and celebrate engaging in the process of accumulating your second million dollars. On the other hand, if your desire to have two million dollars was unconsciously motivated by a compulsion to be better than your millionaire neighbor, whom you had made wrong, then you have been making your "mere" million dollars wrong. Integrating that make-wrong will give you the opportunity to be satisfied with the million dollars you have and will facilitate you in doing something else with your life instead of compulsively driving after that second million. You could also decide to go for the second million anyway, but with clearer motivation. Integration facilitates conscious choice.

Activation and integration can take place at any of the following levels: material manifestation (i.e., contemplation of something in the "outside" world), the mind, or the body. We shall use the example of Joe and his car, from an earlier section, to illustrate how he could cause integration working at any of these levels. Integration is integration, and it makes no difference at which level it occurs, when you integrate you integrate on every level simultaneously.

Suppose Joe notices that he is making his station wagon wrong. If he changes his mind and decides to love his car unconditionally, that is the same thing as Joe becoming humbler with regard to that particular thing. The make-wrong duality clears up.

If Joe notices that he is living beyond his means and does a State-Your-Complaint Process (described in detail in Part III), the process would generate the "reminder": "In every moment I always have exactly what I truly want most." If he follows through with the "proof" part of the process he will establish new contexts and thus eliminate the make-wrong duality by working at the level of his mind. (If you eliminate the graduations on a scale, you don't have a scale anymore.)

The easiest and most straightforward way for Joe to collapse the duality is at the level of his physical body, i.e., by becoming aware of the *feelings* he has about getting the "wrong" car, and then *enjoying those feelings.* This is much easier than it might seem; in Part II of this book, in the chapter on the Fourth Element of Rebirthing, we describe in detail how to do this. Enjoying what a make-wrong duality feels like collapses (integrates) the duality because *there is no difference between changing the context in which one holds one's feelings about a certain thing and changing the context in which one holds the thing itself.* When it feels just as good to be at zero as it does to be at 10, there is no scale, and everything is once again enjoyed for its own uniqueness. This is the manner in which Rebirthing collapses duality. It causes integration at the level of the physical body.

Here are two more examples of how this works. This point is extremely important to you if you intend to maximize your happiness and effectiveness.

Suppose you decide not to like punk rock music (or any other kind of music). What you have signed yourself up for is to have an unpleasant feeling in your body whenever you hear or even think about that kind of music. If you hear the made-wrong music sometime, feel the made-wrong feelings it gives you and then allow yourself to enjoy that feeling, that is exactly the same as switching to a context in which you enjoy the music itself.

Suppose that you are driving on the freeway and you get a flat tire. You may have an initial reaction of frustration. If you allow yourself to experience those feelings of frustration and enjoy them, this is the exact same thing as enjoying changing the tire; you will be more efficient than if you are making it wrong.

The only alternative to celebrating something is to divert part of your energy to hiding from your feelings about it, keeping your spirit body away from contact with those feelings. Rebirthing is the art of bringing the spirit body back into full contact with the physical body. Celebration of one's life causes increased aliveness in the physical body in every case.

People sometimes try to motivate themselves to cause change by making what they've got now wrong, e.g., "If I give myself a hard enough time maybe I'll get better." This is actually a terrible way to cause motivation for two reasons. First, if you do it you'll be miserable. Second, any time you make your present moment situation wrong you will automatically withdraw awareness from the details of that situation. A common form for this withdrawal to take is "going off into the future" thinking of the relief you'll get when it's all over. The details you are withdrawing from by not staying "in present time" may be essential to dealing with the situation effectively.

Motivation is actually already built-in to being a human. You already have motivation to increase your experience of everything that you value. (More about this in Chapter 55.) Celebrating a desire to do something is known as "enthusiasm." You can change a tire, or do anything else, more efficiently if you are enthusiastic about it. Enthusiasm for climbing out of a hole (for example) has to include gratitude for being in the hole in the first place. Celebration of the hole itself facilitates your being aware of more of the details that will make your climb easier and more enjoyable.

Making the situation wrong will automatically divert part of your energy to handling the unpleasant emotions you will have.

EMOTIONS

Emotions themselves are generally a result of resisting something. The emotion will only continue being an emotion for as long as you continue resisting it. If you allow yourself to surrender completely to an emotion, and enjoy it, it will integrate and you'll suddenly find yourself in a good mood. An integrated emotion is not exactly an emotion. Some examples:

Happiness means surrendering to what is so. In the models we use, happiness is not considered an emotion.

Sadness comes from resisting a past change or from resisting the fact that something you are experiencing now is passing irrevocably into the past. When a change that happened in the past is made wrong, it is interpreted as "loss". If you surrender to your feelings of sadness you will end up with a pleasant memory, enjoyable feelings, and gratitude. If you resist a pleasant memory you will get sadness.

Anger is a result of resisting your "purpose," by which we mean something you feel you must do. For instance, suppose you are watching the Super Bowl and you are happily munching potato chips and drinking beer. Right when things are getting pleasurably tense and an important play is happening, somebody rings your doorbell. If you are clear that your purpose is to watch the game and you ignore the door, then you will be happy, not angry. If you are clear that answering the door is more important than watching the game and you surrender to that task you will be happy, not angry. But if you think you are obligated to answer the door and what you really want to do is watch the game, then that despicable dolt who rang your bell had better watch out! If you include your anger in your enjoyment of the present moment, you will again be happy with your visitor. Integrated anger is purposefulness. Resisted purposefulness is anger.

Fear comes from imagining a future possibility and resisting it. When fear integrates, what you have is certainty that you will do whatever it takes to prevent anything that is not in alignment with your goals from happening. Either you realize that you had nothing to fear or else you become enthusiastic about preventing it. If you try to feel safe without preparing for the future, you will experience either fear or suppression. Fear is extremely important to effectiveness. If you are persisting in doing something that is likely to cause some bad result for you in the future, you *ought* to feel afraid. Suppressing fear prevents you from taking appropriate action and is therefore very dangerous. All it takes to integrate fear is to experience it in detail and include it in your celebration of your existence in that moment; if you do that, the rest will happen automatically. Integrated fear is enthusiastic preparation for the future. If you resist preparing for the future you will get fear. There is further discussion of the appropriate use of fear in Part VI of this book.

Frustration and boredom are closely related to anger:

Frustration is a result of resisting humility. If you try to do something and you get the wrong result, you have a choice: be humbled or be frustrated. Humility means having a good attitude about your limitations, your humanness. Frustration means trying to insist that you don't have any limitations, even when you've just butted your head against one at 60 MPH! If you surrender to frustration you will get humility. If you resist humility you will get frustration.

Another word for humility is "self-esteem." Some people interpret "high self-esteem" to mean having an exaggerated sense of self-importance or having a big ego. They think that they display high self-esteem when they look, to themselves and others, like they don't have any psychological problems left. This is obviously not a very good way to go about it, because it does not create a context of loving oneself unconditionally, and because it does not create any context for letting suppressed negativity surface in a gentle way. Humility means accepting fully that you are a human being and loving yourself for that. It eliminates feeling superior to people or inferior to people. It also facilitates a person in doing whatever work there is to do, rather than leaving it to someone else who is not "superior to the task." If there is any higher virtue than humility, we do not know what it is.

By the way, the safest thing in the world to procrastinate is humbling yourself. Rest assured that if you put it off long enough the Universe will do the job for you!

Boredom is a result of resisting emotional activation. It usually occurs when you procrastinate doing something that you know is going to bring up some emotion that you are avoiding. When you can't think of anything better to do, but you still refuse to do the thing you are avoiding, you get bored. Next time you're bored, notice what emotion is really right below the surface and plunge into it! You won't be bored for long and you'll get your work done, too! Surrender to boredom and you'll always get activation. Resist activation and you'll always get boredom. Boredom is an extremely good thing to integrate. People are often at their most destructive when they are driven by suppressing boredom. Remember that our emotions exist for our pleasure and convenience.

INTEGRATION WITHOUT USING ANY TECHNIQUES

In normal day-to-day living, people do occasionally integrate without knowing anything about it. The best example of this is that most adolescents make their parents wrong for all kinds of things; when adolescents grow up and start dealing with adult situations, they gradually make their parents less and less wrong. Whenever they stop making their parents wrong for something they get massive integration with all the benefits usually associated with integration. Unfortunately, most people who don't know any techniques for causing integration suppress a whole lot more than they integrate.

By the way, if you are still making your parents wrong for some things, then you are very fortunate indeed! It means that no matter how wonderful your life is now, you can make it much better in a straightforward and relatively easy way. If you clear everything up with your parents, then you will also have cleared up most of the important stuff with yourself! In Part IV of this book you will find some suggestions for improving your relationship with your parents.

Rebirthing is the most efficient way to integrate a make-wrong duality because Rebirthing works at the level of physical patterns of energy. Your mind will fool you for years at a time but your body won't fool you at all. Your feelings are always right there just waiting for you to explore them and celebrate them. The breathing component of Rebirthing exists to facilitate you in feeling your suppressed feelings.

You cannot have happiness in opposition to anything. Rebirthing, bit by bit, eliminates your specific oppositions.

Integration always makes a person both happier and more powerful. Happier because it means the person is making less wrong in each moment. More powerful because it frees the person from compulsive, subconsciously motivated behavior.

The message in all of this is actually very simple: You are alive in this moment whether you like it or not; if you resist life you will be miserable and weak; if you surrender willingly to the challenge of life you will be happy and free.

Rebirthing is the advanced science of converting resistence to enthusiasm.

PART II

REBIRTHING — THE SCIENCE OF ENJOYING ALL YOUR LIFE

Part II of this book is a comprehensive description of state-of-the-art Rebirthing methodology, a result of the authors' combined decade of research over the course of Rebirthing thousands of people. It is written in much detail yet in a highly readable style. It starts at the beginning, with no assumption that the reader has had any previous experience with Rebirthing, other than reading Part I of this book, yet it is absolutely thorough. It is written both for the professional Rebirther and for anyone who is interested in Rebirthing.

We present this material with the certainty that it will be of great, practical value to every professional Rebirther because it is unique in its content, presentation and completeness.

We know with equal certainty that anyone who reads it will gain much practical insight that will aid them in many real-life situations, whether or not they ever get Rebirthed. Furthermore, for those who do elect to be Rebirthed, this information will in every

41

case make their Rebirthing experience more effective and more pleasurable, regardless of the Rebirthing style of their particular Rebirther.

We present detailed information on dry Rebirthing, on Rebirthing using warm and cold water, and on several other advanced Rebirthing techniques.

A logical question for anyone who has never been Rebirthed to ask at this point is: "Will reading and understanding this material give me enough information to enable me to Rebirth myself?"

The answer is yes and no. It will give you all the information you need, but information is not all you need.

If you wanted to learn to fly an airplane, you wouldn't just buy a plane, buy an instruction manual, read it and take off. For the same reasons, we urge you to seek the aid of a competent professional Rebirther, such as one of those we list in the back of this book.

There is no actual *danger* involved in trying to Rebirth yourself first without a Rebirther. You couldn't harm yourself with Rebirthing if you tried. The worst thing that could happen is that you would become acutely aware of suppressed feelings and then feel stuck with them, unable to integrate them. Such an experience wouldn't hurt you but it might make you very uncomfortable, for a matter of hours or days. If you get Rebirthed by any trained Rebirther, there is virtually no chance of getting stuck in uncomfortable feelings for more than a few minutes.

Rebirthing is the most valuable thing we have ever heard of for anybody who has a mind and voluntary control of the breathing mechanism. What we really urge you to do is to read this section two or three times and then get Rebirthed by a competent professional Rebirther as soon as possible.

CHAPTER 7

The Five Elements of Rebirthing

Anything that has been made wrong and suppressed can be integrated using the technique of Rebirthing. Rebirthing uses the feelings in the physical body to gain access to the mind. Everything you have ever made wrong and suppressed has left a signature of energy in your body that has stayed there, in suppression, waiting for you to let it come to your attention and integrate it into your sense of gratitude and well being.

Rebirthing is not the only way to integrate suppressed material, but it is the most efficient way. Since it bypasses the mind, it avoids the delays involved in figuring anything out.

The Five Elements of Rebirthing are the exact "how-to" of causing integration using the method of Rebirthing. Although Rebirthing is a single process, it can best be described in terms of five components.

Whenever all Five Elements are fully present, integration must occur. Whenever integration occurs, regardless of the method used for causing it, all Five Elements must be fully present. Any time integration is not occurring, at least one of the Five Elements is surely absent.

Rebirthing was invented, and taught extensively, before the Five Elements were discovered. Rebirthing using the Five Elements is enormously more efficient than Rebirthing without them. When

43

the Rebirther and the Rebirthee both have a thorough understanding of the Five Elements, integration of each pattern of suppressed energy can be caused, at will, as soon as the Rebirthee becomes aware of it.

The period of time that begins with the onset of circular breathing and concludes with an integration is known as a "breathing cycle". One way to describe the difference that the Five Elements make in Rebirthing is that their use shortens the breathing cycle. When the Five Elements are used very skillfully, each breathing cycle may be only a few seconds in duration.

Integrating sooner, instead of later, is useful not only because more can be accomplished in each session (it can) but also because integration can be caused when each pattern of energy is still at a subtle level of manifestation, which makes the process much more comfortable and pleasant for the person who is being Rebirthed. No matter how intense something was when it went into suppression, it can be integrated when it is still at a subtle level during a Rebirthing session. If it is not integrated when it is still subtle, and if the Rebirthing continues, it will become less and less subtle, i.e., more and more intense, until the Rebirthee is finally forced to surrender to it, at which point the pattern of energy either disappears or becomes pleasant. When the Five Elements are not used in the Rebirthing technique, "forced surrender", in the face of intensity, is the method of achieving results with Rebirthing.

A Rebirthee who learns to integrate subtly from the very beginning will have a much greater sense of comfort and safety with the Rebirthing process. This sense of comfort and safety, in turn, will result in a greater willingness to allow suppressed material to surface and a greater sense of enjoying it and thus integrating it, once it has surfaced.

For the above reasons, we recommend that the Five Elements of Rebirthing always be used by both Rebirther and Rebirthee and that the efficiency of integration during Rebirthing always be the first objective.

The Five Elements of Rebirthing are:
1. Circular Breathing
2. Complete Relaxation
3. Awareness in Detail
4. Integration into Ecstasy
5. Do Whatever You Do Because Everything Works

We shall explain each of the Five Elements in detail.

CHAPTER 8

Circular Breathing —The First Element of Rebirthing

In Rebirthing, a breathing technique is used to give you access to your patterns of suppression at the level of your physical body. The kind of breathing that is used is called "Circular Breathing."

Circular breathing means any kind of breathing which meets all of the following three criteria:

1) The inhale and exhale are connected together so that there are no pauses in the breathing.

2) The exhale is relaxed and not controlled at all.

3) If the inhale comes in through the nose then the exhale also goes out through the nose, or, if the inhale comes in through the mouth, then the exhale also goes out through the mouth.

Circular breathing results in "complete circuits of energy" in the body—a balancing of "prana" and "apana".

PRANA

Prana is the life force energy in your body. "Prana" is the Sanskrit term used in Indian Yoga philosophy. In Chinese it is called *chi,* in Japanese it is called *ki.*

There are many sources of prana: food, sunlight, water, air. Air is the most important source of prana. You can go for many days without food, water, or sunlight, but under ordinary circumstances you can go for only a few minutes without air.

Prana is not the same thing as oxygen. Oxygen is carried to the cells of the body by the red blood corpuscles. Prana travels through the body in subtle energy channels, known as nadis. The main vessels of the flow of prana are the well-known acupuncture meridians, but every cell of your body that is alive is nourished by the subtle channels of prana.

Prana can be likened to electricity. Negative current flows to a light bulb, the free electrons are converted to light and the positive current flows back to the source. Similarly, prana travels to the cells of the body and nourishes them and *apana* flows back to the source.

Circular breathing sets up a condition in the body that is analogous to alternating current. On the inhale, prana flows to all the cells of the body and on the completely relaxed exhale, all the apana flows back out again, thus completing the circuit. (This is not how people usually breathe.) The result of cycle after cycle of complete circuits of energy is that the breather can *feel* the flows of energy, *including blocks in the flow of energy that are caused by previous suppression. This results in activation of old patterns of suppressed make-wrong and gives the person the chance to integrate them.*

THE VARIOUS KINDS OF CIRCULAR BREATHING

There are many kinds of circular breathing, differentiated from one another by the following factors: volume of the inhale, speed of the inhale, whether the breath is taken and discharged through the nose or the mouth, and whether the air is taken into the lower, middle or upper portion of the lungs. Any kind of circular breathing will result in gaining awareness of suppressed patterns of energy but each of these factors has a particular result and different kinds of circular breathing are especially useful in particular rebirthing situations.

THE VOLUME OF THE INHALE

The volume of air that is taken can be likened to the volume control on your stereo. To get maximum enjoyment of the music on your stereo you don't want the music to be so loud that it's blasting out your eardrums or so soft that you can't hear it. In Rebirthing you listen to the music that your body is making and maximize your enjoyment of it, and the same principle applies. If you can't feel the patterns of energy in your body enough to explore the details, then increase the volume of air that you're taking. If the pattern is coming up too intensely for you to be able to enjoy it, then decrease the volume of air.

The idea that Rebirthing is about "confronting your suppression" makes no more sense than the idea that listening to your stereo is about confronting your music. If you want the music to play a little softer that is not saying that you don't like the music. Similarly, if you enjoy a pattern of energy in your body that doesn't mean that you want it to be awesomely intense. Life can be enough of a confrontation without making your Rebirthing process a confrontation, too.

THE SPEED OF THE INHALE

In Rebirthing you want to come fully into the present moment and keep a balance between two things you do with your awareness: Being aware of everything in your experience and focusing on the most prominent pattern of energy. In other words you maintain a balance between focusing and defocusing of your attention. Taking the inhale slowly increases the ability to focus, and taking it fast increases the awareness of the overall experience.

This is significant because when something has been activated, and before it integrates, it is the most important thing that is happening. After it integrates, it is neither more nor less important than anything else. Until you have gained enough awareness of the pattern to integrate it, you want to maximize your focus, so slow breathing facilitates that. Once you are thoroughly aware of the pattern, then speeding up your breathing will tend to speed up the integration.

It is important to note here that any discussion of the speed of breathing in Rebirthing is referring to the speed of the inhale, not the exhale. The exhale should never be controlled. Sometimes a fast inhale will result in a fast exhale and sometimes in a low exhale; and sometimes a slow inhale will result in a slow exhale and sometimes in a fast exhale. Let your body decide. It is not important for the inhale and the exhale to be of the same duration.

THREE KINDS OF CIRCULAR BREATHING

There are three main combinations of volume and speed, each with its own specific application.

FULL AND SLOW

Full and slow circular breathing is best when you are first starting your Rebirthing session or if you have just integrated one pattern of energy and you are starting to move into the next one. The large volume of air makes you more aware of the pattern and the slowness makes it easier to focus on it.

FAST AND SHALLOW

Fast and shallow circular breathing is the best when a pattern is coming up intensely. The shallowness makes the pattern easier to be with and the speed speeds up integration. When using this type of breathing, it is very important to focus intently on the details of the pattern.

FAST AND FULL

Fast and full circular breathing is best when a pattern is coming up that tends to take you out of your body (sleepiness for example). The large volume of air tends to hold you in your body and the speed speeds up integration. Further details about integrating this kind of pattern are presented in the section entitled "unconsciousness," in Chapter 10.

NORMAL BREATHING RHYTHMS

As a general comment regarding breathing rhythms, your breathing during Rebirthing will ordinarily be rather moderate with respect to the three types of breathing we have just described. There will probably be times, however, when more extreme forms of each of the breathing rhythms just described will be most useful. Once you become very experienced, your breathing will tend to adjust itself perfectly, simply as a result of your increased confidence in the process.

NOSE OR MOUTH?

Regarding nose versus mouth breathing, the general rule is "whichever feels better is better." The only exception to this is that sometimes it is desirable to maximize the flow of air into the body (during activation of suppressed anesthesia, for instance). At that time breathing through the mouth is preferred because the mouth is a larger opening.

UPPER OR LOWER PART OF THE LUNGS?

In deciding whether to take the air into the upper part or the lower part of the lungs, the main principle is, if you are focusing on a pattern of energy that is manifesting in the head or in the upper part of the body, then breathing in the upper part of the lungs will make that easier; if you are focusing on a pattern of energy that is manifesting in the legs or in the lower part of the body, then breathing into the lower part of the lungs will make that easier. There are exceptions to this principle, however. Whenever anything gets suppressed, an inhibition goes into the breathing mechanism; otherwise breathing would bring it right back out of suppression. It is possible that something that you are feeling in the lower part of your body has its corresponding breathing inhibition in the upper part of your lungs or vice versa. We encourage you to experiment and use your intuition. Often the Rebirther can observe that a person is avoiding breathing into a certain area of the lungs and then assist in the activation of more material by directing the person to breathe there.

REBIRTHING USING THE FIRST ELEMENT ONLY

If you didn't know anything about Rebirthing except how to do Circular Breathing, and if you kept at it long enough, eventually you would achieve integration. Probably you would have a very uncomfortable experience. The breathing would activate material which you originally suppressed because it was unpleasant. Without using the other four Elements, the material would be just as unpleasant this time around. If you kept doing Circular Breathing, the material would not go back into suppression but would keep becoming more and more activated. Eventually you would either stop doing Circular Breathing, in which case the material would gradually go back into suppression, or else you would decide that it was never going to go away anyhow, in which case you would surrender and integate it. The other four elements enable you to surrender right from the start, which turns Rebirthing into an extremely pleasant experience of going into deeper and deeper states of Ecstasy as layer after layer of suppressed discomfort integrate.

TETANY

"Tetany" means the involuntary tightening of muscles during Rebirthing. It occurs most commonly in the hands, next most commonly in the facial muscles around the mouth, and sometimes anywhere else in the body. Tetany is not dangerous and not even especially uncomfortable unless one struggles against it. Probably 90% of everyone who has been Rebirthed has had at least a little bit of it.

Tetany is caused by controlling the exhale. Either forcing the exhale or holding on to the exhale can cause it. If the exhale is controlled, the apana does not get the opportunity to leave the body fully and if the person is bringing in large amounts of prana with the inhales, then the build-up of apana can be considerable. The build-up of apana causes the muscles to contract.

People go into tetany when they have "control patterns", i.e., when they have self-delusion built up to such an extent that they feel they have to control everything to prevent the delusion from being shattered. Such people will try to control the exhale even if you tell them not to. Controlling the exhale weakens the effects of Circular Breathing and anybody who does Circular Breathing will realize this, at least subconsciously. If a pattern is coming up that the unconscious mind deems too threatening to the conscious mind's self-delusion, then the person may start controlling the exhale in order to hide. This results in tetany, which itself can serve as a marvelous smokescreen for hiding from what one fears. A control pattern may manifest physically as a band of tension that squeezes the exhale involuntarily. Tetany is a result of resisting disillusionment.

Tetany can be substantially reduced or prevented altogether if one realizes deeply that the truth is ultimately more pleasant than self-delusion anyway. If you are the Rebirther and your Rebirthee goes into tetany, gently remind the person that there is nothing to resist but bliss. Most assuredly, remind the person to relax the exhale and to relax in general. If it comes up strongly, then have the Rebirthee concentrate on the sensations that go with it, and suggest that the person breathe fast and shallowly. Avoid making the tetany wrong. Often it will integrate very quickly.

HYPERVENTILATION

Hyperventilation is not necessary to the Rebirthing process. The cause of hyperventilation is forcing or "blowing" the exhale. If the breathing is done properly, there will be no hyperventilation, even if the fullest and fastest breathing is used.

THE "BREATHING RELEASE"

You may hear Rebirthers use the term "breathing release" or "breath release" from time to time. This is rather old-fashioned Rebirthing terminology for the following event: intense activation of negativity, usually fear, associated with the taking of the first breath as an infant, accompanied by acute discomfort with the breathing process and followed by an integration that makes a noticeable improvement in the Rebirthee's normal breathing.

Despite the fact that most Rebirthers who have been trained up to now (January, 1983) have been trained with this concept, it is rather misleading because of the following implications: that intense activation has something to do with producing the result, that something bad (trauma) goes away, and that it happens once for each Rebirthee.

A clearer model of what actually happens to a person's normal, day-to-day breathing as a result of Rebirthing is this:

As we have mentioned, making anything wrong *feels* unpleasant and once something is made wrong, the mind tends to blame the unpleasant feeling on whatever it is making wrong rather than on the make-wrong context in which it is holding it. This blame results in the mind thinking that as long as what it is making wrong exists, the mind must protect itself from consciously experiencing the unpleasant feelings that the made-wrong thing creates. The strategy for accomplishing this protection is to reduce the flow of prana to the areas where the unpleasant feelings are manifest, which is rather like turning down the dimmer switch on your bedroom light when you want to go to sleep. To do this it is necessary to inhibit the breathing mechanism, because otherwise normal Circular Breathing would activate the feelings the mind is trying to suppress. Thus, whenever the mind makes something wrong, the body puts an inhibition into the breathing mechanism. All of the preceding occurs for virtually all human beings. It can be diagrammed like this:

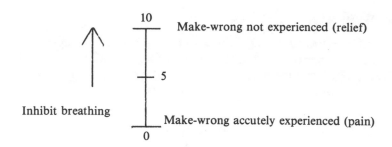

FIGURE 9: THE ORIGIN OF
INHIBITED BREATHING AS A
STRATEGY FOR SUPPRESSION.

Different instances of suppression create combinations of breathing inhibitions of the following main types: congestion of the sinuses; constriction, tension and excessive closing of the larynx, thus restricting the flow of air and interfering with the normal rhythm; chronic inflammation of the bronchi (bronchitis); spasms of the smooth muscle of the bronchi (asthma); inhibited use of the diaphragm and the external intercostal muscles, thus limiting the volume of the inhale and interfering with the normal rhythm; chronic tension of the diaphragm and the external intercostal muscles, thus "holding on" to the exhale and interfering with the normal rhythm; chronic tension and excessive use of the internal intercostal muscles, thus forcing the exhale and interfering with the normal rhythm; the "bunching" of the various fascia involved; and others. In addition, habits such as tobacco and marijuana smoking irritate the lungs and inhibit breathing. Habitual positioning of the body in postures not conducive to good breathing and habitual lack of cardiopulmonary exercise also play roles in inhibiting the breathing. The unconscious mind controls the whole process.

Consciously choosing to do Circular Breathing thwarts this suppressive strategy and facilitates integration of the make-wrong into the person's experience of Ecstasy.

Whenever a person integrates anything, the breathing becomes freer. The "classical breathing release" occurs when a person integrates make-wrong of the first breath, but this does not need to involve *intense* activation any more than integration of anything else needs to do so. When all Five Elements are in use, integration of anything is quick, pleasurable and subtle. Everyone experiences as many "breathing releases" as they do integrations.

CHAPTER 9

Complete Relaxation —
The Second Element
of Rebirthing

It takes a lot of effort to keep something suppressed! Many times, small movements, muscle tightenings, the changing of positions, fidgeting, etc., are the distractions necessary to keep supressed material from coming to a person's awareness. When the whole body is relaxed, the areas that will not relax come much more readily to conscious awareness.

In general, we recommend that the Rebirthee get into one comfortable position and keep relaxing into that position without moving, fidgeting, or scratching itches, throughout the whole session. Many times we have seen unscratched itches become surprising and important patterns of energy. In dry Rebirthing, lying on the back, legs uncrossed, palms up at the sides, in a position of complete vulnerability, is usually best. Instead of moving or scratching, one gets a chance to really feel what it feels like to *want* to do these things. This is one of the best ways we know to activate material quickly and integrate it subtly.

Sometimes people get very relaxed during a Rebirthing session; then suddenly they start to feel like they are so relaxed that if they get any more relaxed, they'll jump right out of their skin! When this happens, it means that a new pattern of energy is starting to be activated. At this point is it a good idea to keep relaxing.

SUBTLETY

One of the most important reasons to use the Five Elements is that they enable a person to integrate material at a much subtler level than would otherwise be possible. Complete relaxation is very important to this because commonly the first awareness that a person has of some suppressed energy is awareness of an area of the body that will not relax. It is much easier to feel the subtle flows of energy in your body when you relax completely.

Relaxation is very important in the actual moment of integration, as well, because at that moment, energy that has been made wrong and held away from the body's normal energy is reaccepted and the very cells of the body drop their struggle against it. A good way to describe Rebirthing is "a relaxation technique so effective that the tension never comes back".

POSITIONS

Obviously Rebirthing does not have to be done on one's back. When people are integrating massive fear or massive sadness, it is often best for them to curl up in a little fetal ball. When anesthesia is being re-experienced, often sitting and sometimes even standing are helpful. Sometimes a particular position will particularly activate a particular pattern of enery. More advanced Rebirthees are often Rebirthed in hot or cold water and various positions are good in hot and cold water Rebirthing, too. In very advanced sessions, we have guided Rebirthees into integration while they were engaging in driving a car or eating in a restaurant or other activities. This is known as "ambulatory Rebirthing" and is described in a later chapter. In all cases, however, Complete Relaxation is of key importance in bringing about integration.

Another way to point out the purpose of Complete Relaxation is to say that the breathing causes an increase in the flow of energy in the body and you can either relax into it and let it heal you or you can attempt to resist it and have the effort of resisting it make you more tense.

CHAPTER 10

Awareness in Detail — The Third Element of Rebirthing

During Rebirthing, one wants to bring one's awareness as much as possible into the present moment to explore everything in the here and now in the greatest possible detail. The best way to do Rebirthing is kinesthetically, i.e., focusing on the feelings that come to your attention in your body. When we use the term "pattern of energy," we are mainly referring to feelings, but a pattern of energy can be anything. It can be tingling in your toes, cats yowling in the alley, or remembering the smell of your grandmother's cookies. A quick definition for "pattern of energy" is: any discrete experience that is part of a person's subjective reality in a given moment in time.

All "feelings" and "emotions" are kinesthetic (physical) in nature and that is how most people experience them. Some people do not experience them physically, due to years of suppression, but Rebirthing makes it easier for anybody to feel and enjoy their feelings.

The Third Element means that you notice what feelings you have, notice where they are manifest in the body, and then focus on those areas and explore every detail of what the feelings feel like.

In the course of a Rebirthing session, the patterns of energy change. Suppression is in layers, rather like the layers of an onion, with each layer covering up the layers beneath it. When a pattern of energy integrates, it either disappears or ceases to be important. Integrating one layer usually activates the next layer down.

Patterns of energy also change because sometimes component parts of a larger pattern get activated separately. For instance, if you were integrating a suppressed experience of being dropped by a nurse when you were an infant, first might come fear, then the thought that you can't trust women, and then pain, and then it might all come together as an integrative memory. Often when components are coming up separately, awareness will switch around among them for a while.

It's a good idea to keep awareness of the whole body while Rebirthing. As a natural process, some things will come to a person's awareness more than others. Whatever comes especially to the Rebirthee's experience is exactly what the Rebirthee should most put awareness into, to experience in detail, at that moment. In other words, whatever asks for the most attention should be given the most attention.

It is also best to be aware of "external" things, rather than try to screen them out. Obviously people get activated by things in their environment so the jet noises, or the rowdy children, or the sound of other people Rebirthing nearby are important parts of a Rebirthing session. Trying to screen them out would make them distractions.

Any time something starts to "distract a Rebirthee," the "distraction" is actually the pattern of energy that is coming to the attention of the person right then—the one to focus on and experience in detail.

UNCONSCIOUSNESS

There are many types of patterns of energy that, by their nature, tend to take you out of contact with your body. Sleepiness is an obvious example. Ordinarily if you relax completely and focus on your feelings of sleepiness, you will just fall asleep. In order to integrate, however, one wishes to relax completely, feel one's sensations and stay in touch with one's body. "Unconsciousness," as we are using the term here, means anything that make you unaware of the patterns of energy in your body.

Generally, the way to integrate any type of unconsciousness in Rebirthing is to do full-and-fast Circular Breathing and to focus fully on the sensations that accompany the condition of unconsciousness, even getting very self-indulgent with the sensuality of the feelings. It is impossible to fall asleep while doing very full, very fast Circular Breathing.

[*A personal note from Jim Leonard:*
It is possible to integrate any type of unconsciousness that comes up in Rebirthing. I once went for five days and five nights without sleep, just using Rebirthing to integrate the causes of my sleepiness. When I would start to get sleepy, I would Rebirth my way into the feelings of sleepiness. Pretty soon they would stop being sleepiness and turn into something else: loneliness, fear, boredom, etc. I found that integrating these emotions left me rested.]

Apart from the things we have already mentioned, there are other strategies that are specific to specific types of unconsciousness. The basic types of unconsciousness that arise in connection with Rebirthing are: those with a quasi-physical basis such as sleepiness, tiredness, intoxication and such things as hypoglycemia; those that center around resisting what the Circular Breathing is bringing up, such as drifting off into fantasies and thoughts, "chit-chat-ananda" (talking instead of Rebirthing), drama (wanting to act out one's emotions instead of surrendering to them), going off into one's mantra or white light (some people who have practiced certain types of meditation extensively do this); epilepsy; suppressed anesthesia; chronic lack of contact with feelings (very suppressive people); and suspended breath.

TIREDNESS AND SLEEPINESS

If someone is going unconscious because of being awake until six o'clock in the morning or because they just left work after unloading 1500 crates of watermelons, it may be best to let the person sleep for fifteen minutes or so first. We suggest that the Rebirther discuss this with the Rebirthee first. Some people are greatly refreshed by short naps and others aren't. Also, some people will not like being allowed to sleep during a Rebirthing session for any reason. It is never necessary to have the Rebirthee sleep; sometimes it makes things easier.

INTOXICATION

It is possible to Rebirth someone who is drunk or intoxicated on almost any substance. The Rebirther should do whatever it takes to keep the Rebirthee breathing as fully and as rapidly as possible.

HYPOGLYCEMIA

People who have been diagnosed as having reactive hypoglycemia (low blood sugar), or who have diagnosed themselves as having it, usually develop habits to prevent the onset of the feelings associated with it or to alleviate these symptoms once they occur. If these feelings (spaciness, weakness, discomfort and helplessness) come up during a Rebirthing session, we suggest that the hypoglycemic relax into the precise sensations and breathe moderately full and fast, until the feelings integrate.

[Personal note from Jim Leonard:
I used to be hypoglycemic myself, and I had some very good integrations of that state which seem to have left me free of that disease.]

FANTASIES AND THOUGHTS

Sometimes people immerse themselves in thoughts and dreamlike fantasies during a Rebirthing because they think that the thoughts and fantasies are more interesting or more important than Rebirthing. We recommend that the Rebirther let the Rebirthee know that it is fine to have thoughts and fantasies, but that they don't cause integration very efficiently. Sometimes the ideas that come up during Rebirthing seem brilliant at the time, but often aren't. The ideas that are worthwhile will probably come up for exploration later. Sometimes it may be helpful for the Rebirther to write down for the Rebirthee something in particular that the Rebirthee wants to remember, thus allowing the Rebirthing to proceed. Often a good instruction for someone who is drifting off into thoughts and fantasies is, "Notice what every thought *feels* like." Sometimes people drift off into thoughts and fantasies involuntarily. Full and fast breathing usually prevents this. People who drift off a lot may do well to Rebirth in hot or cold water.

CHIT-CHAT-ANANDA

Sometimes it is important for the Rebirther and the Rebirthee to communicate during a Rebirthing session. Some Rebirthees, however, use conversation as a distraction from their feelings. The technical term for this is "chit-chat-ananda". When a Rebirthee does this, we recommend that the Rebirther say, "No more talking until the end of your Rebirth" in a firm manner.

DRAMA

"Drama" means acting out one's feelings instead of relaxing and feeling them. Drama such as crying, screaming, crawling around, etc., is OK and not to be avoided when it comes up spontaneously, but it does not cause integration. Indeed, very often it distracts a Rebirthee from feeling what's happening and thus makes the integration take longer and be more difficult than it needed to be.

Expressing an emotion is not the opposite of suppressing it. If you have suppressed anger, you will do better to take responsibility for it and apply the Five Elements to it than to go around expressing your old hostility to everyone you meet. The expression of an emotion can be the distraction necessary to keep it suppressed.

We recommend that the Rebirther gently remind the dramatic Rebirthee that it is possible to enjoy anything and encourage the Rebirthee to relax completely and continue breathing. If a Rebirthee is being dramatic in a way that includes tensing the throat, such as yelling, sobbing, or gasping, it is a good idea to tell the Rebirthee to relax the throat.

Some simple ways we like to express this idea are: "Expression does not end suppression," "Drama does not release trauma," and "The most dramatic results are produced by the least dramatic Rebirthing."

Laughter is usually not drama but rather a sign of integration. More about this later.

SUPPRESSIVE MEDITATION

There are many kinds of meditation and some of them are almost the opposite of Rebirthing. These are the types that are about "transcending" one's emotions. Although we are sure that people derive all sorts of benefits from these meditations in general, during Rebirthing they are inappropriate because they make it more difficult to bring oneself fully into the body. We recommend that the Rebirther inform the excessively meditative Rebirthee that Rebirthing can be thought of as a variety of meditation in which a person meditates on the feelings in the body. Full and fast breathing usually works well here, as do hot and cold water Rebirthing.

EPILEPSY

If a Rebirthee has a history of epilepsy, it is possible that epileptic symptoms may appear during a Rebirthing session. It is important that a Rebirthee with a history of epilepsy understand this before embarking upon a Rebirthing session so that the Rebirthee realizes that the Rebirthing is providing an opportunity to integrate the symptoms instead of thinking that something has happened to cause an epileptic attack. Rebirthees with a history of epilepsy should let their Rebirther know about this and make sure that the Rebirther is willing to assist them with it. They may also wish to consult their personal physician before starting Rebirthing, and Rebirthers may wish to require that they do so. An unexpected epileptic attack can be a frightening experience for the Rebirthee and for the inexperienced Rebirther if there hasn't been some communication about it beforehand. Full and fast breathing on the part of the Rebirthee and extreme patience on the part of the Rebirther are recommended. The authors know of no case in which harm has come to a Rebirthee as a result of epileptic symptoms arising during a Rebirthing.

ANESTHESIA

General anesthesia may enter the body at birth, during surgery, when giving birth, or if it is abused as a recreational drug. The memory of anesthesia is stored in the mind and in the cells of the body until released by the energy experienced during Rebirthing sessions. As the Rebirthee breathes and relaxes, energy begins to flow in the body to a degree not usually experienced. This energy chases out anything unlike itself, including the deadness induced by the suppressed anesthesia.

As the Rebirthee becomes more and more conscious of the memory of the anesthesia, this memory produces the same result that the anesthesia had on the way in, which is that it begins to make the person unconscious. After a couple of Rebirthing sessions in which the person has begun to experience the memory of the suppressed anesthesia, there commonly will occur a session in which the person relives the memory of the anesthesia by actually smelling it and tasting it. Sometimes the room is filled with the odor of the anesthesia that is being breathed out.

When suppressed anesthesia is coming up strongly, which feels rather like heavy intoxication, the best breathing is the fastest, fullest breathing possible, since anesthesia both is a very strong pattern of energy and makes it difficult to maintain awareness of the body. If the goal is to produce the maximum result as quickly as possible then the Rebirthee should keep breathing as fast and full as possible, no matter what, even if it means standing up or bathing in cold water to maintain consciousness.

When activation of suppressed anesthesia is the cause of unconsciousness during Rebirthing, it is almost never a good idea (in terms of producing efficient results) to let the Rebirthee fall asleep, although keeping the Rebirthee awake can require a great deal of gentle discipline on the part of the Rebirther.

LACK OF CONTACT WITH FEELINGS

Some people are so suppressive that they just don't feel. They experience themselves as minds floating through space, directing the body. The paradox is that these are probably the people who have the most to gain from being Rebirthed, and yet they are often the most difficult to Rebirth because the technique requires that most of the suppressed material be accessed kinesthetically, through feeling.

A simple test to find out if someone is like this is to ask, "When you are angry, how do you know that you are angry?" Most people will answer in terms of some kind of feeling in some part of their body, but some other people will give a five-minute speech about what kind of *thoughts* they call anger.

This type of very suppressive person will not usually get much result from dry Rebirthing, but will usually respond very well to warm water Rebirthing. We usually don't start people off with wet Rebirthing, but we do with these people.

SUSPENDED BREATH

Suspended breath is not really a form of unconsciousness in the same sense as the forms of unconsciousness that we have already discussed. Since suspended breath can easily be confused with unconsciousness, we are including an explanation of it here.

Suspended breath is really an integrative technique that is used in some cases by the unconscious mind. It is the result of a kind of negotiation process among various parts of the person. It occurs when some parts are too afraid to let something come up and other parts want it integrated. The solution? Remove the person out of the body, establish the right conditions for integration, return the person to the body and integrate it.

What this looks like from the outside is that the person is breathing along fine and then very suddenly stops breathing and goes very far out of consciousness. When people have suspended breath, they do not respond even to loud noises or vigorous shaking. When the person returns to the body, they usually experience a brief period of panic before relaxing enough to integrate. Sometimes the Rebirthee will not have any recall of what happened during the period of suspended breath and sometimes the Rebirthee reports intrauterine or past-lifetime memories or other interesting experiences that were recalled during this state.

The best thing to do about a suspended breath is nothing, except to assist the person in feeling safe and comfortable during the first few moments of re-entry.

It is not possible for the Rebirthee or the Rebirther to *cause* a suspended breath.

Occasionally a Rebirthee who wants to stop breathing in order to avoid something may try to fake a suspended breath. The Rebirthee can obviously do whatever the Rebirthee chooses, but faking suspended breath makes things proceed more slowly and with greater difficulty. The skillful Rebirther is *very* hard to fool.

ADVANCED TECHNIQUES FOR
DEALING WITH UNCONSCIOUSNESS

Sometimes quite a bit of firmness is necessary on the part of the Rebirther when the Rebirthee is experiencing a lot of unconsciousness. It is best to be firm and yet keep a sense of humor and gentleness about it.

When a Rebirthee is going through unconsciousness, it often helps for the Rebirther to have the person sit up and Rebirth. Often it works well for the Rebirther to tell the Rebirthee, in a firm yet humorous manner, what the Rebirther intends to do about it if the

Rebirthee doesn't keep the breathing connected while sitting up, like this: "If you don't keep your breathing going sitting up, then I'm going to have you stand up; if you don't keep your breathing going when you're standing up, I'm going to have you stand on one leg; if that doesn't work, I'm going to fill up the bathtub with cold water and put you in it. I bet *that* will keep your breathing going!" Although it is best to explain this procedure to the Rebirthee in a half-joking tone, it is also a good idea to actually *do* these things, if it is necessary. Half the value of this plan of action is that each of those steps does, in fact, make it easier for the person to stay in the body and keep breathing. The other half of the value is the threat, which greatly increases the Rebirthee's motivation. These measures are not really unpleasant for the Rebirthee, but they *sound* unpleasant to a person who is going through unconsciousness.

It is important to point out that it is impossible to *make* a person Rebirth. Another good technique for dealing with a recalcitrant Rebirthee who is going through unconsciousness is to get the person to stand up and look the Rebirther in the eye (temporarily suspending the Rebirthing) and for the Rebirther to ask the Rebirthee, "Do you want to sleep or do you want to Rebirth?" The Rebirther then supports the Rebirthee in doing whichever thing the Rebirthee chooses.

YOU ARE ALWAYS FEELING SOMETHING

In every moment there is one pattern of energy or another happening in the body. It is not necessary to wait for the breathing to bring something up; start applying the Third Element immediately when you start Rebirthing. Whenever a Rebirthee reports that, "There is nothing happening" during the Rebirthing session, that is self-delusion—there is *always* something happening. This kind of self-delusion often results in ignoring a pattern of energy until it gets very intense. This can be prevented if the Rebirthee will apply Awareness in Detail to the patterns of energy while they are still subtle.

Sometimes the oldest, most deeply held (and, therefore, most important) patterns of suppressed energy may be the most difficult to acknowledge, for the same reason that a fish may have a hard time acknowledging that it is in water, i.e., if water is all that you had ever known it may be hard to notice it. However, these patterns can be felt and Circular Breathing greatly helps with this.

EXERCISE TO HELP YOU GAIN MASTERY
OVER THE THIRD ELEMENT

This exercise will help you increase your contact with your body and increase your ability to shift your awareness from one part of your body to another. You can practice this exercise any time, anywhere. While waiting for the subway, when you're "on hold" on the telephone, just before you go to sleep at night, and just after you wake up in the morning are all excellent times to practice it. Do it repeatedly. Start off doing it slowly, then gradually increase the speed until you can do it very rapidly, yet very thoroughly.

Focus all your awareness on each of the following parts of your body, at the point of maximum sensation in each one, in the order given. We have selected the points carefully, but of course you can modify the process to suit yourself. Adding more points to the exercise, to make it more thorough, is an excellent idea, once you have mastered these.

Left big toe
Sole of your left foot
Left ankle
Left knee
Left hip
Right big toe
Sole of your right foot
Right ankle
Right knee
Right hip
Anus
Genitals
Navel
Solar Plexus (diagram)
Heart
Left shoulder
Left elbow
Palm of your left hand
Tip of your left index finger
Right shoulder
Right elbow
Right wrist
Palm of your right hand

Tip of your right index finger
Throat
Back of your head
"Third eye" point (between the eyebrows)
"Crown chakra" (center of the top of your head)

You will find that doing this exercise will help you relax and will build up the energy in your body, as well as making it easier for you to Rebirth yourself.

CHAPTER 11

Integration into Ecstasy— The Fourth Element of Rebirthing

The Fourth Element is the Element that is the most fun to talk about. It is said that, "The truth will set you free." This is true. There is nothing more imprisoning than lying—especially lying to yourself. If you are lying even a little bit then you will not be completely freed. To make the old axiom absolutely clear so that it will be of great practical value, we state it as "The whole truth will set you absolutely free immediately in every case." An important corollary is, "If you thought you told yourself the truth and it didn't make you free, then you know that you didn't tell the whole truth yet."

You will never be free as long as you are making something wrong; this point we discussed in detail in Part I of this book.

There are two main ways that the mind creates bondage for itself by not telling the truth: 1) by not acknowledging consciously that something exists (suppression), and 2) by denying that what exists is pleasurable and beneficial (make-wrong). Elements 1, 2, and 3 eliminate suppression and Element Four eliminates make-wrong. The elimination of make-wrong and suppression free the mind to do its job of creating happiness and power effectively. Integration is the truth that sets you free.

66

The Fourth Element is called Integration into Ecstasy because even though the Experiencer experiences everything ecstatically, the mind does not always do so; this element is about *causing* the mind to do so. The minds of most people celebrate a few things but generally make anything wrong that doesn't fit their preferences. The Ecstasy Principle says that people actually enjoy everything whether their minds say so or not, because existence itself is fundamentally enjoyable. Integration into Ecstasy means integrating everything into your conscious mind's acknowledgment that you are ecstatic.

Mechanically, what happens in the Fourth Element is that you switch anything that you have been holding in a negative context, which means a context in which it is made wrong, to a positive context, in which it will be celebrated. Anything you do that facilitates your *feeling good* about what you had made wrong will cause this change of context.

We have covered the theory behind the Fourth Element of Rebirthing thoroughly, in Chapters 4, 5 and 6. Integration into Ecstasy is not a theory, however, it is an Element of Rebirthing, so what really matters is its practical application. The rest of this chapter is about how to feel good about everything that exists.

There is no single way of applying the Fourth Element that is universally best. Different people will do it differently; the same person will do it differently at different times. We will therefore present several methods:

GO DIRECTLY FOR ENJOYING
WHATEVER IS COMING UP

The main thing to know about this method is that, while it is enjoyable to ride a bicycle and it is enjoyable to eat a cantaloupe, you do not enjoy these things in the same way. If you tried to enjoy riding a bicycle in the same way that you enjoy eating a cantaloupe, you would not get very much enjoyment. Similarly, if you try to enjoy a throbbing sensation in your toes the same way that you enjoy a spinach salad, it won't work.

There are infinitely many ways to enjoy absolutely anything; all you have to do is find one that is convenient.

We have already pointed out that at least two parts of you are already enjoying everything that you experience. All you have to do is become consciously aware of this enjoyment and the pattern of energy will integrate.

There will probably be some things that come up during Rebirthing that you will have a difficult time enjoying immediately. That is why we give you so many methods for applying the Fourth Element.

BE GRATEFUL

The way to use the Fourth Element that seems to work the best for the most people is gratitude. Everyone has an experience of being grateful for existing, for being here to experience anything. Most people have a boundary to their experience of gratitude, however, and only acknowledge being grateful for some things and not for others. The Fourth Element says: The present moment is all you have—be grateful for every detail of it!

If you focus on something and simultaneously bring yourself into the present moment and experience your gratitude for your existence, then that gratitude will spontaneously expand to include the thing you are focusing on.

Not everyone is willing to *acknowledge* that they are glad that they exist, however, so this method of application does not work for everyone all the time.

THE MOST NEGATIVE CONTEXT
THAT WORKS TO CAUSE INTEGRATION

The most negative context that causes integration is, "This is really awful but it's here in this moment whether I like it or not."

This is the context of "forced surrender" that we mentioned earlier. If you are ever Rebirthing while you're in a foul, cynical mood, you will find this application very handy.

ENJOY IT QUICK BEFORE IT INTEGRATES

If you ever find yourself wishing that something would "hurry up and integrate", just remind yourself that everything in your experience is passing away quickly enough and what you had better do is enjoy it while it is here.

AT LEAST IT'S SHOWING UP
AT AN APPROPRIATE TIME

Let's say you are experiencing massive fear during a Rebirthing. Aren't you glad it's coming up now instead of when you're talking to a tax auditor?

One of the major advantages of getting Rebirthed at regular and frequent intervals is that doing so provides a safe and appropriate time and place for you to experience and integrate your emotions. If you are a busy person, we can assure you that this can be the height of luxury! You can use that feeling of luxury to help you integrate.

BLISS OUT ON THE MIRACLE OF ITS EXISTENCE

It is just as miraculous that anything exists as it is that anything else exists. This is true both in the context of momentary time and in the context of linear time.

In momentary time, there is no cause and effect, so it is miraculous that anything exists at all.

In linear time, everything that is happening now is the result of an unbroken chain of cause and effect that goes back to the Big Bang, at least according to most modern scientists. When you play pool, whatever the balls do on the table is the result of how you stroke the stick into the cue ball; everything in the Universe is the way that it is now because of the exact way that the primordial fireball flew apart at the Big Bang. That this process occurred in a way that resulted in your existence and in the existence of whatever you are contemplating is infinitely miraculous!

This means you can bliss out on anything, which is exactly what we suggest you do.

EXERCISE ON MIRACULOUSNESS

This exercise will help you to perceive your world as miraculous. Do it as often as you conveniently can.

Select anything that is part of your experience. At first a physical object of some kind will work the best, but when you have facility with the exercise, you can easilyapply it to any sound, physical sensation, thought, etc.

Contemplate the object. Now think about everything that had to happen to make this object be here, in this moment, exactly the way it is. Keep tracing back through these events, until you get to the Big Bang, or any other moment of creation.

Now contemplate the events that led to the creation of your own physical body, tracing these events back to the Big Bang (or whatever) also. When you get to the Big Bang this time, go forward toward the future and trace the paths of creation of both you and the object to the present moment. Consider everything that had to happen in order for you and this object to both come into existence, and then to come together, with you contemplating the object exactly as you are now doing. Consider the transitoriness of your relationship with this object, the specialness of this moment.

Notice your feelings as you do this process. When you have a sense of the miraculousness of your experience, select another object and do the same thing with it. Keep doing this forever. When you have the ability to do this with absolutely anything that ever comes into your awareness, so that you have the sense that everything is a miraculous gift from the Universe and that you love everything unconditionally, then you are well on your way to complete mastery of the Fourth Element and complete mastery of Rebirthing.

COMPARE IT ONLY TO ITSELF

This statement does not make logical sense, but it works. If you compare a paper cup to a fine crystal champagne glass, the paper cup will seem like a piece of trash; if you compare the paper cup to itself, it will appear to be what it is, a perfectly good way to convey water to your lips. Similarly, if you are having tetany in your hands and you compare that to what your hands usually feel like, the tetany will seem hurtful; if you compare the tetany only to itself, it will seem like what it is, a perfectly enjoyable feeling of energy in the hands.

Pain is a context. The content of the experience is just intense energy. Calling intense energy "pain" only means that you are making it wrong. No matter what is happening in your physical body, if you surrender to it and compare it only to itself, you will experience intense pleasure instead of intense pain.

ACKNOWLEDGE THAT YOU ARE RECEIVING
BENEFIT FROM HAVING IT COME UP

You are much better off being aware of what is happening in your mind and body than being unaware. Acknowledge that it's good for you to be experiencing it and be grateful for that.

NOTICE THAT THE PATTERN OF ENERGY
IS AT LEAST INTERESTING

Allow yourself to be very curious about the pattern of energy and fascinated by it. Amazement is often a positive enough context to cause integration.

GIVE ALL PARTS OF YOURSELF UNCONDITIONAL LOVE

If you love a child unconditionally, it means you love that child, whether or not the child does what you want. Give this kind of love to yourself, including the parts of you that has been engaging in make-wrong, or that have been feeling strange or painful.

EXTEND UNCONDITIONAL LOVE TO ALL PARTS OF YOUR EXPERIENCE

Dedicate yourself to loving every moment of your life, 100%, no matter what. If you love everything that exists, merely because it exists, then you will integrate everything.

BE VERY ENTHUSIASTIC ABOUT EVERYTHING

If you are afraid, allow yourself to explore the fear and relax into it; if you are sad, get enthusiastically sad; etc.

NOTICE THAT WHAT YOU ARE EXPERIENCING IS FUNNY

Humor is the result of integrating a paradox. Any time a joke is funny, it's because the joke presents two contradicting lines of thought as both being true simultaneously. Since everything that exists is paradoxical, everything that exists is funny, if you think about it that way.

Laughter is the expression of the pattern of energy that happens in your body when you integrate a paradox. When laughter occurs during a Rebirthing, it is one of the surest signs that something has been integrated.

If you find any way to hold what you are experiencing in a context where it's funny, you will integrate it.

A FOURTH ELEMENT GAME

Here is a game that will help you understand the Fourth Element. It's called:

Creating Your Own Reality

Rules: 1. Create things that already exist.

2. Put things where they already are.
3. Be flamboyant, mystical, and pompous about it.

Thus:

"I *command* the Universe to put a book about Rebirthing into my hands, *NOW*!"

"Let there be *light* to shine on this book!"

"I command the earth to bring forth *trees!* And let them be grouped together in *forests* and also scattered about singly and in small groups in people's *yards*!"

Play this game when you are getting Rebirthed; thus:

"Let there be tingling in my hands!"

"I *command* that there shall be a craving for *hamburgers* in my *mouth* and *throat* and *stomach*."

"Let there be *doubt*!"

And so on.

In other words, pretend that you are intentionally creating your experience the way it is because you like it that way. Acknowledge yourself—You have created a perfect universe!

AN ADDITIONAL NOTE ON REBIRTHING INTEGRATION

Integrating a pattern of energy does not necessarily make the pattern of energy go away. Some patterns of energy go away when they integrate and some do not. Here's an example of one that does not go away: Often a person who has had a fair amount of experience with Rebirthing will notice for the first time exactly what it feels like to have air passages going through the head. The passageways are rather complex and most people do not feel them very much. When people first notice the feelings associated with air passing through the sinuses and other passages, they often report that it feels "cold, dry, weird and unpleasant". When this pattern of energy integrates, it does not go away, it becomes a source of pleasure that one feels from then on. An example of a pattern of energy that does go away when it integrates is tension. When tension integrates it relaxes, or goes away, much like one's lap goes away when one stands up. Even with tension, however, the way to integrate anything is to love it unconditionally the way it is. Trying to make something go away is exactly how to prevent integration.

CHAPTER 12

Do Whatever You Do, Because Everything Works—The Fifth Element of Rebirthing

[*A personal note from Jim Leonard:*

The Fifth Element looks almost like it doesn't say anything, but it is actually the most important of the Five Elements.

At first, I tried to use just the first Four Elements of Rebirthing, but it didn't work. People lay there *trying* to integrate things, instead of actually integrating them. When I invented the Fifth Element, people started integrating immediately, as I reasoned they would. The purpose of the Fifth Element is to integrate trying to integrate. It eliminates "should" from the other four Elements. The Fifth Element is meant to be taken literally.]

With most things you do in life, increasing your capacity to do it right will give you more of the result you are seeking. With Rebirthing, it doesn't work that way. It is impossible to do Rebirthing wrong. If you try your hardest to do Rebirthing wrong, that just means that "trying to do it wrong" is becoming activated in your Rebirthing. If you try to do it wrong enthusiastically enough, it will integrate and you'll move on to the next thing.

One of the hardest ways to cause integration is to try to integrate something in order to make it go away. Instead, surrender to the fact that it isn't integrated.

People usually think of verbs as "action words" and this can lead to confusion about what it means to integrate. The verb "to integrate" sounds like you are doing something, but actually you are ceasing to do something—you are ceasing to make something wrong. Similarly, the verb "to relax" sounds like doing something; you don't *do* something to relax, you *cease* to contract your muscles.

When you integrate something, you cease to make it wrong, cease to hide from it. You relax into acknowledging that it always was perfect, even when you insisted that it wasn't.

If Rebirthing had to be done perfectly in order to work, it never could have been invented. There is no blueprint, picture or diagram of a perfect Rebirthing session. The point is: no one can apply the first Four Elements perfectly; we are grateful for the fact that it is not necessary to do it perfectly in order to get the results of Rebirthing abundantly. The results are perfect no matter what anyone did to cause them.

Integration is much easier than suppression. Your mind and body have to work very hard to keep something suppressed and if you just set up approximately the right circumstances for integration, you will integrate.

The first Four Elements are models, anyway, and reality does not perfectly fit the models. Even if you *were* able to rigidly apply the first Four Elements perfectly, not everything would integrate that way. Some things will integrate when you are holding your breath; some things will integrate when you are moving around; some things will integrate when you are out of your body; and some things will integrate when you are making something wrong. Although perhaps only 1% of all patterns of energy will integrate outside the ordinary limits of the first Four Elements, if you were too rigid, you would get stuck when you came across that 1%.

Another corollary of the Fifth Element is that, since you don't have to do it right, it is safe to experiment. For instance, if you're in a situation where this book says you should breathe slow and full, but your intuitive sense tells you that you should breathe fast and full, then go ahead and do so.

Since you are in a state of Ecstasy before doing anything, while

doing it, and after doing it, how could you do anything wrong?
Even trying to do it right works!

Developing mastery of the Five Elements of Rebirthing is easier than learning almost anything else in life. Rebirthing is so natural for people that it is actually easier to *do* it than it is to *not* do it. Rebirthing is easy, yet it is also one of the most rewarding activities a person could ever engage in—now *that's* a good deal!

THE YOUNGEST REBIRTHEE

[*A personal note from Phil Laut:*

In several places in this book we have stated that Rebirthing is a natural, organic process that anyone can do. The process is so natural that it is not necessary to do it perfectly to get the results. One way to make Rebirthing harder, in fact, is to try to do it right.

In 1980 I Rebirthed an infant who was thirty minutes old at the time. I had attended the birth of the grandson of a friend in San Francisco. It was the first time I had attended the birth of another person. Birth is a miraculous event, and witnessing a birth is a delightfully intense experience that I suggest for everyone.

After the newborn had emerged from the birth canal, and had learned atmospheric breathing lying on his mother's stomach with the umbilical cord still attached, I filled the bathtub with warm water and invited the father to sit down in the tub so we could bathe the newborn. The mother agreed to this plan and after the umbilical cord was cut, I placed the newborn on the father's lap in the warm water. As you can imagine, I did not have the opportunity to explain any of the information contained in this book about Rebirthing to the newborn. As soon as I got his attention, I connected my breath and continued to meet his gaze. The newborn imitated my breath pattern for approximately thirty minutes without my saying a word. We just looked at each other and breathed together. The newborn experienced a mild amount of observable tightness in his hands and arms, but kept right on breathing until his body was completely relaxed and he was grinning broadly.]

CHAPTER 13

Affirmations About The Five Elements of Rebirthing

In this chapter, for the first time in this book, we are giving you affirmations to work with. We know that many of our readers are already at least somewhat familiar with affirmations, and that many of them are not. An affirmation is basically a good thought to hold in your mind. In Chapter 28 of this book we give you detailed instructions for using affirmations effectively. If you wish, you can read that chapter now and then come back to this page.

The following affirmations are ones that we have found especially helpful in developing facility with the Five Elements:

FIRST ELEMENT:

My Circular Breathing is easy, self-regulating, pleasurable and continuous now and forever.

SECOND ELEMENT:

All parts of me know that it is always safe to relax and I am relaxing completely now.

THIRD ELEMENT:

Everything that exists is bliss and I am experiencing my infinite varieties of bliss in full detail now.

FOURTH ELEMENT:

It is easy and normal for me to enjoy everything now.

FIFTH ELEMENT:

Anything I could possibly do leads inevitably to integration.

CHAPTER 14

Completion

There are two kinds of completion to discuss: completion for a particular Rebirthing session and completion for the entire process.

COMPLETION FOR THE SESSION

Our definition of the completion of a session is: the point during a session when all of the following three criteria have been met:
1) A satisfactory amount of suppressed material came to the surface and got processed;
2) Everything that got activated also got integrated, i.e., the Rebirthee is feeling completely wonderful;
3) Both the Rebirther and the Rebirthee acknowledge that the first two criteria have been satisfied;

There are some professional Rebirthers who end sessions based solely on the amount of time elapsed. We are sure that these people have good intentions (such as a desire to make Rebirthing available to as many people as possible each day) and we don't want to make them wrong, but we do not support doing it that way. Ending Rebirthing sessions according to a clock is called the "boiling an egg" approach. Although Rebirthing is a fairly precise science, its point of completion is just not as predictable as that.

You may experience a little bit of residual tingling or even a bit of disorientation at the end of a complete session (these things pass quickly) but you should not be left with any heavy, incomplete emotions or any especially unusual physical sensations.

It sometimes happens that a thoroughly complete Rebirthing session leaves a person in a state of unusual sensitivity. This can be exquisite—the sounds of the birds, the color and fragrance of flowers, all the delights of being alive can be more vividly experienced than ever before. It may also leave you somewhat more vulnerable to emotional activation than usual. For this reason, it is usually nice (but not necessary) to be able to relax in a reasonably serene environment immediately following a Rebirthing session, especially following your first few sessions.

COMPLETION FOR THE PROCESS

Most people have a *lot* of suppressed negativity and it would be unreasonable to expect even the most powerful techniques to clear that up overnight. It is a process extending over many years, even for the best of us. The foregoing is the "bad news". There are two important items of good news: first, every time you integrate anything you will feel better and often *much* better; second, every time you integrate anything the next integration will be easier. You will reach a point where integration happens habitually and spontaneously. In time, you will welcome every hint that you might have more stuff to clear up because it will mean that however good your life already is, it is about to get even better.

We do not know what the end result of Rebirthing might be. The ultimate completion, if there is such a thing, is beyond any ordinary person's wildest dreams; that seems certain.

CHAPTER 15

Warm and Cold Water Rebirthing

Once a person has been Rebirthed enough times to have developed the ability to integrate anything that comes up in an easy, comfortable and efficient way, we recommend several sessions of warm water Rebirthing. When warm water Rebirthing becomes consistently comfortable, we recommend one or more sessions of cold water Rebirthing.

WARM WATER REBIRTHING

When Rebirthing was first invented, it was always done in warm water. At first they even thought that the warm water itself was what caused the results.

Nowadays, we know of no Rebirther who consistently starts clients off with warm water Rebirthing. Gentleness is always a prime consideration in Rebirthing, especially in the first few sessions. Starting someone off in warm water would not generally be gentle enough, but once a person gets used to experiencing unusual patterns of energy, warm water Rebirthing can be very gentle indeed. We do start people off in warm water if they have very little contact with their bodies and their feelings, however.

The reason warm water is used is that it speeds up the activation of suppressed material. During a breathing cycle, material always comes up initially at a subtle level of manifestation, and then, if it is not immediately integrated, it gradually becomes less and less subtle; more and more intense. Warm water accelerates that process. If a person is skillful at integrating, this is advantageous because even more can be accomplished in the same amount of time. If a person is not so skillful at integrating, then warm water Rebirthing is likely to be rather miserable, which has no advantage.

There are other advantages to warm water Rebirthing as well. Because it is warm and wet and the Rebirthee is floating, suspended by the Rebirther, it simulates, somewhat, the womb. Thus, womb and birth memory tend to be especially well re-activated.

Warm water Rebirthing is conducted in a hot tub, large bathtub, or natural hot spring, where the water temperature can be maintained at 98°-102°F (36°C-39°C) and there is enough room for the Rebirthee to stretch out and for the Rebirther to sit or stand comfortably in the water.

There are three basic positions that are good for warm water Rebirthing. These differ in the degree of activation produced. In order from the most activating to the least activating, these are: 1) Floating face-down, breathing through a snorkel; 2) Floating on the back, face out of the water; 3) Sitting on a bench in the warm water.

The Rebirther is present to provide physical support for the body of the Rebirthee and to provide moral support as the Rebirthee relaxes into suppressed feelings, memories and body sensations that come up to the level of conscious awareness.

Although almost everybody experiences greater activation when Rebirthing in warm water, there are exceptions. We have Rebirthed people who are actually less activated by warm water Rebirthing than by dry Rebirthing. Also, occasionally, it may be more activating to float on the back than face-down, because the face-up floating position activates some particular patterns especially well.

Many people who have a great deal of experience at Rebirthing themselves have a consistent preference for warm water Rebirthing.

COLD WATER REBIRTHING

For most people, cold water Rebirthing is even more activating than warm water Rebirthing.

One explanation for this is that while warm water Rebirthing tends to activate memories of birth, cold water Rebirthing tends to activate thoughts and feelings (memories?) of death.

Cold water Rebirthing is an appropriate step after the Rebirthee has gained confidence with warm water Rebirthing. The key to success with cold water Rebirthing is gentleness. The gentle and pleasurable way to do it is to fill a bathtub with water as cold as is comfortable for you. At first you may find it necessary to include a substantial portion of hot water in order to get a comfortable temperature. Once the tub is full, stand outside it and connect your breathing in a comfortable, relaxed rhythm. Very gradually immerse your body in the water. You may find that you need to go an inch or so at a time in order to allow yourself to integrate the fear that the cold water brings up. You can tell whether you are proceeding slowly enough by whether your body feels cold or begins to shiver. When you go slowly enough, the only part of your body that feels cold is the part that has been wetted by the water but that is not immersed. If any part of your body that is immersed, or any part that is dry feels uncomfortable, then you know that you have gone too fast. If this happens, the best procedure is to get out of the water, dry off, and start over.

Cold water Rebirthing, once you master it, is an incredibly invigorating experience. The body automatically produces additional energy to keep you comfortable in the cold water and the increased energy lasts for a substantial period after you get out of the water.

CHAPTER 16

Self-Rebirthing

Really Rebirthing is a self-help technique and you are actually Rebirthing yourself even when a Rebirther is assisting you. ,We use the term "self-Rebirthing" to mean Rebirthing yourself without the assistance of a Rebirther.

An excellent goal for everyone beginning the Rebirthing process is to develop enough facility with the process to produce the results well on their own.

At some point in their Rebirthing process, virtually everyone becomes able to do this. Memories of birth and other material may continue to come to the surface during Rebirthing sessions for years, whether Rebirthing with a trained professional Rebirther or not. The certainty that the Rebirthee possesses about his or her ability to use the Five Elements of Rebirthing eases and facilitates the integration of any remaining suppressed material.

In our combined decade of experience, neither of us has ever heard of anyone who could do self-Rebirthing well without first starting off with an experienced Rebirther. Sometimes people have spontaneous Rebirth experiences without even knowing what they are doing, but they, too, cannot generally recreate that experience consistently. When Leonard Orr first invented Rebirthing, it is true that he used himself as a guinea pig, and over many months of experimentation he did achieve some success. However, he reports that it wasn't until he had trained some other people to be Rebirthers that he was finally able to get a decent Rebirthing, himself.

We also recommend that every Rebirther have the goal of training every client well enough that the client achieves the ability to do consistently successful self-Rebirthing.

WHY PEOPLE HAVE DIFFICULTY WITH SELF-REBIRTHING—AND WHAT TO DO ABOUT IT

We have noticed five main reasons that people have difficulty with self-Rebirthing. These are: 1) Not knowing enough about the technique; 2) Not creating time to do it; 3) Inability to change contexts; 4) Self-deception regarding completion; 5) Inability to cope with loneliness. We shall discuss these problems and their solutions, in detail. Before doing that, however, we wish to remind you that all such difficulties are the result of making something wrong and a remedy for all of them is getting Rebirthed sufficiently by a competent Rebirther.

NOT KNOWING ENOUGH ABOUT THE TECHNIQUE

There is considerably more to know about Rebirthing than can possibly be conveyed to or received by the rational mind. Any Rebirther who has had an active private practice for, say, at least a year, has seen things come up in people's Rebirthings that neither you nor we can even imagine. One of the first things a new Rebirther notices is that each person is completely unique to Rebirth. Rebirthers learn to respond intuitively to situations, and we suspect that all Rebirthers are frequently amazed at their own uncanny ability to do the right thing at the right time without their conscious minds figuring anything out. Rebirthers develop this talent through years of training, by Rebirthing other people, and by developing greater contact with their own unconscious minds through Rebirthing themselves. When you have Rebirthed yourself several times in the presence of a professional Rebirther, you will get to know yourself well enough to be able to deal with yourself effectively in most self-Rebirthing situations. Probably the best thing you could do to gain enough knowledge of the technique to Rebirth yourself consistently on your own would be to become trained to be a Rebirther yourself.

NOT CREATING ENOUGH TIME TO DO IT

We have met many people who would be perfectly capable of being effective self-Rebirthers, were it not for the fact that they only think about Rebirthing themselves when an emotional upset arises. This is perfectly human. The difficulty with this approach is that Rebirthing is at its best when the integration can take place while the emotions are still at a very subtle level of manifestation. Especially when you are first starting to Rebirth yourself, after having several sessions with a Rebirther, we recommend scheduling in self-Rebirthings on a regular basis. In many cases it is very helpful to schedule one-hour sessions of self-Rebirthing daily or almost daily, and a more extensive Rebirthing, by yourself or with your Rebirther, once a week. Build this into your regular schedule. If you are really serious about integrating your suppressed make-wrongs, then we suggest that you never go more than three weeks without an extensive session. We have found that going longer than three weeks gets almost everyone "out of practice" with integrating and makes the process more difficult.

If you are doing daily hour-long sessions, a good way to do it is to buy a timer with an alarm that you can set for one hour and then make sure that you keep Rebirthing for the entire hour, at least.

Even if you become very competent at self-Rebirthing, get an assisted session periodically, at least quarterly.

If you are good at Rebirthing yourself then you are probably good at Rebirthing others also. If you can find a Rebirthing "buddy" who is similarly skilled, then you can derive great benefit from trading Rebirthings often.

INABILITY TO CHANGE CONTEXTS

A good thing about having a Rebirther is that your Rebirther is probably not activated by the same make-wrongs that you are at the same time. This means that your Rebirther probably has positive contexts available for whatever you are making wrong during your Rebirthing.

You will learn to hold everything in a positive context. This is an ongoing process. Every time you Rebirth it will get easier.

If you are Rebirthing by yourself and something that comes up seems just plain bad, we suggest that you pause a moment to review the techniques of integration in our chapter about the Fourth Element of Rebirthing. Then do whatever you do and it will work.

Affirmations to assist you with this are:

1. I celebrate everything.

2. I have the practical wisdom to integrate anything into my experience of the pleasure of being alive.

3. My gratitude for being alive is so great that it includes everything.

4. I have the practical wisdom to change my way of thinking whenever it is to my advantage to do so.

SELF-DECEPTION REGARDING COMPLETION

Since Rebirthing eliminates, bit by bit, the tendency to suppress, it also eliminates the tendency toward self-deception; self-deception is fundamental to make-wrong and suppression. During self-Rebirthing it is easy to decide, upon activation of a pattern of energy, to quit Rebirthing and do something else. "Oh, I'm complete enough, time to go eat a piece of that chocolate cake in the fridge." Needless to say, this is not helpful.

Every suppressed pattern of make-wrong energy has with it a ritualistic means of suppression. Activation of the pattern of energy will often arouse the desire for the suppression. Integration of that pattern of energy requires using enough discipline to continue Rebirthing instead of indulging the desire.

One paradox of Rebirthing is that you are complete when you feel like you could pleasurably go on doing it forever. If you feel like you would like to be complete, then you are not.

AFFIRMATIONS:

1. I always continue Rebirthing until everything feels perfect.

2. I would always rather integrate than suppress.

INABILITY TO COPE WITH LONELINESS

Loneliness is human. In the womb we have no sense of being alone. At birth we become alone for the first time. Almost everyone makes this aloneness wrong at birth. Aloneness that is made wrong is loneliness.

When you have a caring human being present during your Rebirthing it makes it much easier to re-experience this primal loneliness in a safe and integrative way; when you self-Rebirth it is likely that you will experience unbearable loneliness at least once and probably you will experience it many times as layer after layer of it arises. You will have to cope with it and integrate it.

Like almost everything else in life, this is a good-news/bad-news joke. The bad news is you will have to experience your loneliness, by yourself. The good news is that when you integrate this loneliness you will become more powerful than you ever imagined possible. You will become a leader.

Some affirmations that will help you with this transition are:

1. I love everything about my loneliness.
2. I love everything about my humanness.
3. I am enough.
4. Rebirthing by myself is always one of my favorite pleasures.

CHAPTER 17

Rebirthing and Health

While it is true that Rebirthing works starting from any condition of mind or body (within reason), it is also true that it is easier to Rebirth efficiently if you are in a good state of overall physical health. The reason for this is simple: if you are ill, your illness will provide the main patterns of energy in your body and you will spend your Rebirthing time mainly focusing on these. This can be excellent for easing the discomfort and speeding the healing of the illness, but it reduces the extent to which you will be able to get into the subtler patterns of energy. We strongly recommend doing everything practicable to maintain yourself in a state of excellent health, particularly if you wish to be highly successful at self-Rebirthing. Additionally, Rebirthing tends to enhance the benefits and pleasures of other holistic health practices, such as yoga, tai-chi, Rolfing, fasting, good diet, etc. It makes a good massage a lot better. If you're ever receiving acupuncture, try applying the Five Elements of Rebirthing while the needles are in! We have observed that the beneficial effects that Rebirthing has on the breathing mechanism tend to increase physical endurance while running, hiking, cycling, etc.

CHAPTER 18

Ambulatory Rebirthing

Ambulatory Rebirthing means Rebirthing while you are engaging in any other activity: driving your car, talking on the phone to your parents, selling something to someone, etc.

There are some things that will tend to be activated while you are engaging in your regular activities rather than while you are lying down Rebirthing in the presence of your Rebirther. You can Rebirth while engaging in any activity, provided you are good enough at the technique.

When you have had enough experience with Rebirthing to know that you can integrate absolutely anything that ever comes up, you will welcome all your emotions. Every emotion gives you access to something that you have made wrong and suppressed. This means that however good your life has become, you can make it even better now that you are experiencing this emotion!

We will explain each of the Five Elements as it applies to ambulatory Rebirthing:

First Element: Usually slow-full circular breathing is best. You can do this kind of breathing in the presence of almost anyone without them noticing consciously that you are doing anything. It is also the kind of breathing that usually best facilitates coming into your patterns of energy. If you are by yourself and you are feeling very activated, you can use fast and shallow circular breathing. If you are by yourself and you are tending to go unconscious, you can use full-fast circular breathing—this is very useful when you need more energy than you feel you have.

Second Element: Relax every muscle that you are not using for what you are dong.

Third Element: This is of key importance to effective ambulatory Rebirthing: bring yourself completely into present time, as though this is the only moment that exists. Often during periods of heightened activation you will experience a strong desire to do whatever you usually do to suppress the emotion that is coming up. Enjoy that desire for itself!

Fourth Element: Just notice that you are glad that you exist and that whatever you are experiencing is completely miraculous. Know that everything is evolving as it should.

Fifth Element: Stay on purpose. You can integrate a pattern of energy even while you are engaging in whatever you usually do to suppress it, if you do it all very consciously. This is tricky, however, because it is so easy to just go "unconscious" on it and suppress it completely.

Ambulatory Rebirthing is one of the great pleasures of life and should be a major goal of every human being.

CHAPTER 19

Your Relationship with Your Professional Rebirther

Your Rebirther has two main purposes: to facilitate and to educate. By "facilitate" we mean helping you to integrate your suppressed material as pleasurably and efficiently as possible, during each Rebirthing session. By "educate" we mean teaching you how to Rebirth yourself and how to use other, related self-improvement techniques effectively.

Remember that Rebirthing is a self-help technique and the Rebirther doesn't produce the results, *you* do.

WHAT A REBIRTHER IS

A Rebirther is simply someone who has expertise at helping people Rebirth. The main thing all Rebirthers have in common is that they have all been Rebirthed, themselves. Anybody who is effective at facilitating the technique is a Rebirther.

Rebirthers are not licensed by the state, and are not necessarily college-educated. There is no need for anything like that. There is absolutely no way to harm someone using Rebirthing and absolutely no one ever has been harmed by it. People who aren't certain of their ability to facilitate the technique skillfully are extremely unlikely to try Rebirthing people professionally for a simple reason: The Rebirther gets suppressed material activated during a Rebirthing session, too. If the Rebirther can integrate his or her own activation pleasurably and effectively during a session, then that is enough expertise to be skillful at helping someone else Rebirth. If the Rebirther cannot integrate his or her own activation pleasurably and effectively during a Rebirthing session, then that so-called Rebirther is going to have a very agonizing experience, a phenomenon known as "burn-out." The power of the process itself discourages unqualified people from attempting it and eliminates them swiftly if they do.

Almost all professional Rebirthers have taken thorough training in facilitating the process, and have been Rebirthed extensively themselves.

Because the personal relationship between the Rebirther and the Rebirthee is one of unique intimacy, and because the sanctity and integrity of that relationship is so essential to successful Rebirthing, professional Rebirthers do not engage in sexuality with their clients.

For similar reasons, Rebirthers maintain professional confidentiality with regard to anything that their clients tell them or experience during their Rebirthing sessions. Rebirthers may discuss interesting cases among one another, but when they do so they are careful not to reveal their clients' identities.

Almost all professional Rebirthers are self-employed businesspeople. There are some ministers, some physicians, and some licensed therapists who do it. Some holistic health centers employ Rebirthers on their staffs.

HOW TO CHOOSE YOUR REBIRTHER

The first step is to find out who is doing Rebirthing in your area. In the back of this book is a listing of Rebirthers whom we know to be excellent. Other than this you will have to look for their advertising or figure out some other way to find them. You are usually most likely to find Rebirthers in or near big cities.

Some Rebirthers will be better for some clients, other Rebirthers will be better for other clients. This is largely a matter of rapport. Your main criteria for choosing your Rebirther should be that you feel comfortable with the person and you feel confidence in the person's ability to facilitate the process for you. You will have to talk with the person on the phone or in person to determine this.

We definitely recommend that you not choose your Rebirther on the basis of price. Some Rebirthers charge as much as twice the fee of some other Rebirthers, and may well be worth twice as much to you. Rebirthing with even the most costly Rebirthers in the world is not really very expensive when you consider the value Rebirthing can have for you. Similarly, do not assume that paying a higher fee will get you a better Rebirther. Get Rebirthed by the Rebirther you most want to work with and pay as much or as little as that person charges. If you feel you simply cannot afford your preferred Rebirther's regular rate, you can probably negotiate either a barter, a reduced fee, or make some other arrangement with that person. Most Rebirthers are motivated primarily by service, rather than money, and have become skillful, over the course of their practice, at making sure that both Rebirther and Rebirthee are satisfied with whatever deal they arrange. You may want to pay your Rebirther more than he or she asks; it is never considered a faux pas to do so.

Some areas have Rebirthing organizations which have various qualifications for membership and/or qualifications for various levels of membership within the organizations. In these areas there are also excellent Rebirthers who choose to operate independently of these organizations. Keep in mind that you are looking for the Rebirther who will be best for *you* and the person's standing within any of these organizations may or may not have any bearing on that.

USEFUL QUESTIONS IN CHOOSING A REBIRTHER

In your initial conversations with your prospective Rebirthers, here are some questions that we recommend asking:

1) Tell me about your approach to Rebirthing.
2) How long have you been doing it?
3) What training have you had?
4) What are your thoughts about Immortalist Philosophy?*
5) How do you decide when a session ends?

You will learn a great deal about the Rebirthers from how they answer these questions and you will also be able to begin establish-

---

*The authors' thoughts about Immortalist Philosophy are in Part V of this book.

ing the needed rapport with the person who will ultimately Rebirth you.

It should be noted here that "Rebirthing" is not a registered trademark and there are a few people who are doing things completely unrelated to the technique we describe in this book and yet call what they do "Rebirthing." Some of these people may be doing something worthwhile; others may be dangerous charlatans. You will have no trouble distinguishing these types from "real" Rebirthers when they answer the above questions.

In addition to asking the above questions you may want to ask for references, i.e., the names and phone numbers of two or three recent clients who would be willing to talk briefly about their experiences. If you have something particular you want to work on in your sessions, you can ask "What has been your experience of Rebirthing people who _____?" You might want to make a point of *not* asking how much each person charges until *after* you have made up your mind about whom you want to Rebirth you. That way you can make sure that money will not be prejudicial to your decision.

Telephone conversations are probably the most efficient way for you to do your "comparison shopping." Some Rebirthers offer free or inexpensive "Introduction to Rebirthing Seminars," which have one or more Rebirthers talking about Rebirthing to one or more prospective clients. If you want to meet a prospective Rebirther in person alone, we suggest taking the Rebirther out to lunch or dinner as a good way to do this.

WHAT REBIRTHING SESSIONS MIGHT BE LIKE FOR YOU

In general, we recommend that you get at least ten sessions from the same Rebirther. This does not necessarily have to be the person you started with, if you have some good reason to switch. But do get ten sessions from one person.

The reason for ten sessions is that it is enough for you to get a good idea of what the process is and how it applies to various types of suppressed material. The reason for doing them with one person is that that person will get to know you well and will, for that reason, be much better at facilitating and educating you.

Your goal should be to become competent at producing the result on your own. If you have not yet developed that ability at the end of ten sessions, get more. Some people learn to do it faster and some learn to do it slower.

Your experience of Rebirthing will be unique to you. No two people Rebirth alike. In addition, no two of your sessions will be alike because once something integrates it doesn't come back and each pattern of energy feels quite different to Rebirth into.

Almost everyone integrates a lot of material in the first session and then integrates more and more material faster and faster as the sessions progress.

In your first session you will be getting acquainted with your Rebirther, with the technique and with parts of yourself that you've been avoiding. You will be surprised at the power of the breathing.

The first five sessions (approximately) may include some restimulation of suppressed anesthesia, some tetany, some dramatic reactivation of old emotions and/or memories, and all kinds of other strange and wonderful experiences. Most Rebirthers give their clients affirmations with each session and you will be getting started on these. As layer after layer of suppression disappears, you will begin to get a feeling of the vastness of yourself, and to view this vastness with reverence and humility.

The second five sessions (approximately) will most likely be more subtle and more powerful as you gain facility with the process. Your Rebirther may recommend some hot-tub sessions. You may begin experimenting with self-Rebirthing. Perhaps you will get some birth or womb memory. You will enjoy these sessions more and you will notice more profound effects in your life.

CHAPTER 20

Group Rebirthing

Rebirthing is often done in groups, with several people all Rebirthing at the same time. Some Rebirthers will only allow someone to participate in a group Rebirthing if the person has been Rebirthed before. Others are willing to let people start off in groups. There are actually advantages to each approach.

The advantages of starting off with private sessions are that you get the Rebirther's undivided attention and you have complete privacy. Quite possibly you will get a more thorough Rebirthing this way.

The advantage of starting off in a group is that you will get to experience immediately the enormous variety of things that come up and integrate during the Rebirthing process. It is natural for anybody to conclude after their first Rebirthing experience that they know what Rebirthing is like. Since the second Rebirthing will be quite different from the first Rebirthing, expectations that it will be like the first session could conceivably get in the way somewhat. When a whole roomful of people are all going through different kinds of things during Rebirthing, a person is less apt to make premature conclusions about the nature of the process. Additionally, there is a wonderful synergy that is created in a group Rebirthing that actually assists with both the activation and the integration of everyone's material. Group Rebirthing is also usually less expensive.

Follow your Rebirther's advice regarding group Rebirthing. We strongly recommend getting ten private sessions even if you do some group Rebirthing also.

There are two main formats for doing group Rebirthing: one is where everybody lies down and Rebirths at the same time, the other is to have everybody pair up with a partner and take turns Rebirthing each other. We have done it both ways and both ways work. The advantage of having people pair up is that each person gets more assistance while going through the process. Also, while assisting your partner in Rebirthing, you get some practical experience of what it is like to be a Rebirther. Doing group Rebirthing in pairs, however, inevitably takes about twice as much time. When you are considering participating in a group Rebirthing, always find out which format is to be used and how much time each person will have for his or her own process. Make sure it *feels* right to you before doing it.

CHAPTER 21

Buddy-System Rebirthing

Autonomy is the essence of Rebirthing, ultimately. Rebirthing is definitely not about becoming dependent on a professional Rebirther. However, assisted Rebirthing sessions continue to be highly useful to people long after they develop the ability to Rebirth themselves effectively, for the same reasons that the support of our fellow humans is so important to all of us in every area of our lives. One of the most practical ways for relatively advanced Rebirthing students to get assisted Rebirthings on a regular basis is to trade Rebirthings with another Rebirthing student. This has the obvious benefits of saving money and increasing one's confidence in the process. During self-Rebirthing one functions both as Rebirther and Rebirthee, so any experience that one can get Rebirthing others will increase one's ability to Rebirth oneself. Trading Rebirthings with a friend or spouse is known as "buddy-system Rebirthing," and the person with whom one trades Rebirthings is known as one's "Rebirthing buddy." As you can probably imagine, buddy-system Rebirthing presents not only its own unique benefits but its own unique potential problems, as well.

Almost all professional Rebirthers start off trading Rebirthings extensively before they "go professional," and continue trading Rebirthings with colleagues, spouses and, sometimes, students throughout their professional careers. The authors of this book are certainly not exceptions.

It is common for professional Rebirthers to report that the

people they have the hardest time Rebirthing effectively are their own boyfriends and girlfriends, husbands and wives. The authors of this book have been intrigued by this phenomenon and have done considerable research into its origin.

What we have found is that the major cause of difficulty in trading Rebirthings with one's mate (or anyone) is the control patterns that develop in relationships. People develop subtle and not-so-subtle ways of controlling each other in all their relationships. To freedom-loving people this can appear, at first sight, to be a bad thing, and initially many people find this concept abhorrent and deny that they do it. It *isn't* a bad thing at all, however. People simply want to get what they want in life, and this includes their relationships. Like everyone else, you would rather have your friends and lovers be nice to you than have them kill you. Even with your casual acquaintances you do subtle and not-so-subtle things to ensure the result you prefer. You probably do most of these controlling things unconsciously. Whether it is created consciously or unconsciously, rapport with another person is no accident—it is an intentional creation of the mind.

As an example of how these control patterns can cause trouble in buddy-system Rebirthing, however, consider a man who is trading Rebirthings with his wife and who has a strong preference that his wife be sexually monogamous with him. If he thinks, consciously or unconsciously, that his wife maintains monogamy because of a compulsive adaptation to some suppressed pattern of negativity, and if that suppressed pattern of negativity comes to the surface during a Rebirthing session (if he doesn't perceive that that's going on consciously he does perceive it unconsciously) then he may well have a stake in her not integrating that particular pattern. He may well control her (again, consciously or unconsciously) into not integrating it! This is an easy example to think about, but there are many other similar situations, as well. Obviously this problem is not unique to Rebirthing. Husbands and wives (and friends) commonly try to help each other deal with various problems and emotional upsets in the course of daily living and are often thwarted by an unconscious desire for the person to *not* completely handle the problem.

This kind of control pattern only gets in the way when it goes unacknowledged, undiscussed. When it is discussed openly, both parties can find a way to continue getting what they want through open renegotiation (though neither party may call it that).

Communication, of the right sort, eliminates the problem in every case, at least in the experience of the authors.

We have developed a series of ten short communication processes that go directly to the heart of this matter and are remarkably effective in eliminating this type of problem. Assuming that you and your Rebirthing buddy are experienced enough with Rebirthing to be trading Rebirthings in the first place, these processes will do much to facilitate you in being effective with each other. You may find these processes quite activating at first, though they tend to integrate this activation, as well, and they tend to become easier with practice. Additionally, some people may find them fairly time-consuming at first (in a large seminar they often take between 60 and 90 minutes to complete) but with practice they will take considerably less time (as little as 15 to 20 minutes). They have the added benefit of greatly increasing your closeness with your partner. We recommend them highly.

COMMUNICATION PROCESSES TO FACILITATE CLARITY OF RELATIONSHIP:

In each of these processes, one partner asks a question and the other responds. Where indicated, the person who asked the question replies to each answer. Switch roles where indicated.

QUESTION	RESPONSE
1. Tell me something you like about me.	One item.
2. Tell me something you think we agree about.	One item.
3. Tell me something you want me to know.	5 minutes of saying "Something I want you to know is _____." Only the person who is responding talks during this time.

Now switch roles and repeat all three questions. Then the original questioner continues:

4. Tell me something you've been withholding from me. Acknowledge each response with "Thank you."	Five items. (There's always an infinite number of things that anyone has been withholding from anyone else, simply

because of the time constraints of communication, even if the withholding has no ulterior motive.)

Switch roles and repeat. Then the original questioner continues:

5. Tell me something you'd like to be forgiven for.
   Acknowledge each response with "I forgive you for that."

   5 items.

   (In any process of this type, if you can't think of a response, then say what the response *would* be if you *could* think of one.)

The original questioner continues:

6. Tell me something you'd like to forgive me for.
   Acknowledge each response with "Thank you."

   5 items.

Switch roles and repeat both questions. Then the original questioner continues:

7. Tell me some ways you control me.
   Acknowledge each response with "Thank you."

   5 items.

The original questioner continues:

8. Tell me what you're afraid I'll do if you don't control me.
   Acknowledge each response with "Thank you."

   5 items.

Switch roles and repeat both questions. Then the original questioner continues:

9. Tell me some concerns you have about Rebirthing with me today.
   Acknowledge each response with "Thank you."

   5 items.

Switch roles and repeat. Then the original questioner continues:

10. Tell me some things you like about   5 items.
    about me as a Rebirther.
    Acknowledge each response with
    "Thank you."

Switch roles and repeat.

ADDITIONAL NOTES ON BUDDY-SYSTEM REBIRTHING

Besides the problem of control patterns, which can be eliminated by using the above process before each Rebirthing trade, there are two other main problems that people have with buddy-system Rebirthing:

1. Not scheduling the times to do it. The solution to this is obvious.

2. Not knowing enough about the technique. Both partners ought to get ten private sessions froma competent professional Rebirther. Select your Rebirthing buddies with care, to make sure your partner is competent enough to Rebirth you. If both partners are skillful at self-Rebirthing, there will probably be no additional problems.

Good Rebirthing to you!

Eyegaze Rebirthing

A lovely Rebirthing technique for people who have achieved a high degree of mastery over the Five Elements is eyegaze Rebirthing. This is done by having two people, the co-Rebirthees, sit across from one another as comfortably as possible. They then look into each other's eyes and Rebirth themselves, maintaining full contact with their own bodies but making themselves as sensitive as possible to the other person as well. A wonderful "merging" often results and a good time is had by all.

CHAPTER 22

Why We Recommend Taking Professional Rebirther Trainings

The most experienced and knowledgeable Rebirthers lead trainings from time to time. These are offered in various formats and are usually very reasonably priced considering the wealth of information they contain. If you are interested in a career as a professional Rebirther, then obviously you will need to take trainings. But even if you have no interest in Rebirthing other people, we highly recommend these trainings to you because 1) You will learn a lot of information that will make you better at Rebirthing yourself; 2) You will very likely have excellent Rebirthing experiences during the training; 3) You might meet someone at the training that you would like to have for a Rebirthing "buddy," i.e., someone to trade Rebirthings with on a regular basis; 4) You will almost certainly have an enjoyable time from which you will receive life-long benefit.

The Integrative Rebirthing Process as we describe it in this book is simple and straightforward. It is easy to learn to Rebirth yourself and others. We offer 17 day professional trainings on a regular basis that will provide you with the information and experience that you'll need.

CHAPTER 23

Rebirthing Related to Therapy, Religion and Other Practices of Self-Improvement

Rebirthing and integration are natural, organic processes of the mind and body. Rebirthers can claim no monopoly on them nor on their results.

It is probably obvious to you that we are enthusiastic aficionados of what we are writing about, and are grateful for the opportunity to share this information with you. We heartily recommend that you give yourself Rebirthing. We do not claim that Rebirthing is the only way and are suspicious of people who claim to have the only way.

Rebirthing in no way interferes with the benefits of any therapeutic, religious, or self-improvement experience you have given yourself. Rebirthing enhances the benefits of these practices.

Change is the essence of improvement and Rebirthing makes change easier.

PART III

HOW TO CREATE YOUR REALITY

CHAPTER 24

The Movie Called "Your Life"

"It's all in your mind" is something we have all heard and is a glib and useless statement about any condition or set of circumstances unless you have the insight and techniques to apply it in a practical and effective way. Part III is about simple, practical and effective applications of your mind. This part could also have been called, "How to Think to Produce the Results You Intend" or "How to Solve Problems".

The personal Reality of each person is both a projection and an interpretation of that person's own mind. A useful analogy is that your life is like a movie in which you are the producer, screen writer, director, casting agent, star, and film critic. You finance the production of your life and reap the rewards, you decide on the script and make modifications as it unfolds, you direct the actions of the characters, you decide which roles they play, you decide on the set and the location, you obviously have a central part in the production and then you are the film critic, constantly evaluating, comparing and judging the contents of the movie.

Frequently when people judge the plot as going badly, they either become upset at the events that occur on the screen or they suppress their feelings about the events. They may react dramatically by becoming upset at one of the supporting actors, by berating themselves, by leaving the scene and changing the location of the movie or by pretending that what happened does not matter to them. These actions are ineffectual, however. Popular examples of solving problems this way are: changing jobs, getting divorced, moving to California, getting drunk, etc.

To continue the movie analogy, if you wish to make positive and permanent changes in the movie called "your life," this can be done, not by changing the screen directly, but by changing the film in the projection booth. The projection booth, in this analogy, is your mind, which projects your life onto the screen of your experience, creating results through individual thoughts, which are analogous to the individual frames of a movie. The light that shines through the film is known as Universal Energy, God, Life Force, Infinite Manifestation, and a variety of other names. This energy or light dutifully reproduces on the screen the images on the film, no matter what the images may be.

Obviously but importantly, the one thing you have absolute and instantaneous control of is your thoughts. In Part III, we describe how to use proven techniques to control your thoughts and thereby create your intended results.

We mentioned earlier that your personal reality is both a projection of your mind and an interpretation by your mind. The projection capability of your mind is an expression of human creativity. The interpretive capability (or analytical mode) is are actually the same thing, as can be seen by the fact that different people frequently *create* different interpretations of the same events. It is useful to discuss the mind, however, in terms of three of its functions, namely, its interpretive power, its creative power and its attractive power.

CHAPTER 25

Interpretive Power of the Mind

Most of us are well-trained in our interpretive or analytical skills, having learned to interpret traffic signs and signals, symbols on a printed page or sheet of music, the sounds of a human voice, various touches and body sensations and a variety of smells and flavors. Some interpretations or reactions are so well learned that they are taken for granted and we tend to forget that we create these interpretations and therefore have the right and ability to change them if we wish.

Knowing that the results in your life regarding health, emotional state, job satisfaction, relationships and finances are a projection of your mind and ultimately your responsibility can make you upset at first when you contemplate the results that you have that you do not like. These unpleasant results are called "problems" which are to be "solved." If you have a persistent problem, it is almost inevitable that you disapprove of yourself for having that problem. If you loved yourself with the problem, then your love or acceptance of the so-called problem, coupled with your inherent creativity, would naturally have healed it by now. Another way of saying this is that love is the natural healing force and withdrawing our love from ourselves because of something we call a problem causes the problem to persist.

108

To illustrate this point, we will take the example of a person who has been 40 pounds overweight for 40 years, and who consciously wishes to change this condition. It is highly likely that this person disapproves of the overweight condition and has done so for most of the 40 years. It could be said that the person in this example is conducting an experiment to determine whether disapproval heals overweight.

Since the overweight person is the one who is conducting the experiment, it is also this person who decides when sufficient evidence has been accumulated to prove the point. Most people would agree that our experimenter with 40 years of evidence would be safe in concluding that disapproval does *not* solve overweight; however, that person has the prerogative to continue collecting evidence forever if that person so desires.

PROBLEM SOLVING EXERCISE WITH AFFIRMATIONS

At this point, we are going to introduce the technique of composing and writing affirmations for the purpose of making positive changes in your life. In general, affirmations are the opposite side of the same coin from Rebirthing—Rebirthing is about surrendering to what's so and affirmations are about telling what's so how to be. Affirmations are controlled thoughts. Use of affirmations gives you control of your mind.

In this exercise, make a list of all the conditions that you want to change in your life. This is *not* a list of goals or things you want; it is a list of things that you already have that you don't want. Some examples might be: my poverty, my dissatisfaction with my job, my overweight, the way waiters ignore me, etc.

Now look over the list that you have just made, and draw a circle around the item that you want to change the most. This could be called your most persistent problem. For the remainder of this exercise, you will be dealing just with this circled item.

In solving a persistent problem, the sometimes agonizing realization that *every* solution that you have attempted so far has failed allows you to be inspired to try something different.

The next step is to compose an affirmation for yourself in the form:

IT IS OK FOR _____ TO _____.

Fill in the blanks with the item that you have circled from your list of conditions that you wish to change in your life. Some sample affirmations may be:

   It is OK for *me* to *be overweight.*
   It is OK for *me* to *be poor.*
   It is OK for *waiters* to *ignore me.*

This affirmation is often an excellent way to begin solving a problem. It is much easier to solve any kind of problem when it is OK with you to have the problem to solve. Making a problem wrong makes you not want to think about it. This affirmation reduces make-wrong.

Please understand that you will not agree with the statement in this affirmation at first. For that reason we use the "response column," which is a place to write down your reactions, objections and considerations about the affirmation. This process clears the objections, reactions and considerations from your mind so that the truth of the affirmation can manifest in your life. We suggest that you write the affirmation in three persons: the first person (me), the second person (you), and the third person (your name).

   Here is how it might look:

AFFIRMATION	RESPONSE COLUMN
It is OK for me to be overweight.	I hate being overweight.
It is OK for me to be overweight.	NO!
It is OK for me to be overweight	I wish this were true.
It is OK for me to be overweight	I'm starting to feel angry.
It is OK for me to be overweight.	I don't want to do this.

After filling about one-third of the page, switch to the second person.

Nancy, it is OK for you to be overweight.	No one ever told me this.
Nancy, it is OK for you to be overweight.	No one will love me.
Nancy, it is OK for you to be overweight.	Wanting people to love me when I don't love myself.
Nancy, it is OK for you to be overweight.	This is asking a lot.

After filling about two-thirds of the page, switch to the third person.

It is OK for Nancy to be overweight.	My mother always worried about my being overweight, yet she wanted me to eat, too.
It is OK for Nancy to be overweight.	I'm beginning to feel a little better about this.

It is OK for Nancy to be overweight.   I'm still a little afraid that focusing on this problem will make it worse. Maybe I'm better off ignoring it.

Now, as you write this affirmation over a period of time, you will notice that at first the reactions in the response column have a great deal of reality and validity for you. This is because the affirmation is a new idea and you are using it to reverse a lifetime of opposite thinking. As you write the affirmation more and more, the responses may still be there but you'll notice that they no longer have the reality or validity that they had at the beginning because your mind is becoming accustomed to the new reality of the affirmation.

AFFIRMATIONS ABOUT CHANGING YOUR PERCEPTIONS OR INTERPRETATIONS

1. It is OK for _____ to _____.
2. I am the one who tells my mind what to think.
3. I am now willing to see the perfection in my personal history.
4. It is easy for me to see the loving intention of everyone around me.
5. In every moment I have absolute power to choose my reality and my behavior.
6. I love feeling separate.
7. The more I like what I am, the more I am what I like.
8. I am now my ideal self.
9. Everything I do is always good enough, approved of and accepted.
10. I love everything about _____.
11. _____ is infinitely good.
12. _____ is _____ enough.
13. Everything is better than everything else.
14. I am fine whether or not _____.
15. I am glad I am who I am.
16. I am glad I am the way I am.

CHAPTER 26

Creative Power of the Mind

In this chapter we discuss the creative power of the mind and the process by which thoughts are projected into reality and create results.

If you had a strong belief that people are fundamentally nasty and deceptive, then if you met someone who treated you kindly you would naturally assume that they were deceiving you and had some kind of bad intent. This interpretation of the person's behavior will cause you to behave in ways that cause the person to *become* nasty to you. If you had the thought that you are a bad driver, you would naturally respond to that thought by driving badly. If you thought that you had a tendency to create poverty for yourself, then you would do all the right things to make yourself perpetually poor. There are many excellent ways to explain the phenomenon of thoughts creating reality, including some mystical explanations, but saying that thought creates *behavior* and behavior produces results is straightforward, accurate, and easy to comprehend. Another way of saying this is that you must think before you act. If you walk to the store, first you must think about doing it. Since you are reading this book, you first thought about doing so. The creation of results by the mind can also be stated in terms of increase, by saying that whatever you concentrate your mind on the most will increase the most in your life.

Obviously, it is possible to disagree with this point of view. You can believe that your personal reality has nothing to do with what you think or you can believe that your personal reality is controlled by some process like fate, karma, luck, astrology, coincidence, cosmic curriculum, other people, etc., or some combination of these things, all of which have nothing to do with your thoughts. This leaves you in a position of helplessness about life which in turn creates unpleasant results that will support the position of being unwilling to accept responsibility for the results your thoughts created. In other words, your results will prove you right about not creating your reality.

Your unconsciously held thoughts and beliefs affect your behavior and your creation of results at least as much as your consciously held thoughts and beliefs do. To use your mind effectively to create results you consciously intend, you will often need to become consciously aware of unconsciously held thoughts, so that you can change the ones that are creating something other than what you want. Affirmations bring to the surface any thoughts in your mind that disagree with them. These disagreeable thoughts can then be changed with affirmations.

Once you accept the idea that your reality is a projection of your mind, you begin to eliminate the tendency to feel like a victim and begin to eliminate the desire to prove yourself right about your negative convictions. Accepting that your reality is the projection of your mind is giving yourself the opportunity to create for yourself the things you want in life.

CHAPTER 27

Attractive Power of the Mind

Every one of your conscious and unconscious desires motivates you in subtle and not-so-subtle ways to satisfy it.

One of the most fundamental of your desires is your mind's desire to be right. Whenever your mind thinks that any thought is true, it wants to be right about that and will create proofs in your life that it is right. Without this mechanism, your mind would be unable to function normally, because it would be unable to trust its own data. Your mind will, therefore, guide you consistently toward experiences that prove that your thoughts are correct.

For instance, if you think that salespeople want to cheat you, your mind will guide you toward salespeople who do want to cheat you. Since salespeople who have high integrity are probably in the majority, your mind will have to go to a fair amount of trouble in order to put you consistently in contact with those who do not have high integrity. Nevertheless, the mind's desire to be right is so strong that charlatan salespeople will beat a path to your door, until you change your thoughts.

This phenomenon is known as "the attractive power of the mind" and you can use it wisely to your advantage by choosing wisely what your thoughts and conclusions will be.

CHAPTER 28

How to Use Affirmations Effectively

There are many effective and enjoyable ways to use an affirmation. Here is a partial list:

Proofs (described in detail in this chapter)

Written or typed repetitions without responses

Written or typed repetitions with responses (described in detail in this chapter)

Put the affirmation on a card and carry it in your wallet

Get the affirmation tattooed on the back of your hand

Make a sign and put it in a prominent place

Record an affirmation tape (described in detail in this chapter

Visualize

Work the affirmation into conversations

Say it to someone who will agree

Say it to someone who will not agree

Say it to yourself in a mirror

Say it to God or a picture of Jesus, Krishna, the Buddha, your guru, etc.

Say it while exercising

Read it

Say it mentally

Say it to a partner until the partner is certain that it's true
  for you
Scream it with emotion
Chant it
Sing it
Draw an appropriate cartoon and write the affirmation in
  the thought or conversation bubble

AFFIRMATION PROOFS

The results of an affirmation come in the moment that your mind accepts the affirmation as truth. For those who are able to grasp the techniques involved, proofs are the most efficient way to use an affirmation. An affirmation should always be a simple statement of fact that may or may not be how your mind usually thinks about it. If you can create six or seven ways to prove to your mind that the affirmation is true, and always has been true, then that will produce the desired change, providing you are working with the appropriate affirmation. If there are numerous parts of your unconscious mind that think the affirmation is not true, then you will have to convince each of those parts.

WRITTEN OR TYPED REPETITIONS OF AFFIRMATIONS WITH RESPONSES

This is the most consistently effective method of using affirmations that we know of. It has numerous advantages. Putting the affirmation down on paper makes it easier for you to think about it. Using responses not only enables you to find out what your mind has been thinking (which is essential because using an affirmation will only work if you are changing the right thought) but also is 9/10ths of the fun of doing affirmations (responses allow you to play "detective" or "gold prospector"). Writing or typing an affirmation also requires that you use a large part of your brain and at least two of your senses, which seems to get the affirmation into your mind more thoroughly.

Your mind is unique and your affirmation process will be unique. Your affirmation process will evolve and become very uniquely yours. We present here an excellent way to use repetitions with responses. Feel free to make any modifications that you think will make the process easier, more effective, or more enjoyable for you. We encourage you to experiment.

The following instructions are precise, detailed, thorough and concise. If you find yourself feeling confused or overwhelmed as you read them, enjoy those feelings and see the example that follows the instructions. The example will make this process absolutely clear to you.

1. Be very clear about exactly what you are intending to change.

2. Start off using the best affirmation you have thought of so far to handle this situation. Keep your mind open to discovering an even better affirmation.

3. Make a star or asterisk at the top of the page in the left margin, then write the first repetition of the affirmation next to it.

4. On the next line down, in parentheses, write whatever response your mind had to the affirmation. If your mind didn't seem to have a response, then write down what your mind's response would have been if it *had* had one. Always write down a response to every repetition of an affirmation (except the last one in the set) and never write down the same response to the same affirmation twice in any 24-hour period.

5. Make another star or asterisk in the left margin on the next line down from the response. Make up an affirmation that has a high likelihood of handling the response you just had. Write it after the star you just made. If the response you had was completely positive, then you are either fooling yourself or else you are not using the right affirmation. If your mind already *completely* accepts the affirmation you are using, then there is certainly no reason to be writing repetitions of it! Always handle your responses immediately with a new affirmation or with several affirmations if they are needed. Further on in this chapter, we give details on how to make up good affirmations. The star in the margin exists to help you locate your new affirmations easily; only make a star for the first time you write any affirmation. If you keep your affirmations in a notebook and you use this star system, it will always be easy for you to find a wealth of excellent affirmations just by looking for the stars on each page.

6. Now write another repetition of the *original* affirmation. Of course, this time you do not make a star in the margin because you have already done so once. Even though you will be making up many excellent affirmations, and you may be eager to try

them, you will usually be best off doing a complete set of the original affirmation, rather than jumping from affirmation to affirmation. If you feel *strongly* pulled to switch to the new affirmation, you can do so, of course. Trust your intuition.

7. Again write down whatever response your mind gave to this repetition and then make up another new affirmation to handle the new response. Then do another repetition of the original affirmation, etc.

8. After doing three repetitions of the affirmation in the first person, switch to the second person and continue as before. After three repetitions in the second person switch to the third. After the third repetition in the third person, do one final repetition in the first person, *without a response.* You have now completed a set of ten repetitions of the affirmation and you have created nine new affirmations. If you felt a burning desire to respond to the last repetition of the affirmation, then we recommend that you immediately do another set of ten with that same affirmation in the same way. Otherwise, you may wish to do a set of ten with one of the new affirmations you just created, or you may wish to go do something else. If you decide you want to go do something else, and the something else happens to be a suppressive activity, then we suggest that you either Rebirth yourself or continue writing affirmations. If you decide to suppress your feelings anyway, then we suggest enjoying the suppressive activity 100%! Affirmations do tend to activate emotions and if you do your affirmations diligently and wisely, they will also enable you to integrate those feelings.

EXAMPLE OF TYPING REPETITIONS OF
AFFIRMATIONS WITH RESPONSES

Suppose Carl decides that he wants to quit smoking cigarettes. A good affirmation for that is "I already completely satisfied all desire to smoke; I now choose to breathe only clean fresh air forever." His affirmation set looks like this:

*I already completely satisfied all desire to smoke; I now choose to breathe only clean fresh air forever.
(balderdash! This is never going to work!)
*I have the practical wisdom to eliminate any unwanted habit by using affirmations.

I already completely satisfied all desire to smoke; I now choose to breathe only clean fresh air forever.
(ha! In fact, I want a cigarette right now!)

*I am effectively cultivating my desire to breathe only clean fresh air, now and forever.

I already completely satisfied all desire to smoke; I now choose to breathe only clean fresh air forever.
(grumph! I can't even imagine myself not smoking!)
*I always do think of myself as a non-smoker.

Carl, you already completely satisfied all desire to smoke; you now choose to breath only clean fresh air forever.
(nobody tells me what to do.)
*All parts of me gratefully receive all good suggestions from anyone.

Carl, you already completely satisfied all desire to smoke; you now choose to breathe only clean fresh air forever.
(ahh! After all this smoking, I deserve to die anyway!)
*I choose to live forever in perfect health, I deserve to live forever in perfect health, I am living forever in perfect health.
*I forgive myself for smoking in the past.
*I am grateful for the cleanness and freshness of the air here and now.

Carl has already completely satisfied all desire to smoke.
Carl now chooses to breathe only clean fresh air forever.
(namby-pamby doo-dah-day, he lives happily ever after, grumph!)
*I already satisfied all desire to be cynical. I now choose to be grateful for all my manifold blessings.

Carl has already completely satisfied all desire to smoke.
Carl now chooses to breathe only clean fresh air forever.
(Carl's a schmuck and he couldn't quit smoking if he tried.)
*I have already successfully quit smoking!
*I have infinitely high self-esteem about my humanness.

Carl has already completely satisfied all desire to smoke.
Carl now chooses to breathe only clean fresh air forever.
(yeah, Carl's a pretty good guy. He deserves the pleasures

of smoking.)

*I am an infinitely good guy and I deserve to breathe clean fresh air.

*I have already completely satisfied all desire to smoke; I now choose to breathe only clean fresh air forever.

TIPS ON TAPES

Affirmation tapes are an excellent way to use affirmations. You can listen to tapes while you are engaging in many other activities, even while sleeping, so they can be a real time-saver. The unconscious mind receives the affirmation directly, whether or not the conscious mind pays any attention to the tape. Here are some suggestions that will make your affirmation tapes maximally fun and effective:

1. Use either a very high quality endless loop tape (lesser quality can cause problems in your tape player eventually) or else a C-30 tape, i.e., a tape that records fifteen minutes on each side. A longer tape will be more troublesome to record and more troublesome to improve when you think of better affirmations to record on it, which you probably will.

2. Record affirmations after you have worked out the majority of your negative responses with written repetitions.

3. Make sure that every component of a tape-recorded affirmation is positive. A good way to think about this is that an affirmation should only be recorded if you could turn on the tape at any part of the affirmation and still get a completely positive message.

4. Make sure that there are no puns or multiple meanings in a tape-recorded affirmation that could be interpreted in a negative way by your unconscious mind. If you are talented enough to create affirmations that have puns and multiple meanings that are all positive messages, then these are especially good to record.

5. Use the tone of voice that you would use if you were saying the affirmation as a simple statement of fact during a conversation with a friend.

6. Gentle, pleasant music playing in the background of your tape is helpful but not necessary. Music with 60 beats per minute is ideal.

7. According to some knowledgeable psychologists, your tapes will be most effective if you record four-second messages with four-

second pauses between them. This is also helpful but not necessary.

8. It is a good idea to have all the affirmations on one tape be related to the same general topic.

HOW TO CREATE EXCELLENT AFFIRMATIONS FOR YOURSELF

Throughout this book we provide you with a generous supply of affirmations on a variety of topics. We suggest that you use the ones that you like the best and the ones that upset you the most. We usually give the affirmations in the first person and leave it to you to construct the second- and third-person forms. In addition, we tell you, in this section, everything you need to know to create excellent affirmations for yourself.

1. Be concise, honest, and direct in telling yourself what the problem or response is that you are creating the affirmation to handle. If you are a beginner at creating affirmations, it may be to your advantage to state the problem you are handling in the shortest possible sentence that really expresses it.

2. Be creative and wise. This comes with practice and you can also develop it by using affirmations.

3. Simple inversion usually works fine. "Simple inversion" means stating the opposite of the problem or negative belief in a concise way. For instance, if you think, "I'm not good enough," the affirmation would be, "I am good enough."

4. Develop a rapport with your own mind. State the affirmation in the words that your mind already thinks in.

An obvious characteristic of the affirmations in this book is that they are written in English. If a language other than English was spoken in your environment during a formative period of your life, we heartily recommend that you try translating your affirmations into that language and write them or record them in that language. This is a useful technique even if you no longer have any recall of that language and you have to use a bilingual dictionary to perform the translation. We have worked with many people who were exposed to a language other than English only as infants and who, as adults, speak and understand only English. These people have been amazed, gratified, and transformed by the power of using affirmations in the language of their infancy.

5. With few exceptions, you will get the best results if you state every part of the affirmation in positive language.

6. Include your own name in the affirmation except where it's awkward. Usually the best name to use (if you've used more than one during your life) is the name you were called by your family when you were a child.

7. Use conversational language and tone in your affirmations whenever possible.

8. State the affirmation in a way that will bring up both your "highest" and your "lowest" thoughts, your "best" and your "worst" feelings. Feel free to be outrageously positive.

9. Keep the affirmation as short and simple as possible. When you will be handwriting the affirmation, you will especially want to keep it very short. When you will be typing it, it can be a little longer. Tape-recorded affirmations can be the longest. Usually anything that you can say in a long affirmation can be said better in a short affirmation.

10. Do not use language that in any way implies that you are changing from a bad situation to a good one. Always use the following mode for stating it, or one that is equivalent: '' _____ ____ is already perfect, and ____ is getting even better every day.''

We offer several examples of affirmations we do *not* recommend, and an alternative way of stating the same thing that is simpler and more positive:

NOT RECOMMENDED	SIMPLER, MORE POSITIVE FORM
1. I am recovering rapidly from my illness.	1. My body is healthy and is rapidly becoming even healthier.
2. My business competitors suffer the worst in the current recession.	2. Everything supports the success of my business.
3. If I feel upset, I force myself to think of something else.	3. My mind and emotions are a source of pleasure for me.
4. My negativity only stays stuck as long as I refuse to forgive.	4. My natural tendency to forgive makes everything better.

SOME ADDITIONAL SUGGESTIONS ABOUT USING AFFIRMATIONS

1. The more you use affirmations and the more you Rebirth, the more you will eliminate your general "negative mental mass" and the faster all your affirmations will work for you.

2. Plunge right into your greatest areas of negativity even if doing so brings up the feelings you most want to avoid.

3. Use good judgment regarding who you tell about your various affirmation projects. Some people will be supportive and some people may not be. Cultivate friendships with people who will support you.

4. The more you adopt the attitude that you are doing affirmations because they are a fun hobby, rather than because you need to do them, the better they will work for you.

5. Be very loving and patient with yourself and with your process.

6. If you notice that you have a large number of responses to an affirmation, you might as well make a "response inventory" at the outset, rather than put one response down for each repetition. Just write the affirmation once at the top of a sheet of paper and then write down all the responses you have to it and then create affirmations to handle the responses. Then do repetitions.

7. When you are first starting an affirmation project to change your thoughts about some broad area of your life, a good first step is to make an "affirmation inventory," which means that you write down all the affirmations you can think of that pertain to that subject. Then do repetitions of the ones you like the best and the ones that upset you the most.

8. If you wish to be extremely thorough with one affirmation, then we suggest that you do an "affirmation diet," which means writing or typing seven sets of ten repetitions for seven days in a row.

9. Sometimes the results of an affirmation become manifest immediately *after* a person *stops* using the affirmation. For this reason, we generally recommend that you stop working with any one affirmation after seven days of continual use.

10. If you are like most people who use affirmations, you will always be amazed when your affirmations work, no matter how many times you have seen them work before. Any time an affirmation fails to produce obvious results within ten days (maximum!) of when you started using it, that means you have been using the wrong affirmation. You need to discover which of your thoughts is creating the situation the way it is now, and then change *that* thought, in order to produce the results effectively and swiftly.

CHAPTER 29

Solutions to Common Problems that People Have with Using Affirmations

We have over twelve years of combined experience in assisting people with using affirmations. We have noticed that there are certain problems that commonly prevent people from getting the immediate results that affirmations can give. In this chapter, we present solutions to these problems.

We offer two general aids before we get into specifics.

MOST ESSENTIAL AFFIRMATION—
ALL STATEMENTS ARE EQUALLY TRUE

Remember that affirmations are not hocus-pocus magic: they are a way to change contexts. The purpose of "All statements are equally true" is to make it easier for your mind to change contexts. Another way to say this is that it frees your mind from the struggle to prove that it is right. There are an infinite number of contexts or points of view that you can hold about your life; use of this affirmation reduces make-wrong.

KNOW WHAT YOU ARE CHANGING

Applying and enjoying the ideas and techniques in this book will be much easier for you if you think of your life as a pleasurable journey, rather than as a struggle to improve yourself. Any journey begins where you are and knowing where you are is an important piece of information necessary to get you where you are going. For example, if you are in Los Angeles and you wish to go to Chicago, but you tell yourself that you are in Dallas, then you will end up in Seattle. Any time you feel that an affirmation is not producing the result you intend, a good first thing to look at is whether you are using an affirmation that changes the thought that is causing the problem you want to change.

SPECIFIC SOLUTIONS TO SPECIFIC PROBLEMS

It is often a good idea to do affirmations about the affirmation process itself. For each problem, we give affirmations that we have known to work in solving it.

Problem—"Affirmations won't work."
Solution Affirmation—"My affirmations are always working and creating the wonderful results I intend."

Problem—"Affirmations are hard work."
Solution Affirmations—"Playing with affirmations is always one of my favorite pleasures."
"I forgive my teacher for making me write sentences for punishment."

Problem—"I don't have enough time for affirmations."
Solution—If you are very busy we recommend carrying a small notebook around with you at all times so that you can write affirmations while waiting for people to show up for appointments, while you are waiting for the subway, or at other odd moments during the day. You can also develop a habit of writing affirmations for fifteen minutes every morning before going to work. Use the affirmation, "I always have time for affirmations."

Problem—"I am afraid of the negative thoughts and feelings that come up for me when I use affirmations."
Solution—Get Rebirthed. Use the affirmation, "It is safe and fun for me to see what I have been thinking."

Problem—"My affirmations are not true," or "I am kidding myself with affirmations."
Solution—Reread Part I of this book. Remember that a "lie" means lying about the *content;* an affirmation is for

changing the *context*. A change of context is not a lie. Invent four or more ways to prove that your affirmation is true. Keep working with the affirmation, "All statements are equally true."

Problem—"I can't think of good affirmations to handle my responses."

Solution Affirmation—"My creative mind has the practical wisdom to create an abundance of excellent affirmations for every occasion."

Problem—"Good things don't come from my mind, they come from God, or other people, or from working hard, etc."

Solution Affirmation—"My mind is united with the process that creates my reality."

Problem—"Why bother?"

Solution—Read Part VI of this book and use the affirmation, "My goals are important and are worth doing what it takes to attain them."

CHAPTER 30

Some Useful Types of Affirmations

MOST ESSENTIAL AFFIRMATION:

All statements are equally true.

SIMPLE INVERSION:

If the negative thought is "I'm too old to change," then the affirmation might be "I'm young enough to change."

AFFIRMATION MODES (FILL IN THE BLANKS WITH SOMETHING POSITIVE):

All parts of me _____.
_____ whether or not _____
_____ whether or not my mind thinks so.
(We list many, many affirmation modes, along with a process for using them, in the next chapter.)

AFFIRMATION FORMATS (FILL IN THE BLANKS WITH ANYTHING AT ALL):

I love everything about _____.
_____is infinitely good.
(The chapter after the next is on affirmation formats.)

INTEGRATION AFFIRMATIONS (COLLAPSE DUALITIES):

I love everyone and everyone loves me.
I am always completely lovable no matter what.
I always include everything about myself in my high self-esteem.

MONKEY WRENCH AFFIRMATIONS (THEY THROW A
MONKEY WRENCH INTO THE WORKS OF YOUR MIND):

Everything is better than everything else.
Everybody is more enlightened than everybody else.
Every feeling feels better than every other feeling.

FORGIVENESS AND GRATITUDE (THESE CAUSE VERY
RAPID HEALING. THEY BOTH DO THE SAME THING BUT
GRATITUDE GOES FARTHER):

I forgive everyone who ever did anything wrong.
I am grateful for everything everyone ever did.

SHORT-CUT AFFIRMATIONS:

The purpose of my mind is to entertain me with comedy.
Everything I ever experience is a manifestation of God's infinite
  love for me.
Everything is evolving as it should.

CHAPTER 31

101 Affirmation Modes

Scattered throughout this book, you will find affirmations that apply to whatever topic is being discussed. In this chapter we present 101 affirmation modes which you can use to speed the creation of any result you intend. We recommend that you use this list of affirmation modes as a process, like this: start by choosing *one* important, positive result, then read aloud through the list and put your intended result into the blank in each affirmation. You will need to modify slightly the form in which you express your intended result, to get it to fit the grammar of each mode. For example, the word "success" will fit some modes, while in others you will switch to "succeed" or "successful." Saying them out loud to yourself is excellent and saying them out loud to a friend is even better. This process takes about 10 minutes to complete. Remember to breathe and relax:

1. _____ exists for my convenience and benefit.

2. _____ is a source of pleasure for me.

3. It is easy for me to _____.

4. Everyone benefits from my _____.

5. Everyone facilitates me in _____.

6. It is safe for me to _____.

7. I am already _____, and
   I _____ more every day.

8. I have the practical wisdom to _____ .

9. All parts of me are doing what is most appropriate for me to
_____ .

10. I am the right age to _____ .

11. I am the right size to_____ .

12. I have the right genetic characteristics to _____ .

13. I am the right sex to _____ .

14. I have the right looks and mannerisms to _____ .

15. I have more than enough power to _____ .

16. I have great talent for creating_____ .

17. I am highly attractive to _____ and _____
is highly attractive to me.

18. I deserve _____ .

19. It feels natural for me to _____ .

20. I know how to _____ .

21. I have a success consciousness with_____ .

22. Now that I know that I can enjoy everything, I know that I
will enjoy doing what it takes to create _____ .

23. I am grateful that it is my role to create _____ .

24. My natural tendency is to _____ .

25. _____ is certain to improve my relationships
with everyone.

26. I have more than enough energy and enthusiasm to _____
_____ .

27. I know how to get the support of the right people to _____
_____ .

28. I have more than enough perserverance to _____ .

29. I have more than enough time to _____ .

30. I have what it takes to _____ .

31. I have plenty of _____ .

32. It is good for me to _____ .

33. It is good for me to have _____ .

34. It is good for me to be _____.
35. I forgive myself for not already having more _____.
36. I forgive myself for not _____ in the past.
37. I forgive myself for not being more _____ than I am.
38. I love everything about _____.
39. All parts of me now cooperate in _____.
40. I am highly motivated to _____.
41. I am more than good enough to _____.
42. I am willing to do whatever it takes to _____.
43. My mother approves of my _____.
44. My father approves of my _____.
45. My entire family facilitates me in _____.
46. My friends approve of my _____.
47. _____ improves my sociability and my sense of humor.
48. _____ increases my freedom.
49. I already have the right thoughts to create _____ and I am creating more of the right thoughts to create _____ all the time.
50. I forgive myself for having doubts about _____.
51. _____ makes me more prosperous.
52. My desire for _____ is approved of by God and society.
53. God obviously intends for me to _____.
54. I have the practical wisdom to _____ and still remain humble.
55. _____ is proof that I am a good person.
56. _____ proves I am smart.
57. I know that I will _____.
58. Everyone knows that I will _____.

59. I easily visualize _____.

60. I am grateful for the _____ I already have.

61. I am exactly the kind of person who _____.

62. My family tradition facilitates me in _____.

63. Now is the right time for me to _____.

64. My rituals and habits are naturally aligning themselves even more for me to _____.

65. _____ feels absolutely perfect to me.

66. I am absolutely certain that I want _____.

67. _____ proves that I am loving and compassionate.

68. The government facilitates me in _____.

69. Society facilitates me in _____.

70. The economic situation facilitates me in _____.

71. The world of Infinite Intelligence already has my ideal _____ waiting for me.

72. I have the physical ability to _____.

73. I have more than enough skill and know-how to _____.

74. I have more than enough strength and stamina to _____.

75. Even my most rebellious parts support me in _____.

76. _____ fascinates me.

77. _____ makes me feel light.

78. I acknowledge myself for _____.

79. I am clear enough to _____.

80. I am using _____ to improve my service.

81. It is safe, easy, comfortable, pleasurable, and profitable for me to _____.

82. I am patiently and diligently perfecting _____.

83. _____ supports my honest self-expression and my honest self-expression supports _____.

84. _____ increases my aliveness, my prosperity, and my enjoyment of life.

85. I have a right, nay, a duty to _____.

86. It is infinitely miraculous that I exist, so manifesting _____ is obviously easy.

87. _____ is right for me.

88. _____ is sure to be satisfying for me.

89. From the dawn of time, it has been foreordained destiny that I _____.

90. _____ is a proper thing for a person of my social position to be involved in.

91. _____ is worth whatever it takes.

92. _____ makes me even more sexually attractive.

93. I have the practical wisdom to create an excellent plan for achieving _____.

94. I am absolutely determined to achieve _____.

95. I am completely enthusiastic about doing everything and anything that brings me closer to_____.

96. I am prepared for _____ and I am preparing myself even more for _____.

97. I am already on-purpose with _____ and I am putting myself even more on purpose with _____ whether or not I feel like it.

98. _____ is certain to give me even more enjoyment than what I am doing now.

99. My _____ increases the perfection of the Universe.

100. Everything that has ever happened has made a contribution to my _____.

101. The Universe rejoices at my _____.

Say these affirmation modes, containing your intended result, aloud to yourself or to a friend at least once every morning and once every evening until your result manifests.

Additionally, you can write the ones that you like the best and the ones that upset you the most.

Here is an example of how to modify the wording of your intended result to fit the various modes. We use the example of perfect health. Here's how you say the first ten affirmation modes to achieve perfect health:

1. Perfect health exists for my convenience and benefit.

2. Perfect health is a source of pleasure for me.

3. It is easy for me to achieve and maintain perfect health.

4. Everyone benefits from my achieving and maintaining perfect health.

5. Everyone facilitates me in achieving and maintaining perfect health.

6. It is safe for me to achieve and maintain perfect health.

7. I am already perfectly healthy and I become more perfectly healthy every day.

8. I have the practical wisdom to achieve and maintain perfect health.

9. All parts of me are doing what is most appropriate for me to achieve and maintain perfect health.

10. I am the right age to achieve and maintain perfect health.

Chapter 32

Affirmation Formats

The difference between an affirmation format and an affirmation mode is that a mode requires putting someting *positive* into the blanks, whereas an affirmation format produces a positive affirmation no matter what you put in the blanks. Filling in the blanks with "negative" expressions and then writing the affirmations extensively is an excellent way to process your thoughts about things that you have a large emotional charge on.

1. It is OK for _____ to _____.

2. I love everything about _____.

3. _____ is infinitely good.

4. _____ is _____ enough.

5. I am fine whether or not _____.

6. _____ exists for my convenience and pleasure.

7. I am infinitely grateful for _____.

8. I forgive _____ for _____.

9. _____ is pleasantly amusing for me.

10. I receive infinite pleasure and infinite benefit from _____.

11. I am grateful for the existence of _____.

12. _____ inspires me.

CHAPTER 33

Liberation From Double Binds

In this chapter we describe a method of using affirmations to liberate yourself from double binds. We define a double bind as a situation in your life in which you feel stuck. If you examine the stuckness, you will probably find that you are giving yourself only two choices, neither of which is satisfactory.

How to use this process:

1. Make a list of things in your life that make you feel stuck.

2. For each of these items, identify the specific double bind that is operating.

3. For each double bind, create an affirmation that eliminates the duality.

EXAMPLES:

AREA OF STUCKNESS	DOUBLE BIND	LIBERATING AFFIRMATION
1. I hate my job.	Work at my job or go broke.	I have the practical wisdom to make my living in ways that are pleasant for me.
2. I'm stuck with my boyfriend even though he's a jerk.	Stay with my boyfriend and suffer with him or leave him and suffer alone. (Loneliness or dependency)	I am continuously replacing my relationships with better relationships. (Note that this could mean better relationships with the same people or better relationships with better people.)
3. I have to compete to get what I want.	Win and beat the other person or else lose.	Everything everyone experiences satisfies everyone's desires.
4. I hate being told what to do.	Conform or rebel.	I do what I know is right and that creates harmony with everyone.

CHAPTER 34

The State-Your-Complaint Process

The State-Your-Complaint Process is a technique that allows you to cause integration of suppressed make-wrong dualities, working at the level of the mind rather than at the level of the body. It has advantages and disadvantages compared to using Rebirthing.

ADVANTAGES OF THE STATE-YOUR-COMPLAINT PROCESS

- It allows you to decide consciously exactly what you are going to integrate. In Rebirthing you have to let your body decide. If you have a particular thing you want integrated, a particular Rebirthing session might work on that or it might work on something else. The State-Your-Complaint Process allows you to work on anything you want.

- Understanding how the State-Your-Complaint Process works is tantamount to understanding integration itself.

- Sometimes the process facilitates getting a person through certain types of unconsciousness tht arise during Rebirthing, if the unconsciousness is caused by avoiding feeling what is coming up. The State-Your-Complaint Process "bypasses" the body, somewhat like Rebirthing "bypasses" the mind.

138

DISADVANTAGES OF THE STATE-YOUR-COMPLAINT PROCESS, COMPARED TO REBIRTHING

- It is less efficient than Rebirthing because it involves "figuring things out." While each integration in Rebirthing may take only a few seconds, each integration in the State-Your-Complaint Process will take from 15 minutes to one hour.

- You will usually need another person to help you with it. It is too easy to delude yourself to be able to use the process consistently effectively on your own.

- It doesn't always work. Rebirthing is so simple that it always works. The State-Your-Complaint Process only works well for people who have strong, intelligent minds, good facility with the process, good understanding of integration, and a strong dedication to truth for its own sake. Our experience has been that nobody can make the process work 100% of the time.

- It isn't always "ecological". We call a solution "ecological" when all parts of a person accept it. In Rebirthing, if one part of the unconscious mind integrates and another part gets upset about it, the upset part will simply come up next to get integrated, i.e., it will be the next pattern of energy to become activated. When the person reaches completion for the session and everything feels good we know that all of the integrations have been ecological. With the State-Your-Complaint Process it sometimes occurs that integrating something "in isolation" upsets the balances of other parts of the mind. The solution for one problem may create more problems elsewhere. Nobody has the time to do layer after layer of State-Your-Complaint Process. This problem doesn't nearly always arise, and if it does you can always use Rebirthing to restore the ecology.

In spite of these problems, the State-Your-Complaint Process is a very useful tool and a very efficient way to cause integration, when it works. There is never any harm in trying it and even if it doesn't completely handle the problem it will always give valuable insight.

HOW TO DO THE STATE-YOUR-COMPLAINT PROCESS

There are three main steps to causing integration using this process:

Step 1: State your complaint; make it simple and exact.

Step 2:   State the exact same thing in a positive way.

Step 3.   State the positive thing in step 2 as a reminder that says it's true all the time in all situations, and then prove to yourself that the reminder is true, in enough ways to cause your mind to accept it absolutely.

EXAMPLE OF A SUCCESSFUL APPLICATION OF THE STATE-YOUR-COMPLAINT PROCESS

[The following is an experience that Jim Leonard had with applying the State-Your-Complaint Process.]

We will use the actual case history of Steve, the person we mentioned in Chapter 3 who found out that he had the unconscious thought that helplessness made him more lovable.

Step 1:

Steve came to me and told me that he was forty years old and he felt like he was completely powerless to get what he wanted from anybody. He said that whenever he was about to ask anybody for anything, he would feel and act helpless if he could imagine them having the slightest reservations about wanting to give it to him.

It is essential to this process that the complaint be expressed as simply and exactly as possible. Steve agreed to the statement, "I feel and act helpless."

Step 2:

I told Steve to state the exact same thing in a positive way. I explained to him that I did did *not* mean the positive opposite, as is sometimes used in affirmation processes (e.g., "I feel and act powerful"). The content of Step 2 must be the same as in Step 1; the *context* changes.

Steve said that he couldn't imagine any positive way to say it.

I told him something like, "Well, you can give up on anything and not get the result. If you want this to work then don't give up, take your time, and figure out a way to do it."

After several minutes he still couldn't figure it out. The technical term for this is "being stuck in a negative context."

I asked him, "What is the best thing you can say about this condition of yours?"

He thought a moment and then he said, "Well, I guess if people give me what I want even when I'm feeling and acting helpless, then I know that they really love me."

I said words to the effect of "Aha!" and wrote down what he said. We went through several steps of "boiling it down" to its simplest form and finally settled on "I am lovable."

At this stage of the process it is usually a good idea to diagram the duality mechanism and see if it seems right. The way to do this is to draw the scale from 10 to zero and put Statement 2 at 10, its logical opposite (in this case, "I am unlovable") at zero, and Statement 1 at the arrow that indicates the compulsive adaptation. Steve's duality mechanism looked like this:

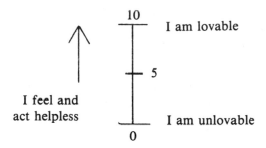

FIGURE 10: WHY STEVE FEELS AND ACTS
HELPLESS.

It seemed obvious to Steve and me that this was in fact what he had going.

Step 3:

I created for Steve the following reminder (which is like an affirmation but I prefer the implications of the term "reminder" in this context): "In every moment I am completely lovable no matter what."

"Start proving it," I told him.

Some of his proofs were: "Lovable means that people have the ability to love me. I am always lovable whether people take advantage of their opportunity to love me or not." "Everything I do is a satisfaction of everyone's desire for me to be doing that." "I love other people when they don't act helpless and so they probably love me when I don't act helpless, too." "All statements are equally true."

After he invented a few of these proofs there was a visible shift in his energy and body language; he obviously integrated the duality.

I saw him again one week later and he told me that the pattern had completely cleared up.

PART IV

YOUR PAST AND YOU

There are two main points we wish to bring out about your past with regards to self-improvement.

The first point is that everything that happened in the past had a part in creating your present, which is your starting-point in creating your future. To the extent that you are making anything in your past wrong, you are also making something in your present wrong, and that inevitably makes you less effective at creating what you intend in the future.

The second point is that although you may have suppressed part of your past, you did survive it. This means that it is completely safe for you to re-explore anything that is in your conscious or unconscious memory.

In this part of the book we examine in detail the events of greatest significance in most people's personal histories. They are primarily important because they are the times when most people made the most important negative decisions about life. The events we explore in this part are birth, infancy, relationship to one's parents, sibling rivalry, and adolescence.

As you read the material in this part, we recommend that you notice which items make you feel sad, fearful, or angry, which items you disagree with and which items you have a hard time paying attention to: these are the most important things in this part for you.

CHAPTER 35

Birth and Its Commonly Suppressed Effects

Birth is an event that we all share in common. Yet it is an event that almost universally is not remembered. Since birth is so commonly suppressed, it may seem a bit strange to you (if you don't remember your birth) that we are even talking about it. You may think that birth is not very important; it is important because all first impressions are important—at birth people make their first conclusions about the nature of life outside the womb.

Most hospital birthing techniques were designed to provide comfort and convenience for the birth attendants, and the newborn are often treated like unfeeling non-entities, and therefore not important. If you feel that birth is not important it may be because you concluded at your birth that *you* were not important.

Often people's attitudes about the newborn are shaped by the belief that the newborn are either too ignorant or not developed enough to be aware of what is going on. Consider for a moment that at the time of your birth you obviously had displayed the innate intelligence to grow a human body starting with just a sperm, an egg, and your mother's willingness to nurture your growth in the womb. What a marvelous job of creation you did! You also had enough intelligence to make many conclusions about the nature of life based on your first impressions of it.

Birth is an experience of unique intensity simply because there is so much happening at once. In this chapter we will examine the common yet miraculous event of birth and some effects that your own birth might still be having on your life.

In general, birth was the only permanent, instantaneous and dramatic change in our reality that any of us has experienced. The growth from egg and sperm, to embryo, to fetus and finally to prenatal infant has been mapped and recorded in detail by modern science as a gradual day-to-day unfoldment. After birth, in the first two years of our lives, we learned to talk, to walk, to feed ourselves and to eliminate in a socially acceptable manner. Although this is a lot to learn in a short period of time, it does occur in a gradual manner.

If you are reading this book, we assume that you are interested in making changes in your life. One of the major benefits of Rebirthing is that the process frees one from the suppressed emotions surrounding one's birth experience. One of these suppressed emotions is fear of change, or said another way, fear of the unknown. Integrating the fear suppressed in the first major change in your life will make it easier to make other changes in your life, whatever they may be.

The major changes that occur at birth relate to: touch, light, sound, atmospheric breathing, relating to the world, relating to other people, physical separation and temperature. We have observed the results of these changes in our own Rebirthing sessions and in those of people we have Rebirthed. Additionally the effects of some of these changes have been described by Dr. Frederick LeBoyer in his pioneering book on gentle birth entitled *Birth Without Violence*.

Once you begin to examine yourself and your mind in an earnest fashion, you quickly become aware of the fact that there are events in your past that you have suppressed. As these events come to conscious awareness, you are able to see the conclusions that you made from those events and how they have affected your life.

The past is over—therefore it does not matter what happened at your birth; it does not matter if the doctor had a moustache, or if you were born in the taxi enroute to the hospital, or whatever. What matters is the *conclusions* that you made about life based on these events. These conclusions are carried forward into the present in your unconscious mind. We have Rebirthed people who have had relatively gentle births, but who made strong negative conclusions as well as people who have had difficult births and made relatively positive conclusions. Rebirthing provides a safe, efficient, pleasurable way for you to re-experience your birth and remove any negative conclusions that you made at that time.

TOUCH

Before birth the infant is encased in amniotic fluid. This saline solution surrounds the body and fills the lungs, preventing them from collapsing before they are needed. This amniotic fluid is the only substance that the skin of the infant touches until the water breaks in preparation for birth. In a normal, head-first, vaginal birth, the engagement of the head into the birth canal is the first tactile experience that is different from being encased in amniotic fluid. The ensuing passage down the birth canal is a roller coaster of sensation—a paradoxical confusion of pain and pleasure. The lubrication of the vernix caseosa which is the thick, slippery substance that covers the skin of the newborn and the remaining amniotic fluid in the birth canal combine to make passage down the birth canal the ultimate in sensual, pleasurable massage. At the same time, the pressure of the contractions, the awareness that something very different and strange is happening and the psychic terror of the mother combine to have an emotional impact ranging from distress to total panic.

Perhaps the most universal conclusion made by people at birth is that pain and pleasure are somehow intrinsically intertwined. This comes from associating the pleasure of embryonic life in the womb with the pain of birth. In human society, the belief in the connectedness of pleasure and pain is pandemic. For example, how many people do you know who work forty hours per week at jobs they don't like, then try to cram a week's worth of pleasure into the all-too-short weekend? How many people do you know who expect something to go wrong whenever things start to go really well? Or who feel guilty about giving themselves pleasure? Or believe that it is necessary to suffer first in order to "earn" satisfaction?

Even some modern religions would have us believe that it is necessary to suffer here on Earth in order to earn eternal bliss somewhere else. It is impossible to suffer enough to earn bliss. The ancient pagans attempted to appease angry gods by believing that if they sacrificed enough goats, this would prevent earthquakes; the trouble with this way of thinking is that no one ever comes along to tell you that you have sacrificed enough goats! The lyrics of many rock and country-western songs portray the idea of confusion between pain and pleasure.

AFFIRMATIONS:

1. Everyone is in a state of ecstasy whether or not anybody tells the truth about it.
2. Pleasure always leads to more pleasure.
3. The more I allow myself to enjoy this moment, the more I will

allow myself to enjoy all future moments.
4. I have the practical wisdom to enjoy everything.
5. I forgive myself for thinking in the past that pain and pleasure
   had anything to do with one another.
6. Thank you, God, for everything. . . .

LIGHT

Before birth, the infant is shielded from light by the mother's
body and by the amniotic fluid. In some delivery rooms, lights of
great intensity are directed on the pelvic area of the mother to aid
the attending physicians. These lights are a shock, to say the least,
to the eyes of the newborn. The application of burning drops to the
eyes shortly after birth does not rank in the top ten of pleasant
experiences either, as those of us who remember our births recall.

Might you have concluded that some things in your life are too
intense for you to look at them?

SOUND

In the womb, the infant experiences many sounds—the mother's
heartbeat, intestinal rumblings, muffled conversations and
environmental noise. All of these sounds are filtered through the
amniotic fluid. By comparison, any loud noises made in the
delivery room after the infant has emerged are an assault to the
tender eardrums. Birth is therefore a dramatic change to the way
that we experience sound.

Does your life sometimes scream obvious truths at you that you
refuse to hear?

ATMOSPHERIC BREATHING

In the womb, oxygen is supplied to the infant by the umbilical
cord. The mother does the breathing for her prenatal infant. Birth
is where we learned to breathe. For many of us, our first breath was
taken after the umbilical cord was cut. This resulted in being forced
to learn to breathe in a do-or-die situation, under fear and panic of
death.

If the umbilical cord is cut before the newborn is breathing fully
and freely, learning to breathe is a terrifying experience in which
the survival of the newborn is threatened. When there has never
been air on the tissues of the lungs before, a gasping first breath

causes searing pain. It is easy to see that if you unconsciously associate breathing with pain, then you will be utilizing a portion of your energy to suppress the memory of the pain every time you take a breath. This not only makes it harder to enjoy your life, it also tends to make your normal breathing shallower and less regular. Proper breathing is so important to good health that this primal fear of breathing can reduce your physical aliveness.

Before the breath can be taken into the lungs of the newborn, the remaining amniotic fluid must be expelled. Often the newborn is subjected to the vertigo-inducing experience of being held upside down to expedite the draining of the fluid. As we have often observed in Rebirthing people, this vertigo often leads to various forms of disorientation that last throughout life until it is integrated during Rebirthing sessions.

Regarding breathing, Rebirthing can be described as taking time out to learn how to breathe. The first time we learned, we were too busy just trying to survive to learn it in a way that suited us. The fact is that everyone already knows how to breathe in a full, effortless and spontaneous manner. Rebirthing, then, will not teach you how to breathe (you already know how); it will, however, free you from the fear that surrounds the memory of the first breath.

The breath is a unique physiological phenomenon. It is subject to both voluntary and involuntary control. You can breathe faster if you do it intentionally or you can run around the block and soon you'll begin to breathe faster whether you intend to or not. The breath is the connection between the invisible and the visible, taking in oxygen and expelling carbon dioxide (both invisible) to nourish our body (the visible). Free and connected breathing is an expression of aliveness and fills the body with life-giving energy called kundalini energy, chi energy, prana, life force and a variety of other names.

RELATING TO THE WORLD

Another change that occurs at birth is the way that the newborn relates to the environment. In the womb, there is a sense of timelessness, a sense of oneness. In the womb our world completely surrounds us. Birth is the first time that we relate to people in the way that we relate to people now. While it may be unnecessary to point out that the way we relate to people now is that they are over there and we are over here, this method of relating is completely different from the way that we did it in the womb. The sense of oneness, of sameness, of unity experienced in the womb are gone and the newborn is confronted with an environment of never-ending variety with no one to explain the rules or what anything means.

For most of us, our first experience in relating to people was with the obstetrician or the midwife who was present at our birth. The first people that we related to were in a position of authority, regardless of their attitude about their jobs. Certainly they were in charge of what happened and they had much larger bodies and much larger vocabularies than we did as newborns. Also, generally our mothers did what these people wanted. For some people, the memory of pain at birth and the memory of the relationship with the obstetrician as the first authority figure in their lives are carried forward unconsciously as patterns of rebellion, non-cooperation and mistrust toward people that are perceived as authority figures.

AFFIRMATIONS ABOUT AUTHORITY

1. I am grateful for everyone who ever acted as an authority figure.
2. I love everything about being told what to do.
3. I am grateful for all the attitudes of everyone who was present at my birth.
4. I received infinite benefit from everyone who was present at my birth.
5. People of higher status than myself are my friends.
6. I am the authority in my own life.
7. I have already completely satisfied all desire to rebel or conform; I now choose to act only in accordance with my own highest thoughts.

PHYSICAL SEPARATION

If the umbilical cord remains attached until the newborn has had a chance to learn to breathe at his or her own pace, then individuation takes place naturally and the newborn learns to experience physical closeness as something natural. The premature cutting of the umbilicus allows the newborn to be whisked away and separated from the mother at this critical period of life when what is needed is a reuniting with the mother whose body has sheltered and nourished the infant for so long.

Nine months is a long time to stay in the same place. Abrupt, unannounced and sometimes painful separation from an environment that has been the only environment known to the newborn is bound to be a shock.

People that we have Rebirthed have reported memories of conclusions made at the time of separation that have shaped the way that they regarded life. Some of these conclusions are: "I can't trust anyone," "If I get what I want, someone will take it away," "I hurt people," "I am unwanted," "I have done something wrong," and "People hurt me."

TEMPERATURE

Temperature in the womb changes very slowly if at all and is between 100-104 °F (37-40 °C). Birth is the infant's first experience of sudden temperature change. If the temperature of the delivery room is kept at 70 °F (21 °C), in order to provide comfort for the adults, then the transition from the womb to the delivery room, without clothing and with wet skin, can be likened to running outdoors from a hot shower with no clothes on. This rapid change in temperature creates fear that is usually deeply suppressed in the cells of the body. The suppressed memory of this sudden drop in temperature is so significant that it is often the first memory of birth to be restimulated during Rebirthing sessions.

The "common cold" recreates the experience of the abrupt temperature change at birth. Even the name of this ailment implies a drop in temperature. Other elements of the common cold that are similar to birth are difficulties in breathing and muscular aches and pains.

CHAPTER 36

Suggestions for Birth Attendants and Prospective Mothers

Although we are neither doctors nor mothers, we have conscious recall of our births and have been with thousands of people who have integrated the suppressed emotions surrounding their birth experience during Rebirthing sessions. In most communities, there are a variety of birthing methods available in addition to the traditional, twentieth-century, hospital birth with its array of equipment and inherent sense of emergency. For a prospective mother, having a baby is an important event. We suggest that prospective mothers and fathers investigate the methods of birth available in their communities before making a choice. To understate the point, choosing a method of birth for your baby deserves at least the degree of earnest consideration and frank discussion that you would give to selecting a new car or a new home. There are several sources of information regarding gentle birth methods listed in the back of this book.

For birth attendants, we recommend that you incorporate an extreme degree of gentleness and patience into the procedures that you use at births. It is important to consider the environment of the womb which the newborn has been used to for a long time and to make his transition to life here a gentle one. Birth attendants and obstetricians who have been Rebirthed report a greater ease and peacefulness in their work as a result of integrating the suppressed emotions surrounding their own births.

AFFIRMATIONS ABOUT BIRTH

1. I have the right to be here.
2. I am glad I was born and so is everyone else.
3. I forgive myself for letting the doctor hurt me at my birth. I now appreciate the doctor's work.
4. I am glad to be out of the womb and now express myself fully and freely.
5. I am now breathing fully and freely.
6. It is safe and pleasurable for me to make positive changes in my life.
7. Change is safe for me.
8. I forgive myself for creating disappointment in my life.
9. My body is a safe and pleasurable place for me to be.
10. I enjoy my life.
11. My life is fun.
12. Pleasure is good for me.
13. I am grateful for all the circumstances of my birth.
14. I love everything about being human.
15. Everyone respects me whether they act like it or not.
16. Everything about my birth was perfect and everything about my life is perfect whether or not I say so.
17. Everything about my birth was blissful for my mother whether she holds it in that context or not.
18. The world is more pleasurable than the womb.

CHAPTER 37

The Implications of Specific Events at Birth

We will describe the effects of specific events at birth, based on our observations of people that we have Rebirthed. Please bear in mind that these are generalizations and do not occur in all cases. We want to remind you that it really does not matter what happened at your birth or anywhere else in your personal history. What does matter is the *conclusions* that you made from past events.

ANESTHESIA

In Part II of this book we discussed what happens when memory of anesthesia surfaces during a Rebirthing session.

Some of the symptoms that are produced by the suppressed memory of general anesthesia are:

1. Heavy use of alcohol. This is an attempt to suppress fear by recreating the deadness, numbness and disorientation of the anesthesia that got the person through the fearful experience of birth.

2. Excessive coffee drinking. This is the result of the desire to function effectively in the world despite the deadening effect of suppressed anesthesia.

3. Fear of heights and fear of falling. This is usually the memory

153

of the uncontrollable "fall" back into the body as the effect of anesthesia wore off.

CAESARIAN BIRTH

In Caesarian birth, the newborn is surgically removed from the mother's womb. Since this method has inherent differences from vaginal birth, the conclusions about life made by people born by Caesarian section are often quite different from those made by people born vaginally. In some major hospitals, Caesarians account for as much as twenty percent of deliveries.

The primary difference between a Caesarian birth and a vaginal birth is that in the Caesarian birth the transition from life in the womb to life as we experience it now is much quicker. People born by Caesarian often have difficulty with processes that are gradual in nature, and with completion of projects in general. Since they were rescued from the womb, they sometimes expect to be rescued from difficult situations and do not take even the most basic actions to solve their own problems. They also often have a pronounced fear of abandonment.

DRY BIRTH

"Dry birth" means that the uterine sac containing the amniotic fluid breaks, releasing the amniotic fluid long enough before birth so that the amniotic fluid does not ease the passage of the newborn through the birth canal. Despite the residual lubrication provided by the vernix caseosa, the journey through the birth canal is more of a struggle than the journey would have been with the additional lubrication of the amniotic fluid. People born of a dry birth frequently conclude that struggle is either essential to survival or fundamental to existence, and sometimes struggle with situations in their lives far more than other people do.

TWINS

From our experience in Rebirthing, the effect of being a twin depends on whether one was the first or second to come out of the birth canal. Typically, the first one feels guilty about leaving its sibling and constant companion of nine months and the second one feels betrayed and angry about being left.

BREECH BIRTH

Breech birth means a vaginal delivery other than head first. This type of delivery is usually difficult for the mother. Her body was designed for head first delivery and a breech birth is out of harmony with this basic design. People who were breech births frequently have a fear of hurting others and/or a pattern of compulsively behaving in a manner they think is wrong or different.

PREMATURE BIRTH

Premature birth means that the newborn was born long enough before full term of pregnancy to require incubation. The suppressed conclusions from a premature birth vary greatly from person to person and often depend on the cause of the prematurity. In some cases the newborn sensed that the mother did not enjoy being pregnant and cooperated in the mother's desire to end the pregnancy as soon as possible. The mother's dislike of the pregnancy could have been caused by any number of factors ranging from sickness during pregnancy, conception out of wedlock, abandonment by the father or not consciously wanting the child in the first place.

People born of premature birth frequently have a greater degree of difficulty with time. This can manifest as compulsive lateness, fear of being late or constantly creating lateness in others.

The incubator experience frequently causes the person to expect warmth, affection and security from the presence of inanimate objects instead of from people.

CHAPTER 38

Rebirthing Clears Up Suppressed Effects of Birth

Rebirthing allows you to re-experience the feelings you had at birth in a gentle way. When you remember parts of your birth during a Rebirthing session, it is a sure sign that you have stopped making those parts wrong and that you have replaced suppressed trauma with conscious joy.

CHAPTER 39

Dear Mom & Dad

You are a loving person and you want to love your parents. If you are someone who has a complete and abiding love and appreciation for your parents and everything about them, then we congratulate you and invite you to savor the enjoyment of your attainment with relish. You can read the remainder of this section as a validation of your loving nature.

If you are someone who would like to increase the genuine sense of love and joy in relating to your parents, we are going to describe the most common sources of difficulties in relating to parents and ways to integrate the suppressed feelings and memories.

Relating this to Rebirthing, the integration accomplished by Rebirthing has the advantage of making it easier to create and accept change in your life, enabling you to view changes as improvements. As we have stated earlier, it is not important what your parents did or how they behaved in the past; the important thing is the *conclusions* that you have formed as a result of their behavior or as a result of their thinking. The close connection that children feel with their parents, especially with their mothers, causes them to imitate their parents. Because of their uninhibited intuitive abilities and lack of social graces, children tend not only to imitate their parents' behavior, but also their thoughts. For the parents the child's loving imitations of the parents' thoughts is a little bit like having their suppressed thoughts acted out by their child in three dimensions, in technicolor and sometimes in loud volume. Parents react to their discomfort in this situation by

157

providing the child with a set of rules, so that the child behaves in a way that is comfortable for the parents. Sometimes these are the same rules that their parents gave them, and sometimes they are exact opposites. These are rules for proper behavior, rules for proper use of time, rules about reward and punishment, etc.

Obviously any conclusions that you made at your birth about yourself, about life, or about how people treat you were carried forward into your relationship with your parents. You tended to interpret their behavior in accordance with those conclusions, and to create their behavior by the creative power of your mind. An example of this is that if you concluded at birth that you were not important, then in your relationship with your parents what they wanted always seemed to be more important than what you wanted.

Parenthood is not an easy job. In fact it is the most important job in the world and also the job for which there is the least amount of practical training available. There is much more education available about how to be a successful anthropologist, botanist, chiropractor . . . to zoologist, than there is practical training about how to be a successful parent. Unless you are willing to see the loving intention of your parents and see that they did the best job that they knew how, you will make them wrong, continue to seek their approval, and suppress the feelings about your relationship with them. These suppressed feelings are sure to cause problems in your relationship with everyone.

Here are some useful ways to increase the love and joy that you experience in your relationship with your parents. Developing and maintaining a good relationship with your parents will increase the love and joy that you experience in *all* your relationships and will also make it easier for you to function as an adult. The techniques that we suggest will work whether you have contact with your parents or not.

THINK OF YOUR PARENTS AS INDIVIDUALS

One characteristic of your relationship with your parents is that they have you outnumbered two to one. Pick your relationship with one parent first and apply these techniques to it. When you see your parents, arrange to spend time with them one at a time. Obviously your parents had a relationship with each other before you arrived on the scene so when you relate to them together, it is also necessary to deal with the way they relate to each other.

VISUALIZE YOUR PARENTS AS CHILDREN

Visualize your parents as children and imagine yourself having a conversation with them. Tell them what you want to say. Imagine them saying what you want to hear.

WRITE LETTERS TO YOUR PARENTS

Write a letter to your mother and a letter to your father on a regular basis in which you tell them the complete truth about how you are feeling about them. After you write each letter, you can decide whether you want to mail it to them. If you do this, even for a little while, you'll start feeling the love for them that you have suppressed.

VISUALIZE YOURSELF AS A CHILD

This exercise will aid you in seeing yourself from your parents' point of view. Sometimes, this is easier to do for people who are parents themselves.

AFFIRMATIONS ABOUT PARENTS

1. I am glad that my parents decided to have children.
2. I am grateful that I chose the family that I did.
3. I love my mother.
4. I love my father.
5. I love everything about my family.
6. My family is a source of pleasure for me.
7. I have and deserve the love and respect of my family.

CHAPTER 40

Infancy Patterns

Infancy is the next step after birth and is a period where the newborn usually spends considerable time with its mother. For the infant, birth is an event of recent (and sometimes not completely suppressed) memory. If you ask a child who has recently learned to talk but has not yet learned that people do not usually talk about birth, the child will frequently give you reasonably clear recollections about birth.

INFANT GUILT SYNDROME

As an infant, your feelings regarding your mother were shaped by the recent memory of birth. One of the most universal conclusions brought forward from birth to infancy is the conclusion that the infant hurt the mother at birth, or even the conclusion that the infant killed the mother at birth, if the newborn was quickly separated from the mother. These conclusions are called "infant guilt syndrome" and result in thinking that your very existence killed the source of your life (your mother), or in thinking that your mother was in pain and it was your fault. The nature of these conclusions was unpleasant and they were therefore suppressed by the infant. We define guilt as the context in which you erroneously conclude that someone is not experiencing infinite pleasure and infinite benefit and it is your fault. Some of the results of infant guilt syndrome in adult life are:

1. Embarrassment about receiving compliments.

2. Feeling guilty when you assert yourself for your benefit.
3. Feeling guilty about doing what you get paid for.
4. Fear about hurting your sex partner.
5. Thinking that getting what you want hurts people.
6. Fear of success.
7. Frequently doing things that you will later feel guilty about.

AFFIRMATIONS ABOUT INFANT GUILT SYNDROME

1. I forgive myself for thinking I hurt my mother at birth.
2. Everything I have ever done has caused infinite pleasure and infinite benefit for everyone.
3. My birth caused infinite pleasure and infinite benefit for my mother.
4. Everyone benefits when I do what it takes to get what I want.

As infants, we felt the effects of infant guilt syndrome most strongly when our mothers were present. Times when mothers were almost always present and that are important to consider are mealtime, bedtime and toilet training.

MEALTIME

All of us have received conditioning about food. This conditioning was started at the very beginning of infancy and repeated several times daily for many, many years. In many homes mealtime is an emotion-charged event. The family gathers together to partake of the nourishment provided by one member of the family as an expression of love. To reject the food is to reject the love of the food preparer. In many families, attendance at meals is mandatory or at least expected. Admonitions to eat are usually accompanied by warnings of grave consequences if they are not heeded. Thus the Clean Plate Club is perhaps the largest unorganized club in the world.

Infant feeding practices establish basic patterns relating to nourishment. The conclusions relating to feeding patterns are evident in adult life in the way that people relate to money. One almost universal conclusion from infant feeding is that all the goodies in life come from one source. This conclusion is acted out when people grow up and want to create an income and do so by getting a job. Having a job is a good idea, but if you think that it is the only way for you to produce an income, you are mistaken.

Many people in our society (including the authors of this book) are successfully self-employed and create incomes without the convention of having a job. It's nice to know that you have a choice. We suggest that you read *Money Is My Friend,* by Phil Laut, published by Trinity Publications, for information about applying the principles of creative thought to your career and finances.

Infant feeding patterns are often the beginning of compulsive eating problems. Frequently infants are held and cuddled during and after feeding. The association between food and love is carried forward into adult life as the compulsive eater eats to feel loved whenever experiencing anxiety or upset. *The Only Diet There Is,* by Sondra Ray, published by Celestial Arts, is an extremely useful book in assisting people in achieving freedom from eating problems.

AFFIRMATIONS ABOUT INFANT FEEDING

1. It is OK for me to receive love and money from various people and places at once.
2. I forgive my mother for her unwillingness/inability to breast feed me.
3. I forgive myself for accepting things I didn't want.
4. I can take it or leave it.

DRINK FROM A BABY BOTTLE

Drinking your favorite beverage from a baby bottle is not only pleasurable, but will assist in integration of feelings suppressed during infant feeding.

BEDTIME

Most parents put their children to bed when the parents are tired. You can discover this for yourself by following around a healthy three year old for a day. By mid-afternoon, *you* will want a nap. As children, we did not have much to say about what time we got out of bed either. A common characteristic about fatigue is that it is contagious. If you sit in the same room with a dozen people and yawn, even discreetly, you can observe that several other people will yawn within a few minutes. The contagious nature of fatigue relates to the fact that it appeared that fatigue was something that we caught from our parents when we were told it was time for bed.

AFFIRMATIONS ABOUT SLEEPING.

1. My energy exceeds my fatigue.
2. My energy exceeds other people's fatigue.
3. Now that I am grown up, I am responsible for deciding the appropriate time to sleep and wake up.

TOILET TRAINING

Toilet training, for a child, is an important step toward personal independence. With diapers, there is little necessity to be aware of digestive eliminations until after the fact. Being successful at using the toilet requires that you become aware of the body sensations that presage the need to eliminate. Like anything, this takes a bit of practice. It is quite possible that, for your mother, waiting in the bathroom for you to learn how to do this was only slightly more pleasant than washing your diapers.

It is easy to see some of the common beliefs about digestive elimination by observing some of the things we were taught about it. Most parents teach their children to wash their hands *before* eating and *after* digestive elimination. If the food is clean before you eat it and dirty after it comes out, what does this say about your body? What does this say about particular parts of your body?

AFFIRMATIONS ABOUT TOILET TRAINING

1. I approve of my body; I approve of everything I put into it and everything I take out of it.
2. My way works.
3. I am grateful to my mother for changing my diapers until I learned to take care of myself.

CASSETTE TAPE ABOUT INFANCY PATTERNS

A one-hour cassette tape entitled "Reclaiming Your Personal Power (Unravelling Infancy Patterns)," by Phil Laut, is available from Trinity Publications and provides additional information.

CHAPTER 41

Sibling Rivalry

Sibling rivalry is about believing that it is necessary to compete for love. It starts with the belief that there is a certain amount of love in the world, but that you are not getting it, and therefore someone else must be getting it. Then the way to get more love is to stop the other person from getting the love they are getting. It is not necessary to have a brother or a sister to have suppressed this context of competition. If you are an only child or have brothers and sisters who are considerably older or younger than you, it is possible that you thought you competed with your father for your mother's love and competed with your mother for your father's love. Sibling rivalry is a pattern of scarcity. Its suppression results in unconscious patterns of behavior such as: constant demands for attention, compulsive competitiveness, believing that if you are not superior then you must be inferior, being judgmental about your peers, fear of being compared to others, or compulsive nonconformity.

AFFIRMATIONS ABOUT SIBLING RIVALRY

1. I am a good person.
2. I love my sister(s).
3. I love my brother(s).
4. I forgive myself for comparing myself to others.
5. I forgive myself for hurting my sister(s) and brother(s).
6. I forgive myself for letting my sister(s) and brother(s) hurt me.

164

7. I forgive my sister(s) and brother(s) for hurting me.
8. I forgive my sister(s) and brother(s) for letting me hurt them.
9. I forgive my parents for blaming me for things that my sister(s) and brother(s) did.
10. I forgive my parents for giving credit to my sister(s) and brother(s) for things that I did.

CHAPTER 42

Adolescence

The primary human experience of adolescence is puberty—the advent of adult sexuality. In American society, puberty is unconsciously associated with events occurring at the same time which lead to independence, like obtaining a driver's license and spending more time away from home. However, the advent of adult sexuality is the essence of the adolescent experience that is independent of culture and comes with having a body. Sex is an embarrassing topic for many people. Sex is an especially embarrassing topic to parents in relation to their children. Ask ten of your friends if they are satisfied with the information that their parents gave them about sex.

Very few adolescents successfully integrate their rampant feelings of sexuality. The idea that sex is dirty usually started during toilet training, as mentioned earlier. Jokes about sex are called "dirty jokes". Even poor jokes about sex are told and enjoyed as a reaction to the fact that sex was often a suppressed subject in the home.

Adolescence is also a time of rebellion and rejection of parents and parental values as a reaction to parental inability to discuss the obviously burgeoning sexuality of the adolescent. Adolescents commonly spend time only with each other and imitate each other to an extraordinary degree. Adolescents who are unsuccessful at imitating their peers are often made to feel like outcasts.

A typical adolescent attitude is "I have it all together, I know everything, and I will do anything possible so that I don't have to prove it." .

AFFIRMATIONS ABOUT ADOLESCENCE

1. I forgive my parents for being afraid to talk with me about sex.
2. It is OK for me to have thoughts about sex.
3. My sexual desires are holy.
4. My sexual desires benefit everyone.
5. I am ordinary and unique, just like everybody else.
6. I belong to that group.

PART V

IMMORTALIST PHILOSOPHY

It could be said that there are two types of contexts: integrative and suppressive (make-wrong). In this part we will discuss the contexts in which you view life and death.

It is appropriate to state at this point that death is a subject not commonly discussed, and in some circles death is not a socially acceptable topic of conversation. While reading the material in this chapter you may experience the activation of some of your suppressed feelings about death. You may even feel threatened by some of the ideas. We have a very good reason for dealing extensively with this topic, however: Your thoughts and feelings about death have a major effect on all your thoughts and feelings about life. We suggest that you pay close attention to your thoughts and feelings while reading this material; welcome even the most unusual and upsetting ones, because they are all telling you something very important about yourself.

People who hold their lives in integrative contexts find it easy and natural to take responsibility for everything they experience. People who hold their lives in make-wrong contexts think of themselves as victims. These tendencies extend to include personal attitudes about death.

167

To a person whose fundamental attitude about life is that of being a victim, it is natural to assume that death is built into cells of the body and is inevitable. For this reason, we will refer to such attitudes as "mortalist" or "deathist."

To a person who celebrates life and takes responsibility for it, it is natural to assume that death, whenever it occurs, is a result of conscious or unconscious desire to die. Because such people believe that death is a matter of choice, and is not necessarily inevitable, we will refer to them as "immortalists."

The system of contexts that goes with the idea that death is a matter of choice is known as "Immortalist Philosophy" and is highly congruent with the philosophy of integration itself.

Adopting Immortalist Philosophy means accepting that it is possible for you to achieve full mastery over your body and your fate and then *doing* the best you can to achieve that.

There is no discernible advantage to concluding that you must die whether you want to or not. Similarly, there is no discernible disadvantage to holding open the possibility that you might achieve full mastery over your physical body and your life.

This is purely a matter of personal choice about thoughts. People have been thinking they had to die, and have been dying, for many centuries now, and it seems to have worked fine for them. Some of our favorite people in history are, in fact, dead, so we definitely won't make you wrong if you decide you must die as well. If you wish to explore alternative thoughts, however, read on.

At this point in your contemplation of Immortalist Philosophy, it makes no difference at all whether physical immortality is actually attainable or not. We are not claiming to offer you eternal life. What we are offering you is an alternative to *thinking* that you must die. The point is that even if you end up dying, you will have a much fuller and more enjoyable life if you live it with the belief that your life or death is a matter of your own choosing. Either you won't die or else death is somewhere in the future; either way, it has nothing to do with you right now. Your *thoughts* about death have *a lot* to do with you right now.

CHAPTER 43

The Five Fundamental Disadvantages of Thinking You Have No Choice About Death

There are five fundamental disadvantages to holding the thought that you must die and therefore have no choice about it. These five disadvantages play a significant role in almost every example of human suffering. The five fundamental disadvantages of thinking that death is inevitable are: fear, helplessness, apathy, limitation and self-deception.

FEAR

If you are like most people who haven't processed their thoughts about death very much, then there are probably make-wrong duality mechanisms in your unconscious mind that have dying as a compulsive adaptation. Some common examples of make-wrong dualities that have dying as a compulsive adaptation are:

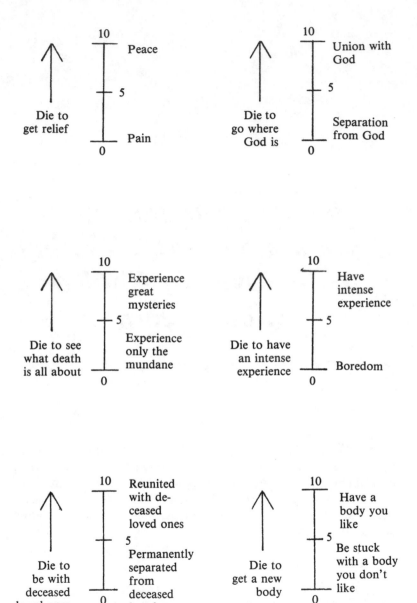

FIGURE 11: SOME COMMON DEATH-URGE
DUALITY MECHANISMS.

This type of adaptation is known as "death-urge". Thinking that death is something outside your control is tantamount to suppressing your death-urge. The result of suppression is that you cannot do anything about your death-urge, and therefore all parts of you that don't want you to die will be in a constant state of fear because of the easy control your suppressed death-urge has over your mind, body and actions. Not only does this fear make it hard for you to relax, it also puts an additional barrier between you and your unconscious mind. As long as you take no responsibility for your death-urge you cannot integrate it, which leaves you with only manifest fear and suppressed fear as options.

HELPLESSNESS

There is no difference between helplessness and thinking that you are not responsible for something. If you take responsibility for something and try to change it, you might succeed, or you might fail and then succeed, or you might fail ultimately. If you don't take responsibility for something, you won't even try in the first place, and so you can only fail. All advantage is on the side of taking responsibility for everything, whether or not you can see *how* you are responsible. Failing to take responsibility for something as important as one's own life and death leads to a pervasive sense of helplessness. This helplessness must color one's every endeavor. Inevitably much energy must be diverted to suppressing such helplessness and that practice perpetuates the helplessness and makes it grow.

APATHY

If you think that it is a certainty that in as short a time as one hundred years from now, you won't be around to reap the benefits of what you do today, that will certainly make you apathetic. Why bother accumulating wealth if you can't take it with you? Why bother conserving wilderness if you won't be around to enjoy it? Why not just kill somebody (yourself for instance) if that person is just going to die anyway? Why bother taking care of your own health, much less the health of our planet? Why bother starting to learn a new foreign language when you're 70 years old?

If you think that your death is inevitable and you think you don't have this kind of apathy, that probably means that you are suppressing this kind of apathy and it is running your life. Pause for a moment and think about the method you might be using to suppress it.

LIMITATION

To say that your death is inevitable is to say that your time is limited. If your time is limited, that means that you have only limited ability to experience anything. This in turn makes you feel like everything is more limited than it actually is. This condition is known as "limited thinking". One example of limited thinking is the idea that wealth is limited. Wealth is actually not limited at all; any time anyone does anything productive that person creates new wealth. If you think that there is a fixed amount of wealth in the world at this moment, then we suggest you go wash your windows and prove yourself wrong. Regarding wealth, greed is the result of limited thinking, too.

If you think that death is inevitable, then you are thinking that your aliveness is limited in terms of time; this will give you the experience that your aliveness is limited right now, which does limit the flow of aliveness in your body.

SELF-DECEPTION

Your unconscious mind receives all of the information that comes through the various senses in every moment. The unconscious mind then decides which part of this information the conscious mind will receive (about 4% according to studies by psychologists). Whenever death occurs, it has a cause. In almost every case, the unconscious mind has received enough information about that cause soon enough to prevent it. If the unconscious mind steers you toward death instead of away from death, that is obviously intentional on the part of the unconscious mind. The belief that death is not a matter of choice results in the conscious mind's failing to acknowledge the unconscious mind's choice to die. This failure is the origin of an especially troublesome form of self-deception. (Note that Rebirthing makes a person more aware of the body and thus significantly reduces this kind of self-deception.)

In addition to the five fundamental disadvantages of thinking that death is inevitable, we have discovered that the belief in the inevitability of death is a major source of:

Sickness
Depression
Suicide urge
Desire to get even
Desire to defend yourself and others

As long as you are living it is impossible to prove conclusively that you are going to die. In spite of this fact, if you are like most people, you allowed yourself to be convinced by some authority figure, when you were at an impressionable age, that your death would certainly come within a relatively short time. We are urging you to consider ending your unquestioned loyalty to death.

For anyone who enjoys having a physical body and who has integrated most of their compulsive death urge, it is natural to have full mastery of the physical body as a most important goal. "Full mastery of the physical body" means maintaining a high state of physical health at all times, under all circumstances, and includes preventing accidents, injuries, illness, aging, and death. It is easy to see that mastery of the body means mastery over the mind, the physical world, and spiritual mastery as well.

Belief that it is possible to attain full mastery over the body, which is to say that death is not inevitable as long as the body is still living, has many advantages. The following chapter is only a partial list and we are sure you will be able to add many more to it from your own personal experience.

CHAPTER 44

Advantages to Immortalist Philosophy

You will find it easier to take responsibility for everything in your life.

You will experience much greater freedom of thought than if you insist on staying stuck in a context where your death is inevitable.

You will feel safe enough to allow your fear of death, and then your death-urge itself, to surface and be integrated.

You will experience less limitation, so you will have both greater self-confidence and greater motivation to accomplish great things with your life.

You will have stronger motivation to take care of your body and your environment.

You will be able to relax more easily.

You will be both more courageous and less foolhardy.

You will have both higher self-esteem and greater respect for others because you will cease thinking that human beings are disposable.

You will be more enthusiastic about developing new skills and learning new things throughout your life.

You will never think of yourself as an old dog, so you will always be able to learn new tricks.

You will experience greater abundance of all of life's riches.

If you experience temporary setbacks you will find it easier to start over.

You will greatly increase your likelihood of actually mastering your body.

You will find it easier to break other negative family patterns as well.

You will have a more loving relationship with God because He won't seem so much like a big guy with a flyswatter.

You will have a better sense of humor because it will give you greater ability to decide which things you will take seriously and which things you won't.

Your more favorable outlook on life will be contagious and you will play a part in making the world a happier, more peaceful, more prosperous place to live.

You will find it easier to forgive because you will expect to outlive any unpleasant experiences you might have.

You will find it easier to Rebirth yourself because you will find it easier to be grateful for everything.

You will be more likely to incorporate new breakthroughs in health-science into your habits.

You will have more time to live it up (and more time to live it down).

As a result of all these things and more, the most important advantage is that you will enjoy your life more.

CHAPTER 45

The Origin of Deathist Philosophy

The origin of deathist philosophy is the thought that, as human beings, we are irrevocably separated from the source of life. Deathists believe that the origin of their bodies is something that has nothing to do with them. Immortalists believe that people choose their bodies. Deathists believe that death is built into the cells of their bodies. Immortalists believe that physical death, whenever it occurs is a result of conscious or unconscious desire to die. As you probably realize, it is impossible to take full responsibility for your life unless you also take responsibility for your thoughts about death.

The urge to die is the urge to suppress taken to its natural end. All parts of a person desire improvement, each part desiring improvement in its own way. One obvious thing to note about improvement is that it is change. The more a person resists change the more that unconscious desire for change builds up. The ultimate result of suppressed desire for change is death; the biggest change a living person can think of. Resisting change may well be the cause of death in all cases and integrating all change may be synonymous with attaining physical immortality.

Relating this to Rebirthing, Immortalist Philosophy makes it easier to derive the benefits available from Rebirthing. Also

Rebirthing makes it easier to hold the context of Immortalist Philosophy. This is because both Rebirthing and Immortalist Philosophy greatly increase the pleasure of being alive.

There is nothing particularly wrong with death, providing that it is congruent with your other goals. Both of us have conscious recall of our most recent, past-life deaths, and we can assure you that it is no big deal.

Life is infinitely merciful and if you do happen to destroy your body, then it will gladly give you another one. Intentionally destroying your body is at least as senseless as intentionally destroying your car. Anything that you plan to accomplish by dying you can probably accomplish faster in some other way.

The concept and philosophy of physical immortality is a logical and ultimate extension of the idea that personal reality is a projection of and an interpretation by the mind. Physical immortality is living as long as you want to and wanting to as long as you do. For the living, death is just an idea or a philosophy. At first, physical immortality is an idea or philosophy, the purpose of which is to counter the philosophy of the inevitability of death, which seems to have achieved a degree of statistical popularity in our society. By the creative power of belief, the statistical popularity of death correlates with the popularity in the belief, expectation, or philosophy of death.

For many people, birth was the most similar thing to death that they have experienced while in the body they now occupy. This is especially true if the umbilical cord was cut before you had the opportunity to learn to breathe on your own.

The paradox of physical immortality is that it is a philosophy that allows infinite manifestation and expression of your personal aliveness and yet it defies proof. What would it take for someone to prove to you that he was immortal—or to make it more personal, what would it take for someone to convince you that *you* are immortal? Being alive is the only proof that you'll ever get. If you think that death is inevitable, then you are the one that has convinced yourself of this belief. It may take some convincing to integrate Immortalist Philosophy, but then what have you got to lose?

SOME IMMORTALIST AFFIRMATIONS TO START WITH

1. I forgive myself for thinking I had to die.
2. I forgive myself for wanting to die.
3. My desire to experience death was already completely satisfied long ago.
4. Since I am a success at life, I am now willing to be a failure at death.
5. I am safe and immortal right now.
6. I am alive now; therefore my life urges are stronger than my death urges. As long as I continue to strengthen my life urges and weaken my death urges, I will continue to live in increasing health and youthfulness.
7. The more I live, the more alive I become.
8. The longer I live, the more alive I become.
9. It is safe for me to confront my fears about death.
10. I choose to live.
11. I forgive all those people who died on me.
12. I love everything about my life.
13. My body is now healthy and every day the health of my body increases.
14. My life span increases every day whether I am aware of it or not.
15. My body is a pleasurable place to be.
16. Improving my health in enjoyable ways is always one of my favorite pleasures.
17. Everything I have ever been through has had a strengthening effect on all parts of me.
18. Since it is a miracle that I am alive in the first place, it is perfectly reasonable to think that I will still be here in 1000 years.

CHAPTER 46

A Comparison of Deathist and Immortalist Philosophies

Philosophers study thought and endeavor to create a coherent and consistent set of beliefs about life. A comparison of deathist and immortalist philosophies is a useful way to begin mastery of Immortalist Philosophy. We present the following chart for easy comparison and then we explore each point in detail.

As you study this chart, please bear in mind that we are presenting deathist philosophy and Immortalist Philosophy in their purest forms. The belief in the inevitability of death has been around for so long that there are many branches of the philosophies that it has developed. Religions that believe in any kind of an afterlife are less deathist by nature than existentialism which represents the ultimate in deathist philosophy. Of course every individual has an individual philosophy. Few people have completed their transformations to Immortalist Philosophy as of A.D. 1983. Not all personal philosophies of people who think they have no choice about death will fit perfectly the models we present, and not all personal philosophies of those who question the inevitability of death will fit perfectly the models we present for Immortalist Philosophy. We are describing general tendencies and we believe we are accurate in how we do that.

ASPECT OF LIFE	DEATHIST PHILOSOPHY	IMMORTALIST PHILOSPHY
Purpose of Life	Avoid ultimate and inevitable failure (death) for as long as possible. Avoid pain or experience pain. Attempt perpetual survival of genetic and philosophical characteristics by having and raising children and by serving others who have similar genetic and philsophical characteristics, often in competition with those of dissimilar genetic or philosophical characteristics.	Expand success, learning and service to infinity. Experience pleasure or avoid pleasure. Reproduce what is best in oneself through service to everyone regardless of their philosophical or genetic characteristics.
Purpose of Relationships	Sacrifice or control. Need/obligate.	Give and receive love.
God	Judgmental. All-powerful and remote being. Demanding of sacrifice.	Source of sources. Always available. The origin of individual personal reality. All loving in creating us. Present everywhere including in all the cells of our body.
Ethics	Determined by factors external to the individual. Situational. Exist to avoid punishment.	Individual. Self-determined. Absolute. Exist to increase love and creativity.
Relationship to group	Sacrifice for group.	Act as an inspirational example to others.
Government	Necessary to protect people from each other.	Largely unnecessary. Exists to make rules to improve the game.
Relationship with One's Body	Attachment to body. Necessary for survival. Dependency and resentment.	Body exists for one's pleasure and convenience.
Money	Scarcity	Abundance

PURPOSE OF LIFE

If you believe that death is inevitable, then your enjoyment and success are obviously limited in time, are a temporary reprieve from their inevitable cessation. No matter how much deathists succeed in life, they know that they must fail completely in the end. The opposite of success is accomplishing nothing, and deathists believe that they inevitably end up accomplishing nothing (we know of not a single dead person who is accomplishing anything of much significance at this time). To deathists the span of life is an infinitesimal portion of eternity, so that their aliveness is an exception to the general rule that they are dead. Accomplishment in life, to a deathist, is merely padding and protection from experiencing their fundamental, inanimate nature. We are aware that deathists do not usually think about it this way, but it is a logical corollary of deathist philosophy and therefore exists somewhere in a suppressed part of the logical mind of anybody who believes people are not responsible for their own deaths.

To an Immortalist, every action produces results that will affect their lives forever. This, coupled with holding everything that exists in a positive context (which is a necessary component of being Immortalist), results in an experience of eternal, expanding success.

To a deathist, the purpose of learning is to help one get as far as possible before the ax falls. To an Immortalist, learning is of eternal value.

Since personal survival is impossible for a deathist, the best attempt they can make at survival is the continuation of their genes and ideas (their bodies and minds, in a certain sense). This is the basis of sociobiology. To an Immortalist, service to all is a natural expansion of their own enjoyment of being alive.

Believing that old age, disease and death are an integral part of life makes life a matter of either suffering or temporary relief from suffering.

To an Immortalist *everything* is pleasurable, so there is only experiencing a particular pleasure or else avoiding it in order to experience another pleasure. If you are reading this book now, you are probably avoiding the pleasure of watching a movie in a theater. If you are enjoying being here then there is no necessity to go somewhere else for enjoyment; you can go somewhere else just for variety.

PURPOSE OF RELATIONSHIPS

In deathist reality, where life has apparently unchosen limitations, it is common for people to look to other people to provide the things that they think that they lack. Once love and safety are experienced in a relationship, there is a tendency to want to hang onto it, due to the belief that love is limited. The belief in limitation results in fear of loss which prevents you from receiving and experiencing the love of the other person. This fear of loss or dependency on the other person results in behavior designed to keep the other person with you, instead of accepting their love and presence as something that is natural and normal. There is then a tendency to obligate them to you so they won't leave, or a tendency to sacrifice for them so they won't leave, or a tendency to control them so they won't leave. The fear of the loss of a partner is an expression of the suppressed fear of death.

To a mortalist, loss is permanent and therefore loathsome, and therefore all change is, to some extent, made wrong. To an Immortalist, who is grateful for everything, "loss" is viewed as a change for the better.

In immortal relationships, neither partner fears the loss of the other. The essence of the relationship—the sharing of love—is more important than the form that the relationship takes. This attitude fosters enormously more freedom and honesty, which in turn create a much safer environment in which to experience and express genuine love.

GOD

In deathist philosophy, there is either no God at all (which makes randomness a sort of god) or else there is a contradiction between God being loving and God destroying your body against your will. Another way of saying this is that God is blamed for death, but no one has the courage to confront Him (Her) (It) about it. It is hoped that God has something better for us somewhere else, but *getting to* that something-better-somewhere-else is dependent upon obeying certain requirements. To make this even more confusing, different authorities on God's laws propound different sets of rules, so how can you be sure about anything?

In Immortalist Philosophy, God is That Which Exists, the Supreme Personality, expressing in Infinite Love, Infinite Intelligence, Infinite Being and Infinite Manifestation. Since God is infinite, almighty and everlasting, surely God has the ability, flexibility and willingness to satisfy everyone's desires for God. Another way of saying this is to say that your experience of God is determined by your thoughts.

ETHICS

In deathist reality, ethics is a set of beliefs that are imposed and enforced with an elaborate system of reward and punishment. If you believe that you are powerless over death, then you are unlikely to believe that you have the right to make up your own rules about life. The elaborate system of ethics varies with the situation, is enforced by other people, and is less than straightforward and simple. For example, killing another person is thought to warrant the award of a medal in certain circumstances, is thought to be an excusable error under different circumstances, and in some circumstances is considered a capital offense.

In Immortalist reality, ethics are the responsibility of the individual. Death is no longer the great escape from being responsible about life. Realizing that death is a choice makes it easier to act in accordance with the ethics that you choose.

We do not encourage selfishness. A person who sees death as a choice is likely to live life as a permanent resident of our planet and as a responsible member of society. Nor does Immortalist Philosophy encourage people to be rebels (except in rebelling against the tyranny of deathist beliefs by questioning the inevitability of death). There is no more satisfaction in rebellion than there is in conformity, since both rebellious and conformist patterns of behavior are motivated by the expectations of others. By choosing your own ethics, you choose to act and behave in accordance with your own highest thoughts.

RELATIONSHIP TO THE GROUP

Mortalists' logic is that since they are going to die anyway, the best thing they can do is to die in a way that preserves the survival of the group. This same kind of limited thinking extends to include every other example of thinking that sacrifice for the group is a virtue. The obvious problem with this attitude is that if everyone in the group is sacrificing then no one in group can be doing very well, with the ultimate example of this fallacy being warfare.

Since Immortalists view everything in life as being a choice, they feel that the best thing they can do for the group is to enliven themselves, prosper themselves, and please themselves to infinity so that the group will see their example and be inspired to do likewise.

GOVERNMENT

The major purpose of government in a deathist society is to protect people from each other and from bad circumstances of all kinds. The basic belief is that people are fundamentally victims who need someone else to take responsibility for their well-being since they are not responsible for their own well-being. So we have military forces capable of blowing up the world to protect us from people who live in other countries and we have police departments, prisons and execution chambers to protect us from our fellow citizens. As you may have noticed, none of these institutions succeed in providing us with security, the end of war or the end of crime.

What is accomplished in a war could obviously (obviously to most people nowadays we hope) be much better accomplished through other means. In the authors' opinions, the thing that makes war attractive to people is the apparent gambling with such high stakes; i.e., it is a victory-or-death situation for the participants. If the participants in a war win, they enjoy feeling that they defeated an opponent who was highly motivated; that is, they prove that they and their kind are superior to people who are unlike them. War is only a gamble to the extent that participants are unaware of their choice about living or dying. A war among Immortalists would be as uninteresting as going to Las Vegas and being certain about getting the cards that you asked for. The point is that the belief in the inevitability of death is the source of war and less organized forms of murder; war and crime are simply ways in which the belief is acted out.

Governments cannot even provide for the financial well-being of their citizens (if you question this, please interview recipients of social security benefits in any country and ask them how they feel about their income) let alone protect them from death. It is unreasonable for us as citizens to continue to expect governments to provide for us what they have for so long proved they are unable to deliver. Individual self-reliance is the only practical answer.

Democracy was the greatest step forward ever made in government. Democracy, however, is tyranny by the majority. The world is not free until everyone is free.

Death is the last tyranny to be eliminated. When all of us take full responsibility for our own lives, government will be perceived to have a very different role.

RELATIONSHIP WITH ONE'S BODY

Deathists regard the body as something necessary for their existence. Depending on their attitudes about existence, this makes them either very attached to their bodies or else desirous of destroying them.

Immortalists view their bodies as highly convenient tools for self-expression in the physical world. They treat their bodies with respect and love rather than as objects of need or obligation.

Having been both deathist at one time and Immortalist for several years now, the authors can tell you without equivocation that it *feels* better to occupy the body of an Immortalist than the body of a deathist.

MONEY

We are living in a highly materialistic society. "Materialistic" means thinking that material things are more valuable than ideas, capabilities, and things spiritual. People who are motivated by money seem to have less motivation to keep their material bodies around forever, and deathists tend to be materialistic. This is rather paradoxical when you consider that money is worthless without having a material body; i.e., if you are alive you are wealthier than all the dead people put together.

Immortalist Philosophy includes having an abundant consciousness about money. The idea that death is inevitable is a limiting idea and a source of belief in limitations about money.

CHAPTER 47

Unravelling Personal Allegiance to Death

Unravelling your personal allegiance to death means being responsible about your life. In this chapter we present techniques that increase your awareness of your choices regarding your thoughts about death. Becoming aware of choices is all that we are really talking about in this whole part of our book called "Immortalist Philosophy."

RECALL THE FIRST TIME YOU WERE
TOLD YOU HAD TO DIE

Relax and recall as many of your early conversations and experiences regarding death as possible. Especially remember the first time anybody ever told you in a convincing way that you had to die; the suppressed feelings associated with this event are at the very core of your most limiting negativity.

Other good things to remember are deaths in your family or among your friends or other people you knew, especially ones that occurred when you were very young. Also recall near-death experiences that you have had in your life: near drownings, falls that knocked you unconscious, auto accidents, violent attacks, war experiences, etc. Focus on the feelings that these experiences bring up and allow yourself to enjoy those feelings.

INVESTIGATE YOUR FAMILY TRADITION ABOUT DEATH

Ideas about death are passed down from generation to generation. It is common for people in a family to die at about the same ages of about the same causes generation after generation. Try to create a "family tree" going back at least four generations and discover what your ancestors died of at what ages. This will tell you a lot about the programming you received regarding what is socially acceptable regarding death.

Talk to your oldest living relatives and try to find out as much as you can about the personalities of your ancestors. Most people who don't engage in extensive self-improvement fit into one of the following four categories: moderate rebels or extreme rebels, or moderate conformists or extreme conformists. These categories tend to have a large influence on patterns of death. Moderate rebels usually outlive their parents, acting out a suppressed desire to see their parents dead. Extreme rebels tend to die at about the same age as their parents. Extreme conformists may die before their parents in a subconscious effort to protect their parents or other family members' from the family's own death-urges.

Investigate the attitudes that your parents have about death and about their bodies. These are probably the same or very nearly the same as your own subconscious attitudes about these things.

There is an excellent chance that you will reap extreme benefits from being a skillful Sherlock Holmes in these matters.

MAKE A LIST OF REASONS THAT YOU MUST DIE OR WHY YOU WOULD WANT TO DIE

Make one list of 5 reasons that you have to die. Make another list of 5 reasons that death might seem desirable to you. These processes may make you feel very uncomfortable, but as we have extensively pointed out, uncomfortable feelings are opportunities to integrate suppressed negativity. Be brave, keep breathing, and be grateful for your feelings. Be completely honest. If you get stuck and can't think of any more reasons, then make the rest of them up using your imagination. When each list of 5 is complete, create affirmations to handle each item on the list. At the end of this process you may feel more alive than ever before.

BE GRATEFUL THAT YOU ARE ALIVE

A very telling question to ask yourself frequently is: Would I be willing to live forever experiencing exactly what I am experiencing in this moment? Death is a result of making life wrong. This question will tell you whether you are making your life wrong enough for you to kill yourself (consciously or unconsciously) in order to escape from your life.

Again make two lists: a list of the 20 things you are the most grateful for and a list of the 20 things you hate the most. Then put each of the 40 items into affirmations in the format "I am so grateful for _____ that I am willing to live forever in order to keep experiencing it." If you expand your gratitude to include absolutely everything then you will expand your aliveness to infinity.

USE REBIRTHING TO UNRAVEL YOUR ALLEGIANCE TO DEATH

The practice of connected breathing used in Rebirthing increases the flow of life-force energy in the body. At the same time, concentrating on your breath naturally brings you into the present moment and heightens your awareness of your aliveness. When a person has enough experience with Rebirthing to be certain that the breath and the energy it generates are the strongest things in the body, then it becomes instinctive to regard any physical symptoms or weakenesses as temporary.

TAKE FULL RESPONSIBILITY FOR RETRAINING YOUR THOUGHTS ABOUT LIFE AND DEATH

Like any new idea, the idea of physical immortality is at first a fragile thing. Despite its obvious attractiveness, there is no reason to believe in it at first. If you have allowed yourself to be convinced that death is inevitable, then physical immortality is a matter of taking responsibility to convince yourself otherwise.

ADDITIONAL COMMENTS ON IMMORTALIST PHILOSOPHY

Immortalist Philosophy is not primarily about living forever. Its benefits are much more immediate than that. There are two main purposes to all of the information in this book: to make you happier and more powerful *now*. Contemplation of physical immortality assists enormously with both the activation and the integration of suppressed make-wrong duality, and thus enormously supports both of those two main purposes. It is natural that the happier and more powerful you are, the longer you will live, and the healthier you will be while you are living. The expansion of your aliveness, happiness and power may be a gradual process, but every step of the way it *feels* good.

Immortalists do not necessarily feel great all the time. They do, however, have a sense of humor and a sense of perspective about their emotions. Life is the most valuable gift you have been given. The ability to feel grateful for your life is more valuable than everything else put together.

CHAPTER 48

Practical Body Mastery

Practical body mastery is learning to listen to your body and learning to take care of it so that it lasts forever. All of us have received a generous portion of social conditioning about our bodies—what to eat, how to eat, when to sleep and so on. The first step is to realize that none of the traditional practices regarding taking care of your body were designed to enable you to keep it forever. There is no scientific evidence that proves that three meals per day enable you to live forever. The idea of three meals per day is taught by people who have never tried anything else. The most important aspect of practical body mastery is the willingness to experiment. It is the willingness to become your own scientist, devising the experiments and then watching the results. An experiment is a departure from regular practice. Several ideas for experiments will be discussed here and you are free to invent your own experiments. The key to success with the experiments is gentleness. If you are accustomed to a diet of brown rice and lemon juice, for example, and you abruptly change your diet to pizza and root beer, you will probably feel sick. One diet is not necessarily better than the other; it is the abrupt change that creates the upset. If you were to change abruptly from pizza and root beer to brown rice and lemon juice you would also feel sick.

FOOD

Food is an area where most people have received a substantial dose of conditioning. Meal time is frequently an emotion-packed event at which the children are informed of the dire consequences that they can expect if they do not eat. This message was repeated three times per day from a very early age until you either decided to comply or stopped paying attention.

Fasting has two purposes The physical purpose of fasting is to cleanse the body. The psychological purpose of fasting is to increase awareness about the suppressed beliefs that you have regarding food and nourishment.

If you have no experience with fasting, it is important to approach this with gentleness. You might try eating nothing one day per week, or eating only two meals per day, or alternating one-meal days with three-meal days. If you have never tried being completely vegetarian for extended periods of time, we highly recommend that you experiment with this. As you do any of these experiments (or perhaps even think about doing them), you will become aware of some of the beliefs that you have about dependency on food. Here are some affirmations to facilitate the process:

FOOD AFFIRMATIONS

1. I no longer support inaccurate beliefs about food and mind.
2. My body is constantly nourished whether I eat or not.
3. I can take it or leave it.
4. I have the right to say no without losing people's love.

TEMPERATURE MASTERY

The abrupt temperature change that occurs for most people at birth creates a widespread association of temperature with discomfort. Some people seemingly never feel comfortable with any temperature and think that they are always either too hot or too cold. Many people associate changes of temperature with illness in spite of the fact that some of the healthiest people on virtually every continent make a cultural practice of heating their bodies to a high temperature in saunas or sweat lodges and then plunging into cold water or banks of snow. What you think will make you ill probably will in fact make you ill. Discovering what thoughts and beliefs you have about temperature and then improving those thoughts and beliefs has a high potential for making you more comfortable and more healthy, as well as more creative at a wider range of temperatures.

Hot and cold water Rebirthing greatly assist in gaining mastery over temperature. Here are some affirmations to help you, as well:

AFFIRMATIONS ABOUT TEMPERATURE:

1. I no longer support inaccurate beliefs about temperature and my body.
2. My body is comfortable in an increasing range of temperature.
3. It is safe for me to relax into the energy that causes me to shiver.
4. I love everything about coldness.
5. I love everything about heat.

SLEEP MASTERY

Sleeping each night is a practice engaged in by almost all of us. It is accepted as a standard practice and not questioned. Examining sleep in regard to the time that we spent in the womb as a prenatal infant provides interesting insights into the practice of sleeping. When we sleep, we demand quiet and darkness, we crawl under covers which exert pressure on the body and which elevate the skin temperature, and it is common for people to want another person present with whom they enjoy cuddling. Some people take it even a step further and enjoy a water bed. All of these conditions plus the fact that sleep is a non-verbal state of consciousness simulate the conditions in the womb. If you regularly sleep every night without thinking about it, the thoughts and feelings that you have suppressed about sleep will stay suppressed because you are obeying them and there is no reason for them to come to your conscious attention. When you begin to change your pattern of sleep by staying up all night, say once per week at first, and allow yourself to breathe through the feelings that come to your attention, you will surely learn some interesting things about yourself and your emotions. It is common for people to integrate suppressed anger or to integrate fear of loneliness by staying up and breathing during periods when they usually sleep.

AFFIRMATIONS

1. My energy exceeds my fatigue.
2. My energy exceeds other people's fatigue.
3. My wakeful environment is more restful than the womb.
4. I am glad to be out of the womb.

EXPLORE HOLISTIC HEALTH PRACTICES

There are so many excellent sources of information on diet, exercise, herbs, bodywork, etc., that there is no point in us going into the subject too extensively in this book. We do suggest that you make a hobby of experimenting with all of these things to discover which ones feel good to you.

CHAPTER 49

Healing and Pain

Healing is the result of integration in your body. It is the result of allowing energy to flow in a portion of your body where it had previously been blocked. There are many efficient methods of healing available. It is up to each individual to select the most appropriate method.

Laying on of hands or massage is a well-known form of natural healing. When someone gently touches a part of your body, you naturally pay more attention to that part and have an increased awareness of the part that is being touched. The increased awareness causes additional energy to flow to that part of your body and the healing process is enhanced.

Healing in Rebirthing takes place in much the same manner, except that it is the willingness of the Rebirthee to relax into the energy flow in the body, instead of the touch of the body worker, that acts as the catalyst. In this sense Rebirthing could be called giving yourself a massage from the inside out.

Pain is held in place by fear. If you allow yourself to relax into the fear sufficiently, you can discover that pain is held in place by specific, suppressed, fearful thoughts. Two of these are fear of worsening and fear of irreparable damage.

With fear of worsening, the person experiences a body sensation, then makes the body sensation wrong and then becomes afraid that it will get worse. The reaction to the fear that it will get worse is to tense or tighten the body as protection against the anticipated worsening pain. The cycle completes when the pain in fact does get worse as a result of the increased tension and the person's fear is validated. Hypochondriacs manifest fear of worsening to an extreme degree.

With fear of irreparable damage, the person is afraid that the pain will cause or has already caused damage that is beyond healing. If you have begun to integrate the philosophy of immortality, you can see that birth (which was irreparable damage to life in the womb) is the last irreparable damage that you need to suffer.

The most important thing to notice about pain is that it is a context. Pain means that there is a sensation that the person is making wrong. A person can make even a normal sensation wrong and experience it as being painful. A person can also surrender to a painful sensation and experience it as pleasurable. To do so is tantamount to integrating the fear that was holding the "pain" in place and facilitates faster healing.

Healing and curing are different. If someone has symptoms that are cured, that means the person has been returned to the same state that existed before the symptoms came to the surface. If the person has not integrated the suppressed thoughts and feelings that caused the symptoms in the first place then the person is in a condition where the symptoms may recur or perhaps recur in a different form. Healing means that the person has integrated the suppressed thoughts and feelings that caused the symptoms.

If you are earnest in your intention to heal yourself, then the information in this chapter about Immortalist Philosophy is of great importance to you. It is axiomatic that a cure is temporary unless the belief in the inevitability of death is healed.

AFFIRMATIONS

1. It is safe, easy and pleasurable for me to allow my symptoms to be dissolved by the energy that makes my body feel good.
2. My aliveness is much stronger than my pain.
3. Everything is more pleasurable than everything else.
4. I am safe and immortal right now.
5. My body has a natural tendency to heal itself.
6. I am always led to people who assist my healing.
7. People I employ support my healing.
8. Doctors and everyone assist me in healing myself.

CHAPTER 50

Aging and Youthing

Aging is a process that is the result of clinging to the belief in the inevitability of death. In this section, we shall present some ideas about aging and youthing. "Youthing," which means the opposite of aging, is a term coined by Leonard Orr, the founder of Rebirthing, and an exponent and practitioner of Immortalist Philosophy.

Some thought-provoking paradoxes about the inevitability of aging: Obviously, our bodies are continuously in the process of replacing their cells. It has been said that every seven years each of us has a completely new body, because all of its cells have been replaced with new cells. If our bodies grow new cells, then in order to age, the new cells have to be older than the cells they replaced. If they are new cells, how can they be older? When a fetus is formed from the body of a 25-year-old father and the body of a 25-year-old mother, do we think of the fetus as being 25 years old? In that case, all of us would be millions of years old. In order to age, you must have the ability to replace old cells with new cells that have characteristics that are different from the ones that they replaced. If you already have the ability to grow cells that are older, then couldn't you just as easily grow cells that are younger? Or the same age perhaps? Everybody gets older you say? How do you know? Do you know everybody?

Most Rebirthers know many people who have restored their bodies to youthful appearance and vitality by using the principles we describe in this book.

Consider the physical and psychological changes that most people expect from the process called aging: Hair falls out, teeth fall out, physical strength decreases, some people experience motor-coordination difficulties in walking and talking, and sometimes incontinence. Are not these the same things that we experienced as an infant? Isn't it possible that aging and senility are a manifestation of a suppressed desire to return to the womb? Is it not possible that integrating memories and emotions of the transition from the womb to our current environment would free a person from the suppressed desire to return to the womb?

In observing anything that is alive and thriving there is no empirical or logical basis for assuming that it will, with certainty, eventually die. The belief that death is inevitable is a *theory* no matter how widespread the belief that it is a law might be. Recently the belief that human beings could not fly was just as widespread. The burden of proof rests on the proponents of such theories of limitation, not on those who challenge them. We offer a challenge: if there is anybody who thinks they can prove conclusively that everyone who was alive in 1720 is now dead, let them come forward with their evidence. Furthermore, if there is anyone in the scientific community who can prove conclusively that everything that is alive now must eventually die, we challenge them to do so.

We, the authors of this book, do not claim to know the future. We do not claim that we have certainty that we, or anyone else, will in fact live forever. This is because we do know that we still have unconscious minds and it is the nature of the unconscious mind that the conscious mind does not know what the unconscious mind contains.

We do know with certainty, however, that people produce their own results with their own conscious and unconscious thoughts. When people produce any result in their lives, including death, it is because they had the conscious or unconscious intention to produce that result.

We have observed time and time again that people reap vast rewards from challenging the assumption that death is inevitable. Holding open the possibility that any barrier can be overcome is enormously more productive than closing one's mind and assuming that any limitation is absolute.

Well, what do you think? The choice is really up to you.

PART VI

YOUR FUTURE
AND YOU

The past and present are by their natures very different from the future. You cannot do anything about the past or the present because they already are the way they are. The future, however, has not been created yet, and it is your choices, thoughts, conscious and unconscious desires and actions that determine what your future will be. Earlier parts of this book have been largely about making peace with your past and present experiences. This part is about choosing your future and creating the future you choose.

You can start anywhere and then arrive anywhere, by following any of an infinite number of courses of action. For instance, no matter where you are right now, there exist an infinite number of possible ways for you to be in Paris, or anywhere else, on June 1 of next year. Where you are now determines the starting point of your journey and that is all.

If you do not know where you would like to be on June 1 of next year, we have processes to help you decide. If you know you want to be in Paris on June 1 of next year but don't know how to get from here to there, then we have processes to help you with that, too. If you don't care where you'll be on June 1 of next year, or you think it's not up to you, or you think it's not worth the bother anyway, then we even offer processes to help you with those conditions. Even if you know where you intend to be, you know how to do it, you are highly motivated and you know that you will succeed, then we expect that somewhere in this part you will still find something that will inspire you, something that will help you deal with someone less fortunate than yourself, or at least something that will amuse you.

CHAPTER 51

Desire

There are two kinds of desire: consciously chosen desire and unconsciously chosen desire that comes about by making something wrong.

Consciously chosen desires are what people want their lives to be about. For instance, you might choose to have the desire to eliminate world hunger, or to become a more prosperous person, or to get a college degree.

Unconsciously chosen desires are always desires for relief from unreal conditions. For instance, if you made your father wrong, and then suppressed it, then you simultaneously created a desire to be unlike your father. But you already are unlike your father! In spite of the obviousness of this situation, millions (probably billions) of people spend substantial parts of their lives acting out unconscious desires to be unlike their fathers.

Unconsciously chosen desires divert much time and energy from pursuing consciously chosen desires.

Integration does not eliminate desire, it purifies desire by eliminating the needless cross-current desires created by make-wrong duality.

Another way to describe an unconsciously chosen desire is to say that it is a pattern of energy in the body with an accompanying thought about what it would take to make that pattern of energy go away.

Integrating a desire means that you allow yourself to experience the desire, in your body, fully, and allow yourself to enjoy that feeling rather than try to make it go away. For instance, if you want a cigarette that means that you have some feeling in your body that you think you can suppress by smoking one. If you allow yourself to enjoy that feeling, then you will not want the cigarette anymore. You can always integrate any desire you choose, providing you are skillful enough at applying the Five Elements of Rebirthing.

With any desire you have four options: satisfy it but don't integrate it, satisfy it and integrate it, integrate it but don't satisfy it, and neither satisfy it nor integrate it. For example, suppose your car is dirty and you have a desire for it to be clean:

If you satisfy the desire but don't integrate it, then you will make the car wrong for being dirty. You will wash it, but you won't be happy until the job is done; then you will get temporary relief, not happiness, because even when it's clean you will still be making it wrong for being in the process of getting dirty again.

If you satisfy the desire and integrate it, then you will enjoy the car while it's dirty, you will enjoy having the desire to wash it, you will wash it enthusiastically, you will be happy when the job is done and you will still be happy even when it gets dirty again.

If you integrate the desire but don't satisfy it, then you will choose to enjoy having a dirty car and enjoy not washing it. This is a fine option if you have something better to do than wash the car. (Of course, this is the best of the four options if you have a desire to do anything harmful.)

If you neither satisfy it nor integrate it, then you will go into ennui, which is described in detail in the next chapter.

CHAPTER 52

Ennui

Ennui (pronounced "on-we") is the sense of futility and boredom that results from operating in momentary time contexts but not linear time contexts. When people complain about feeling helpless, hopeless, frustrated or bored, what they are saying is that they are in a state of ennui and are making it wrong. If you ever find yourself on a seemingly ceaseless roller-coaster ride with highs of listless relief and lows of listless fear, guilt and self-hatred, then you are in a state of ennui. It is a result of procrastination, of putting off tomorrow's problems until tomorrow.

When one surrenders into the present moment, one discovers that one has preferences. You will notice that your preferences are there whether or not you want them to be and whether or not you tell the truth about them. When one doesn't tell the truth about one's preferences, one is well on the way to ennui.

Ennui can also be described in terms of having desires but pretending not to, rather than either integrating them or doing anything to satisfy them.

Ennui also results when a person has fears but doesn't do anything about preventing what is feared from happening. Every fear is the source of a goal—unless the fear is made wrong and suppressed. Integration of fear makes you comfortable with fear, but it only makes the fear go away to the extent that you are doing what it takes to keep what you are fearing from happening to you. For example, everyone who is alive and isn't preventing nuclear war is afraid of nuclear war whether they admit it or not. Saying that it can't happen is just suppression. Fear of nuclear war actually obligates all of us to do the best things we can think of to prevent it. Whether nuclear war will ever happen is not what matters here—the *threat* of nuclear war is what we are talking about. This situation has virtually everybody in the world in ennui.

Anytime you think that what you do doesn't matter, you are in ennui.

Ennui is hiding from one's purpose. To feel purposeless and to be in ennui are two ways of saying the same thing. The only cure for ennui is to look at your preferences and fears, examine your abilities, decide what your purpose is and *get on with it.*

Some people spend their lives waiting for some project to come along that will "ignite their passion." These people are in ennui. What they do not realize is that passion can be, and needs to be, cultivated. The point is that you are going to do *something* during the next six months and "just waiting" is probably not your highest option. Decide what the best thing is that you can think of and then let your natural passion for existence itself extend to include that. You are more likely to think of something better to do while you are doing something productive than while you are "just waiting," anyway.

If you don't usually think of yourself in terms of having a purpose, then you have a fairly severe case of ennui. The following process is designed to break you free of the clutches of ennui.

To use this process, you may find it helpful to work with a partner, preferably someone with a stronger sense of purpose than yourself, but anyone who is willing to tell you the truth unequivocally will do fine.

HOW TO ELIMINATE ENNUI
AND GET ON WITH YOUR PURPOSE
—OR—
THE "FROM ENNUI TO ONWARD" PROCESS

Instructions:

1. Make a list of the 5 most important changes that you want to make in your life. Be specific.
2. Make a list of the 5 things you are most afraid might happen. Be honest!
3. Convert each item in step 2 to its positive opposite. State this

as a goal. (For example, if you are afraid of nuclear war, then convert that to the goal "to be eternally safe from nuclear war.") Discard the list you made in step 2.
4. From the list in steps 1 and 3 pick the single most important item. This is your prospective goal.
5. See if the prospective goal fits the following criteria:
   a. It must be specific.
   b. It must be attainable within 3 months. (For less severe cases of ennui, use a period of 6 months or one year. If you don't already have the next 3 months extensively planned, use the three-month period. If you already have the next twelve months extensively planned, use a two-year period. If you already have the next two years satisfactorily planned, you don't need this process.)
   c. It must be highly important to you.
   d. It must be challenging.
   If the item doesn't fit all of the above criteria, go back to step 4 and choose the next most important item. If none of the ten items fits all four criteria, go back to step 1.
6. Ask yourself "On a scale from 0-100, how certain am I that I am willing to achieve this goal? TELL THE TRUTH!
7. If your answer to the question in step 6 was 99 or less, than say out loud, "What's between me and being certain that I am willing to _____ is _____."
   Just say the stem sentence and then keep talking and say whatever comes to mind. Keep doing this until you achieve a breakthrough, then go back to step 6.
8. Once you are 100% certain that you are willing to achieve the goal, make a list of everything you can think of that you could possibly do to help you achieve the goal.
9. Using the list in step 8, create a logical plan, a series of steps, that will enable you to achieve the goal.
10. See if the plan you created in step 9 fits the following criteria:
    a. The plan must be specific.
    b. The plan must be direct.
    c. The plan must be highly likely to succeed.
    d. The plan must make you feel emotionally activated.
    e. You must be able to start on the plan immediately.
    If the plan doesn't fit all of the above criteria, then go back to step 8.
11. For at least 2 minutes say out loud to yourself, "Something I

have to give up to follow this plan is _____."
This is just to get you clear on the truth about it.

12. Ask yourself, "On a scale of 0-100, how willing am I to start this plan immediately and follow it through to completion?" TELL THE TRUTH!

13. If your answer to the question in step 12 was 99 or less, then say out loud, "What's between me and following this plan is _____." Keep going until you achieve a breakthrough, then go back to step 12.

14. Fit the plan into your schedule, so that you know exactly when you will do each of the steps in the plan.

15. Do it!

CHAPTER 53

Overwhelm

Overwhelm is a close relative of ennui. Overwhelm can be described as the belief that you have more things that you must do than you can hold in your mind at once.

The active life of a busy, productive member of society is an enjoyable and satisfying experience. If you are overwhelmed by it, it is difficult to notice the joy and the satisfaction. Obviously Rebirthing allows you to integrate the sense of emergency and panic about life that was suppressed at birth.

We can think of two other ways out of overwhelm.

The first is easy. Make a list of the things you want to do. This simple practice frees the mental energy that you are using to remember everything and allows you to concentrate that energy on one thing at a time.

The second way out of overwhelm is less easy. Keep doing the things that are in your mind until the number that you have left to do is small enough so that you can hold them all in your mind at once.

CHAPTER 54

Taking Responsibility

You cannot change anything effectively without taking responsibility for it being the way it already is, for your preference that it be different, and for the process of changing it. For example, if you are broke and you want to become a millionaire, to be effective you must acknowledge that *your* thoughts and actions led you to the point of contemplating your lack of money, *you* have chosen to be rich, and that if *you* do not cause large amounts of money to come to you and accumulate then very possibly nobody else will either.

"Taking responsibility" for something means that two conditions are satisfied: 1) you acknowledge yourself as the source of it, and 2) you acknowledge that the situation *the way it already is* is perfect. Acknowledging that you are the source of something without acknowledging that it is perfect is not taking responsibility, it is self-blame. There is a world of difference between saying, "I created this" and saying, "Some messed up part of me created this."

Taking responsibility is the opposite of blame. Blame does not work very well when you wish to create a result. If you blame your lack of money on "the economy," then you will have to wait until the economy changes before your financial situation will improve.

There is no discernible disadvantage to taking responsibility for everything that exists, whether you can see how you are responsible for it or not. If you fully take responsibility for something, then you will either succeed at producing the result you intend or you will fail. If you do not take responsibility you can only fail!

If your conscious mind does not see how it created something, then that means that some part of your unconciousness mind created it. Finding ways in which the thing is perfect will put your conscious mind in contact with the causative part of your unconscious mind, which *already* sees it as perfect. Integration facilitates taking responsibility and taking responsibility facilitates integration. Integration facilitates your ability to cause change.

CHAPTER 55

Values and Motivation

If you have read other self-improvement books or attended self-improvement seminars, you may have been presented with rags-to-riches stories or stories of miraculous healings from dread diseases in order to motivate you to duplicate the results of the person in the story. We have chosen to avoid that approach in this book. Regardless of the results that you have created in the past and regardless of the results that you are now creating, you had motivation to create them or they wouldn't have occurred.

Motivation is the result of values. In other words you are already motivated to increase your supply of the things that you consider valuable and to diminish or eliminate your supply of the things that you consider detrimental. Therefore, if you have a value system that supports you in life, you will never have to worry about your motivation; however, if your value system doesn't support you in expressing your aliveness fully, then you will always be questioning your motivation.

THE CHARACTERISTICS OF VALUE

We will start with two concepts about value.

ONE—THE MOST VALUABLE THINGS IN LIFE ARE AVAILABLE IN INFINITE SUPPLY.

TWO—THE MOST VALUABLE THINGS IN LIFE ARE ETERNAL.

The Creator of the Universe is a benevolent being. Unless you are willing to accept this idea, you are in for a lot of struggle in your life. We are living in a world in which everyone can win. This means everyone regardless of race, religion, nationality, gender, chronological age, socio-economic level or any other form of differentiation that you might consider. This is true because each individual creates his or her own game, creates all the rules and goals of that game, and decides which strategies and tactics to use in achieving those goals. From this stems the idea that the most valuable things are available in infinite supply.

The opposite of the idea that we are presenting is called, "The Theory of Limited Good." The Theory of Limited Good comprises the following line of reasoning: 1) Valuable things are limited; 2) Since valuable things are limited, it takes an unlimited supply of valuable things to be truly secure, and I don't have enough; 3) Other people have all the valuable things that I don't have; 4) The people who have the valuable things that I don't have think that they don't have enough, too, so they are unwilling to give me the valuable things that I need and desire; 5) Therefore, the only way for me to increase my supply of valuable things, which I must do, is to take them away from other people, by using manipulation or force, whether they want me to take them away or not. Note that if you are working at a job you don't like, merely to get your boss to give you money, that is a form of manipulation.

The Theory of Limited Good is the basis of most economic systems. Indeed it is an important premise of many economic systems that value comes from limitation itself! The Theory of Limited Good has obviously resulted in an enormous number of conflicts ranging from domestic disagreements to worldwide warfare.

The best things in life *are* free. It is easy to imagine that there is an abundant supply of things like LOVE, JOY, TRUST, GENTLENESS, CREATIVITY, FORGIVENESS and HONESTY. Even if you believe that only material goods are what are valuable, then consider that production creates wealth and that there is no shortage of production. Even if you are only willing to consider that money is valuable the only way to have a limited supply of money is to stop the flow of money. Obviously there is some definite number that expresses the amount of money that there is in the world at any given moment. However, the circulation of money allows people to use the same money over and over, making the actual supply of money infinite.

If you are taking responsibility for your life, then your ability to get anything that you think is valuable to you is limited only by your imagination. If you think that your imagination is limited, then we suggest that you start keeping a journal by your bed and that every morning you write down in it all the dreams you can remember having during the night. Along with many other benefits that you will probably derive from this process, you will also discover that your imagination is very, very vast.

The idea that the most valuable things in life are eternal comes from the idea of Immortalist Philosophy. If you are willing to contemplate being here forever, then you will find that you are motivated to increase your supply of things that will last as long as you will. Something that lasts forever is clearly more valuable than something that will wear out as soon as the warranty expires.

The idea that the most valuable things in life are both abundant and eternal is quite a contrast to the way many of us were taught to think. Integrating this way of thinking into your life is the beginning of freedom from identification with your external circumstances and conditions—freedom from identifying with your results, your credentials, your possessions and your money. Adopting this value system means, for example, that the ability to heal your body is more valuable than a healthy body; that certainty about your ability to earn $1,000 per week doing work that you love is more valuable than a very large sum of money; the willingness to forgive yourself and others is more valuable than saying the right thing or acting in the right way.

FROM CONDITIONED MOTIVATION TO SELF-MOTIVATION

The freedom and pleasures of being a self-motivated person are that you set your own purpose in life, you choose what your goals are, you evaluate your results and you make corrections yourself where necessary. Conditioned motivation means responding to the conditioning that you have received as though it were the only way, rather than making a conscious choice about it.

AFFIRMATIONS ABOUT VALUES AND MOTIVATION

1. I have the practical wisdom to change my values whenever it is to my advantage to do so.
2. My sense of well-being has nothing to do with _____.

(For instance, "My sense of well-being has nothing to do with my financial situation.")

3. I forgive myself for thinking I needed _____ to motivate me. (For instance, "I forgive myself for thinking I needed disapproval to motivate me.)

4. I am safe whether or not I am in control.

5. The things that are most valuable to me are infinite and eternal.

CHAPTER 56

Purpose

In creating the results that you intend, the first step is to have clarity about purpose. Another way to say this is—How do you expect to get what you want if you don't know what you are doing? A purpose can be thought of as a broadly worded statement that is perpetual in nature and that directs your activities and thinking. A purpose is something that is expressed continuously: *not* something that is achieved once. A purpose is an idea that brings you so much satisfaction and pleasure that you are willing to devote your life to it.

1. Make a list of 10 unique personality characteristics that you like about yourself. For example: my sense of humor, my ability to learn.

2. The next step is making a list of 10 ways that you enjoy expressing these characteristics. For example: teaching, talking, listening, writing newspaper articles, singing in church.

3. The third step is to write a brief statement of your vision of a perfect world. For example: clean air and water, everlasting peace on Earth, abundance and joy for everyone.

4. Step four is to write a sentence in the following form using items that you select from the three previous steps. MY PURPOSE IS TO USE MY ____(insert selected items from step 1)____ AND MY _____ BY (insert selected items from step 2) AND _____ SO THAT (OR TO CREATE) ____(insert step 3)____.

For example: My purpose is to use my integrity, receptivity, willingness to forgive and clear self-expression by Rebirthing, writing and talking to create a body and a society filled with Everlasting Physical Life, love of God and abundance.

Some people find it useful to perform this process more than once to define a purpose that they like, and you may find that you want to modify your purpose from time to time using this process.

For people who have difficulty in accomplishing their goals and for people who find that accomplishing goals is not very satisfying; having a purpose and being committed to its expression adds meaning and direction to their lives. Once you have defined a purpose that you like, we suggest that you write it on a small piece of paper and carry it with you in your wallet or purse. You will find that having a purpose that you like well enough to be committed to will provide focus for your activities and will make the process of coming to decisions much, much easier.

CHAPTER 57

Goals

Goals can be thought of as milestones or signals that you are in a state of continuous expression and realization of your purpose. As mentioned earlier a purpose is something that is continually expressed. By contrast, accomplishing a goal is a particular event that occurs in linear time. We suggest that you have lots and lots of goals. It is a good idea to have goals that seem easy to you and goals that seem to be beyond your reach. It is a good idea to have goals about your body, goals about your relationships, goals about your business and money, goals about skills that you would like to learn, goals about personality traits that you would like to develop in yourself and goals about the world. Another way to look at goals is to make a list of all the things that you would like to be, do and have in your life.

Accomplishing goals requires the ability to hold the image in your mind of your intended result before your goal has manifested in your external reality. There may be times when your external reality will appear very different from the image that you are holding in your mind. This process becomes easier with practice and with the use of the techniques that we describe in this book. One reason that we suggest that you select many goals is to give yourself lots of practice with this technique of holding an image in your mind before the result has manifested. Each time you accomplish a goal, the next one becomes easier.

PROCESS:

Make a list of 100 things you would like to be, a list of 100 things you would like to do, a list of 100 things you would like to have, and finally, a list of 100 things you would like for the world. From the 400 items, select one, decide on a specific day by which you intend to complete its manifestation, make a plan for manifesting it, and do it. You will probably find that in the course of fulfilling one goal you fulfill several others also, whether or not you consciously intended to do so.

AFFIRMATIONS

1. It is OK for me to exceed my goals.
2. I am willling to know what I want; I am willing to ask for it; and I am willing to receive exactly what I ask for.
3. Everything works out more exquisitely than I plan it.
4. Success is natural for me.
5. My strong sense of purpose attracts those people and situations necessary to accomplish my desired result.

CHAPTER 58

Planning

Once you have chosen your goal and have taken full responsibility for manifesting it, you will want to create a definite plan of action. If you were about to embark on a car trip from San Francisco to Miami Beach, you would look at a map and select the route you prefer. Doing so enables you to do three things: to make all of the correct turns, to know when you are on the right course, and to know when you have left the right course. If you do deviate from your chosen course, you do not need to make yourself wrong for it; you can simply minimize the deviation and get back on course in the most efficient way possible, while enjoying the scenery you would have missed if you had stayed on course. It is also usually helpful to set particular target times for completing various segments of your journey.

Planning anything works basically the same way. Without a clear, logical, workable plan you are not very likely to achieve anything very desirable in life. Planning and following a plan are absolutely essential parts of taking responsibility.

Whenever you have a goal, that means that you presently have something else instead of that goal. In order to attain any goal you must give up something that you have now. Using the example above, you cannot go to Miami without giving up being in San Francisco. If you want to become wealthy you must give up your poverty. People often have difficulty achieving their goals because they have unconscious attachments to what they must give up in order to attain them. One useful idea in remedying this situation is that you can enjoy having something be in your past just as much as you can enjoy having it in your present or future. Living can be described as a process of putting more and more experiences into the past, anyway. Enjoying putting things that are in your present permanently into your past is tantamount to enjoying your life. This kind of thinking is very helpful in breaking attachments and getting on with your purpose.

AFFIRMATIONS ABOUT PLANNING

1. I have the practical wisdom to create clear, logical, workable plans.
2. Planning and following my plans are two of my favorite pleasures.
3. I am completely willing to obey the orders I give myself.
4. I enjoy my past as much as my present or my future.
5. I am always willing to put anything permanently into my past whenever it is to my advantage to do so.

INTEGRATIVE PLANNING PROCESS

This process is useful in making any kind of plan, once you are absolutely clear about your goal.

1. State the situation you desire to create. Be specific.
2. State the situation as it is now. Be simple and exact.
3. Make a list of all the advantages you get from the situation the way it is now.
4. For each item in step 3, create at least 3 ways to get the same advantage even after achieving your goal in step 1.
5. Make a list of all the factors that contribute to the situation being the way it is now.
6. For each item in step 5, create a course of action which will either eliminate the factor or adapt you to it in a positive way.
7. Make a list of things you can do that would contribute to your achieving your goal.
8. From lists 4, 6, and 7, create a plan that has a very high probability of succeeding and that you are willing and able to carry out.
9. Fit the plan into your schedule.
10. Do it.

CHAPTER 59

Structures

Structures are planning devices that you create in order to assist you in achieving your goals. Examples of structures are schedules, budgets, marriage, and making an agreement with yourself to do an hour of yoga first thing every morning.

It is important to choose your structures consciously, because if you don't you will choose your structures unconsciously. Unconsciously chosen structures are called "habits".

Creating effective structures for yourself is a fine art. Structures that work for other people may very well not work for you, because your mind is unique and you have different goals and different pre-existing habits. Creativity and the willingness to acknowledge that a structure hasn't been working are essential, as well as having a good attitude about starting over. Remember that you get lasting benefit from a structure even if you use it for only a short while. If you exercise every day for only four days when you had created a structure to do it forever, you are still much better off than if you hadn't exercised at all, not only because of the beneficial exercise but also because you learned something about yourself in relation to structure. Rededicate yourself to your goal, create a new structure utilizing what you learned from the old one, and start over again enthusiastically. This can be a joyous lifelong process and there is no substitute for it in terms of increasing your effectiveness at getting what you want.

All of life can be described in terms of games. You might be playing the Prevent-Nuclear-War game or you might be playing the

Destroy-My-Body-Slowly-With-Drugs game. If you don't choose your games consciously then you will choose your games unconsciously, but you are always going to be playing one kind of game or another. Once you have chosen your game, your structures form the rules of the game. Games do not exist without rules.

CHAPTER 60

Virtues

By "virtues" we mean "those characteristics of you and the way you lead your life that facilitate you in achieving your consciously chosen goals." Cultivating the right virtues in yourself can make your life much easier, much more enjoyable, and much more effective.

Here is a process that will help you cultivate virtues:

THE CULTIVATING VIRTUES PROCESS

1. Write out a clear and concise statement of your goal and your plan for achieving it.
2. Make a list of 5 things about you and how you lead your life that are most helpful in following your plan and achieving your goal.
3. Make a list of 5 things about you and the way you lead your life that most get in the way of your following your plan and achieving your goal.
4. Convert each item in step 3 to its positive opposite. Throw away the list in step 3.
5. Make each item in steps 2 and 4 into an affirmation in the format "I already (am, have, do) _____ and I am (becoming, creating, doing) more _____ all the time.
6. Write each affirmation in step 5 three times, once each in the first, second and third persons. Use these affirmations often.

7. For each item in steps 2 and 4, think of something you can do in your day-to-day life to make that virtue even more manifest. Write these neatly on a sheet of paper.
8. Read the list in step 7 every night before going to bed and every morning just after you get up. Do them as much as possible.

CHAPTER 61

Discipline

Any time you decide in advance to do some particular thing in some particular way at some particular time (which you must do if you want to accomplish very much), then you may have a desire to do something else when that time comes. Discipline means staying with your plan and integrating that cross-current desire. Discipline is a virtue that is cultivated with repetition and is one of the great privileges of being a free human being. Indeed it is impossible to be free without it. Some people think that freedom means the freedom to satisfy their desires, but that is just slavery to desire. Real freedom means being able to choose where you are going with your life and then going there. Discipline means knowing what your goal is and then doing what it takes to achieve it.

Discipline and Rebirthing go hand-in-hand. Without a certain amount of discipline you can never integrate anything because every pattern of energy has an accompanying desire; if you just go off and satisfy that desire you are unlikely to integrate that pattern of energy. At the same time, Rebirthing makes it much easier to have discipline because it allows discipline to be enjoyable rather than merely suppressive.

AFFIRMATIONS ABOUT DISCIPLINE

1. Discipline has entirely good associations in my mind.
2. The purpose of discipline is to increase my freedom.
3. My discipline is a major source of pleasure in my life.

4. I love discipline for its own sake.
5. My discipline shall triumph.
6. I forgive myself for not having discipline in the past.
7. My gentleness is part of my discipline and my discipline is part of my gentleness.

CHAPTER 62

Forgiveness

Forgiveness is declaring a divorce from past behavior and thinking. Forgiveness is an action that takes place in present time which frees you from all claim to retribution. Our idea is that everybody has already paid and exacted more than enough retribution to last for the rest of eternity. When you forgive anybody, especially when you forgive yourself, you free yourself from past limitations on your love and move into the future with a clearer conscience and a clearer mind.

Feeling guilty is a common form of retribution. Whenever you make yourself or anybody else feel guilty, you actually deny the fundamental innocence of everyone. Guilt is a reaction to thinking that you did something wrong in a Universe that is unsafe. (If you are making your behavior wrong, that is an indication that the Universe is not safe for you.) If you think the Universe will punish you for your wrong-doing, then you will think it is wise to punish yourself first and beat the Universe (which is bigger than you) to the punch. There are several ways to describe guilt. Different people experience it in different ways so we'll describe it in a few ways to be sure that you know what we are talking about. Guilt can be described as a context in which you erroneously conclude that someone is not experiencing infinite pleasure and infinite benefit and it is your fault. Guilt can be called lack of respect for your perfection. Guilt can also be described as the idea that you hurt someone or someone hurt you and therefore guilt claims that neither of you create your own reality.

Guilt is also a prime cause of compulsive behavior. Repeating patterns of compulsive behavior like compulsive gambling, compulsive drinking or compulsive criminality are unconscious attempts to justify and feel OK with previous behavior of the same kind. The pattern of compulsive behavior continues until the person forgives himself for it. So, if you are feeling guilty about anything, you might consider that you have punished yourself enough. Guilt is its own punishment and you are the one that decides how much punishment is enough. Just as guilt is its own punishment; forgiveness is its own reward. Forgiveness may not provide you with any direct external benefit, however, the freedom from guilt is more valuable than any external benefit.

FORGIVENESS EXERCISE

Make a list of all the significant people in your life; for example, parents, step-parents, siblings, children, lovers, teachers, grand-parents, aunts, uncles, God, etc.

Now, look over your list and take a moment to visualize the face of each person and to conduct a mental review of your relationship with them. After you have done this, draw a circle around the name of the person that you are the most angry with. Another way to say this is draw a circle around the name of the person who would be the most difficult for you to look in the eye and to say, "I love you."

Now compose a forgiveness affirmation for yourself in the form; I forgive _____ for _____.
Inserting the name of the person in the first blank and what you are angry with them about in the second blank. If you write this affirmation consistently, say a page full for a week or so, please be prepared to accept miracles in your life.

AFFIRMATIONS ABOUT FORGIVENESS

1. I forgive _____ for _____.
2. I forgive myself for letting others hurt me.
3. I forgive myself for hurting others.
4. I forgive others for hurting me.
5. I forgive others for letting me hurt them.
6. I forgive myself for thinking I was separate from God.
7. I forgive God for making my life difficult.
8. I forgive God for giving me the freedom to hurt myself.

9. I forgive myself for pretending to be right when I wanted love.
10. I forgive the doctor for forcing me to breathe at my birth.
11. I forgive everyone who ever did anything wrong.
12. I forgive myself for not receiving what I wanted.
13. I forgive everyone who ever gave me what I didn't want.
14. I forgive_____completely.

INTERNATIONAL FORGIVENESS WEEK

International Forgiveness Week is a week in which everybody in the world can forgive everybody in the world simultaneously. Obviously, this promotes world peace. As it is organized at this time, International Forgiveness Week is the week that contains the full moon of the astrological month of Aquarius. Here are the dates of International Forgiveness Week, as it is now organized, for the next several years: Jan. 26-Feb. 1, 1986; Feb. 8-14, 1987; Jan. 31-Feb. 6, 1988.

Here are appropriate activities for each day of International Forgiveness Week:

Sunday, forgive yourself.

Monday, forgive your family.

Tuesday, forgive your friends and associates.

Wednesday, forgive across economic lines.

Thursday, forgive across cultural lines.

Friday, forgive across political lines.

Saturday, forgive other nations.

For more information about forgiveness or about International Forgiveness Week, write to:

International Forgiveness Week Committee
San Francisco Miracles Foundation
1040 Masonic Avenue #2
San Francisco, CA 94117
U.S.A.

CHAPTER 63

Gratitude

Gratitude is the willingness to be thankful for what you have. Gratitude therefore, includes the willingness to notice what you have. An important aspect of the projection principle of the mind is that the things that you concentrate upon the most in your mind tend to increase the most in your life. If you concentrate on the things that you do not have, your mind automatically creates more things that you do not have. Gratitude is concentrating on the things that you do have, with the result that you increase the things that you are glad you have.

Here is a useful exercise about gratitude.

Make a list of the things that you have that you want:

Make a list of some of the things that you *don't* have that you are glad you don't have:

THE HEAVEN ON EARTH PROCESS

Instructions:

1. Write down five things you sometimes complain about, make wrong, make disparaging jokes about, or otherwise withhold love from. Include anything: people, ideas, feelings, countries, objects, etc.

2. For each of the items make a list of four advantages you derive from its existence in your reality. When you have completed your list of advantages for one item, before going on to the next item, write "I am grateful for the existence of   (the item) ." "(your first name) , you are grateful for the existence of   (the item)   ." Then go on to the next item on your list. Always complete the process for all five items.

3. Repeat the process with another list of five things. Set aside time in your schedule for doing this process as much as possible. Thank you.

We like to describe gratitude as "advanced forgiveness". You forgive another person or yourself when you acknowledge the amount of energy that you are wasting in blaming and making-wrong. Gratitude is the celebration of the lesson that you learned from the experience.

CHAPTER 64

Integrity

Integrity is more than the courtroom definition of telling the truth, the whole truth and nothing but the truth. Integrity is living the *true life* in accordance with your own standards; it is remembering your Divine Identity and forgiving yourself when you forget. Some examples of lack of integrity, then, are staying at a job you detest because you think you need the money, suffering with difficulties in a relationship because you are afraid the other person will leave if you take steps to clear it up or feeling helpless to clear it up.

Telling the truth means verbal expression of what you have decided to make most important in that moment. For example there are moments when we feel angry. Saying, "I feel angry about the condition of our living room" can be the beginning of a conversation that will integrate suppressed feelings. "I feel angry at you about the condition of our living room, because I think you are partly responsible for it" may be a more complete statement of the truth and "I feel angry about the condition of our living room and I am making myself wrong about feeling angry because I haven't cleaned it up" is an even more complete statement of the truth. You have probably noticed that when you state the truth clearly enough, you will experience integration and in the next instant the truth is different.

Everyone has the right to change his or her mind about things. Everyone has the right to make agreements that support their

231

purpose in life and to change the agreements that have already been made. In negotiating agreements, we recommend that you allow for a way to change the agreement, by either party. It is also a good idea to make a review of the agreements that you have already made and renegotiate the ones that do not support you in expressing your purpose. This does not mean that we recommend being haphazard about agreements; on the contrary, if you have made an agreement then it is your responsibility to keep it or to renegotiate a new one, in a high-integrity way, that still satisfies everyone involved. People who follow this practice are very aware of the agreements that they make and are earnest about keeping them.

If you are serious in desiring to have integrity, then it is important to note that having integrity implies a great deal of consistency and means treating everyone with integrity whether they treat you with integrity or not.

CHAPTER 65

Negotiation

Negotiation is the process of making and re-making agreements. Negotiation is being more willing to ask for what you want than to complain about what you have. Negotiation is a process of communication which concludes with an arrangement that results in the satisfaction of all parties.

Much has been written about using power and intimidation to get your way in negotiations. We do not think power and intimidation are necessary, or even desirable in negotiating. The Universe is just and it responds to your desires. Since everyone is already motivated to operate for his or her own benefit, it is unlikely that much in the way of permanent success will be achieved by intimidating people. You can experience and receive the support and co-operation of your associates, friends, customers and creditors if you negotiate on behalf of all parties in the agreement. The practice of each individual negotiating for the benefit of all parties concerned results in agreements that are fun and easy to make and fun and easy to keep. What is required to do this is the willingness to switch contexts and see the situation from each person's point of view.

AFFIRMATIONS

1. It is safe for me to tell the truth.
2. I am willing to know what I want, I am willing to ask for it and I am willing to receive exactly what I ask for.

3. I have the right to say no without losing people's love.
4. When I mean yes, I say yes; when I mean no, I say no.
5. I enjoy asking for what I want.
6. I make and keep agreements that support my purpose.

CHAPTER 66

Service

Service is an attitude that results in behavior that is motivated and rewarded in the same instant. Service is the most satisfying way to relate to being in the world. A service mentality is when the quality of your giving, the quality of your behavior and the quality of your service is more important to you than the quality of the giving, the behavior and service of other people. A service mentality is generosity in action. A service mentality is measuring yourself against your own standards and lovingly making corrections where appropriate.

Service has nothing to do with sacrifice. Service has nothing to do with competition.

Service is also being responsible about receiving. Inaccurate beliefs about giving and receiving often cause people problems in achieving a service mentality. It is common to believe that it is better to give than to receive; and it is common to believe that giving is a premeditated act while receiving is an embarrassing accident. Receiving and giving are one. Without receivers there would be no givers. Realizing that your ideas about giving and receiving are what creates your results regarding giving and receiving make it easier to approach the things that you do with an attitude of service. Claiming responsibility for your own enjoyment and adopting a service mentality turns drudgery into pleasure. Anyone is more successful doing work that they love to do. However, it is a good idea to remember that the work is no more satisfying than the attitude that you bring to it. If you resent giving or resent people who appear to be more successful than you are, then it is possible to turn the most enjoyable work into a struggle.

Take a moment to examine your current beliefs about work and about *your* work. Write down ten thoughts about work in general and ten more things about *your* work in particular.

Take a few minutes to review the lists that you have just made. The thoughts that you have written are most likely the thoughts that mold your attitudes about work and about your work in particular. It is possible that the two lists that you have just made contain some thoughs that do *not* support you in enjoying your work. You can use the simple process of inversion to convert the thoughts that do *not* support you into affirmations which will enable you to change the thoughts you have now.

For example, if one of the thoughts on your list is, "Work is hard," then the affirmation by the process of inversion is, "Work is easy"; or if one of your thoughts is, "My work is something I have to do," then you affirmation would become, "Since I now choose my work, work is fun for me." There is also a list of affirmations at the end of this section to assist you in constructing a positive attitude about work.

The dictionary defines "work" as effort to accomplish something; the dictionary also defines "work" as to function or to operate. The more that you view your work as an opportunity to function in a capacity of providing service in the world, the more enjoyable it will be.

If you don't enjoy your work, then you'll never get paid enough to compensate for this. People who work for money usually don't have a lot of money because they spend money to give themselves the pleasure they think they are missing by working. Even if you accumulate a lot of money by working for money, it is not nearly as satisfying as doing quality work that you love. Additionally, the more that you enjoy your work, the higher the quality will be. When you provide the highest quality of service that you are able to and are willing to expand the quality of your service continuously, customers will beat a path to your door. Word of mouth advertising is more effective and a lot less expensive than advertising that you pay for.

A WRITTEN EXERCISE TO INCREASE
THE QUALITY OF YOUR WORK

Make a list of ten things that you are willing to do to increase the quality of your work.

AFFIRMATIONS

1. My work is appreciated by everyone.
2. I have the right to enjoy my work.
3. It is easy and fun for me to give people what they want.
4. I am the one in charge of my receiving.
5. I forgive myself for accepting things that I didn't want.
6. It is OK for me to be paid for doing work that I love.
7. I love to work.
8. I love to give.
9. The quality of my work increases every day.
10. I enjoy serving people.
11. I am a servant of God.
12. It is fun to work.
13. I am always aware of and grateful for the benefits I am receiving.
14. I am receiving right now.
15. My work is satisfying to me.
16. Any task that is there to do is worthy of my full attention.
17. Whenever I work, I open a channel that brings aliveness from God through me into the physical world and enhances my aliveness in every way.
18. I enjoy completing things.
19. Completion is safe for me.
20. Since by the essence of my nature I am whole and complete, it is easy for me to forgive myself for my incompletions.

CHAPTER 67

Self-Employment

A person who is self-employed is a person who sells his or her services to *many* customers. This is in contrast to a person who is employed by an employer and therefore sells 100% of his or her services to *one* customer.

Self-employment has benefits that are both practical and enjoyable. Working for a company, even a large one, does not guarantee financial security. If you read the newspapers, you know that large companies sometimes declare bankruptcy and even more frequently lay off workers. Successful self-employment is much more secure than depending on an employer.

A person who is self-employed has the benefits of flexibility in scheduling, of setting his or her goals and evaluating progress and making necessary corrections. Successful self-employment requires that you be an effective manager and an effective subordinate at the same time.

We are surprised that the principles of successful self-employment are not generally taught in public schools and that the focus of primary and secondary education is to prepare students for jobs only. Successful self-employment provides a person with a sense of self-reliance and a sense of self-determination that are useful in all areas of life.

Self-employment is an obvious and effective solution to the problem of unemployment.

A successful self-employment mentality requires that you take complete responsibility for your financial situation and is the best financial security there is. It is worth going through whatever it takes to develop the skills and atittudes that create successful self-employment. If you doubt this, ask anyone who is successfully self-employed.

CHAPTER 68

Rebirthing Is A Wonderful Way To Make A Living

We are grateful for this opportunity to share with you our experience of Rebirthing as a profession.

Rebirthing may well be the most delightful profession in the world. It's the best thing you can do for your own process, you can make a good living at it, and assisting people in gaining joyful mastery over their lives is certainly one of the most satisfying and blissful experiences we know of. All professional Rebirthers experience themselves as contributing greatly to the process of making the world a better place to live.

The best thing of all about being a Rebirther is the lasting, close friendships that Rebirthers form with their clients. Both of us are pleased to say that we have many close friends and that a large portion of these friends were originally our Rebirthing clients. People who want to get Rebirthed are generally excellent people to begin with, and the honesty and intimacy of the Rebirther-Rebirthee relationship, combined with the nature of the process itself, definitely foster lasting friendship.

If you want to become a professional Rebirther, the single most important thing for you to do is to master your ability to Rebirth yourself. Take as many trainings as you possibly can from as many different trainers as you can. We recommend continuing to take trainings, periodically, forever, even long after you have developed a successful practice.

If you want to, you can take all the trainings you want and get paid to take them by producing seminars and trainings for the people who lead them. This usually involves handling publicity, enrollment, and logistics for the seminar or training. Virtually all trainers are always looking for more good producers, so you can get an enjoyable experience of being in demand and of being appreciated. If you are good at all, you can create an abundant income, too. Most Rebirthers and trainers have produced numerous events themselves and will be happy to tell you how to get started doing it. You may need to make an initial capital investment to pay for advertising and other expenses for the event, but this is almost never a large amount of money and sometimes is not needed at all; if you use common sense you should make a substantial profit.

As a Rebirther, you deserve an income at least comparable to that of any other professional person, whether or not you have as much college education as they do. This means that you will want to master self-employment. The best way to get started learning about self-employment is to read Phil Laut's *Money is My Friend* repeatedly and make sure that you do everything it recommends.

Rebirthing is an artful science and you will continue getting better at it forever. You are ready to begin Rebirthing people professionally when you experience certainty that you can produce consistently excellent results and that you will operate with utmost integrity.

CHAPTER 69

Acceptance

Acceptance is a context that exists outside the reality of make-wrong duality. Acceptance is the loving contemplation of everything.

There is no such thing as conditional love. The only love there is is unconditional love and we establish our own limitations on our willingness to express and experience unconditional love.

This idea is a confront to what we call "snob mentality," which is the idea that the more discriminating that you are or the more things you disapprove of, the better person you are. The way to be happy is to integrate your judgments and enjoy everything.

It is possible to use disapproval to motivate yourself to accomplish things. However, this does not result in a great deal of joy in the process nor a great deal of satisfaction in the accomplishment. Acceptance makes it easy to accomplish results in a context of joyful participation and satisfying accomplishments.

AFFIRMATIONS

1. I gratefully accept all of life's abundance.
2. I gratefully accept my purpose.
3. I gratefully accept my situation.
4. I gratefully accept all the people with whom I am sharing this planet.

CHAPTER 70

Heaven On Earth

Consider a world where everybody enjoys every experience they ever have and consistently create experiences to satisfy all parts of themselves. It seems reasonable to call such a world Heaven on Earth, doesn't it? We hope that you realize by now that the world already is exactly that way. Yet there are few people indeed who would call the world the way it is Heaven on Earth. The authors of this book do not experience being in Heaven on Earth all the time, either. To the extent that any of us do not experience Heaven on Earth we are obviously making something wrong.

We all take a quantum leap toward Heaven on Earth when we realize, if only intellectually, that we are responsible for everything in our experience, that everything is the way it is to satisfy our conscious or unconscious desires, and that once we stop making something wrong we are free to change it as we will. Surrendering fully to the task of manifesting Heaven on Earth is tantamount to already being there.

Consider the transformation that would occur if everyone negotiated on the behalf of everyone in all their relationships. That would be an end to war and the threat of war. It would also be the end of world hunger.

Consider the transformation that would occur if everyone took full responsibility for satisfying their own needs and wants. That would be an end to unemployment and poverty, surely.

What would happen if everybody celebrated existence itself

243

continuously? Then everybody would be profoundly happy and would integrate all suppressed make-wrongs.

What would happen if everybody gave up attachment to the idea that death is inevitable? The end of disease, aging and death? The end of plundering and polluting the Earth?

Consider the dawning of such an age. Hundreds of thousands of people who realize that they have the practical resources to move themselves, at least, toward these objectives, and are doing so. People who have glimpses, at least, of Heaven on Earth. This is the phase we are in now.

Imagine these hundreds of thousands of people liberating not only themselves, step-by-step, but also sharing the liberating ideas and methods with others. At first they may do so only cautiously, with their most trusted friends, for these are not yet the usual ideas of our societies. But as they gain experience and self-confidence with their own transformations they become more courageous, more dedicated, more compassionate.

There is a movement that is not a movement of joining, but a movement of individuating. Rebirthers are not the only ones who are in this movement. All who are more dedicated to truth than to conformity or rebelliousness are already doing their part to spread it.

The future is up to you. The future is up to us.

Glossary

Every science has its own special vocabulary and the science of enjoying all of your life is no exception. Although most of the words and phrases that we use in special ways are defined in the text itself, we also define them here in order to offer greater precision and more information about them than would be convenient in the flow of the main text. In almost all cases the definitions in this glossary are rather different from the definitions you would find in a standard dictionary—the glossary tells you exactly what *we* mean by the terms we use. We have included only two or three words with definitions borrowed from standard dictionaries; in those cases, e.g., with the word "therapy," we want to make the reader absolutely clear that we are using the word in the ordinary way. Some of the terms in this glossary were coined by the authors of this book; others have evolved to their current meanings through many years of use by self-improvement professionals, not only in Rebirthing, but also in other branches of applied philosophy. Often we do not use these borrowed terms in exactly the same way as their originators use them, so this glossary is an aid in preventing any misunderstanding of our meanings.

We suggest that the serious student of Rebirthing study this glossary not only to gain better understanding of the main text, but also as a useful source of information in its own right.

Words that are italicized are main entries or derivatives of main entries.

ACCEPTANCE: Acknowledging that something exists and *holding* it in a *positive context.*

ACKNOWLEDGE: To *know consciously.*

ACTION: The changing of an *individual's reality* by that individual. Every action is *motivated* by one or more of the individual's own *thoughts.*

ACTIVATION: Partial or total *awareness* of *content* that is *held* in a *negative context.*

ACTIVITY: Any discrete, focused use of the *mind* or body to produce a particular *result.*

ADOLESCENCE: The period of an *individual's* life that begins with the onset of puberty and ends with the assumption of adult responsibilities.

ADOPT (as in "to adopt" a *thought, model* or *context*): to begin *holding.*

AFFIRMATION: A simple *statement* of *fact,* the *purpose* of which is to facilitate the reclassification of a particular item of *content* from *one context to another.*

AFFIRMATION DIET: Writing seventy *affirmations* about a particular topic every day for seven days in a row.

AFFIRMATION FORMAT: An *affirmation* with a blank in it that can be filled in with anything at all and still be *positive.* Compare *affirmation mode.*

AFFIRMATION INVENTORY: A listing of all the *affirmations* one can think of that pertain to a particular topic.

AFFIRMATION MODE: An *affirmation* with a blank in it that can be filled in with anything *positive.* Compare *affirmation format.*

AFFIRMATION PROCESS: A.) An *individual's* use of *affirmations.*

B.) A *process* that utilizes affirmations.

AFFIRMATION PROJECT: A use of *affirmations* to assist one in *manifesting* a *consciously chosen desire.*

AFTERLIFE: The continuation of one's *experience* after one has undergone *death.*

AGING: Replacing the cells of one's body with less healthy cells that interact with one another to create a less healthy body.

AGREEMENT: A *structure* to which one commits oneself as a *result* of *negotiation.*

ALL STATEMENTS ARE EQUALLY TRUE: A *context* in which all contexts are available for use.

AMBULATORY REBIRTHING: Rebirthing oneself while simultaneously engaging in any other *activity*.

ANESTHESIA EFFECT (also loosely called simply *"ANES-THESIA"): Unconsciousness* originating in *activation* of previously *suppressed memory* of having any type of *suppressive* substance in the body, especially ether.

ANGER: The *pattern of energy* that occurs in one's body when one *makes* one's *task at hand wrong*.

APANA: The quasi-physical energy of the body that is created by cells when they use *prana* to carry on metabolism.

APATHY: Indifference to the *results* of one's *thoughts* or *actions,* or to one's future in general.

ATTRACTIVE POWER: The ability to bring oneself together with anyone or anything.

AWARENESS: A.) Access by the *Self* to any particular *model, context, feeling,* etc., etc.

B.) *Conscious perception.*

AWARENESS IN DETAIL: Awareness of all of the details of a *pattern of energy.* The Third *Element of Rebirthing.*

BEHAVIOR: Any way that one's *mind* or body responds to anything in one's *reality.*

BELIEF: A.) An *ecological thought* that is rather perpetual.

B.) Loosely, any *thought* that one has *held* for a long time.

BENEFICIAL: Enhancing well-being. Advantageous.

BIRTH TRAUMA: Negativy created by *making* aspects of one's *reality wrong* at birth.

BLAME: Holding someone or something in a *negative context* because of the *thought* that that person or thing is the creator of something in one's *reality* that one is *making wrong.*

BLISS: A.) *Awareness* of *holding content* in the *context* of *ecstasy.*

B.) The *pattern of energy* that occurs in one's body when one *accepts* the *perfection* of the *Universe.*

BLISS TRAUMA: Negativity created by *fear* of *bliss, sadness* about having lost one's bliss, *making* other people *wrong* for being blissful, or any other way of making bliss wrong. Negativity created by refusing to *accept God's unconditional love.*

"BOILING AN EGG" APPROACH: A method of determining the end of a *private Rebirthing session* that the authors of this book do not recommend. It involves the *Rebirther*

watching a clock and ending the session at a particular time whether or not the *Rebirthing* has reached its natural point of *completion.*

BOREDOM: A *pattern of energy* that occurs in one's body when one is avoiding the further *activation* of an *emotion* that is already partially activated, usually *anger.*

BREAKTHROUGH: Sudden *acknowledgement* of a *beneficial truth.*

BREATHING CYCLE: During *Rebirthing,* the period of time that begins with an inhale and ends with the *integration* of a *pattern of energy.*

BREATHING RELEASE (OR BREATH RELEASE): Permanent improvement of a person's breathing.

BURN-OUT: The phenomenon of an incompetent *Rebirther* becoming very uncomfortable as a result of the Rebirther's own *negativity* becoming *activated* but not *integrated* while the Rebirther is attempting to assist someone else with *Rebirthing.*

CASE: One's main patterns of *negativity.*

CASE HANDLING: Interacting with a person in a way intended to produce a specific *desired* change in that person's *mind.*

CELEBRATE: To *acknowledge* and *hold* in a *positive context.*

CHIT-CHAT-ANANDA: Conversation used as a method of *suppression.*

CHOICE: A.) The ability of the *Self* to select among available *contexts.*

B.) A particular utilization of the Self's ability to select among available contexts.

CIRCULAR BREATHING: Any kind of breathing that meets the following three criteria:
1. The inhale and the exhale are connected together with no pauses.
2. The exhale is relaxed and not controlled at all.
3. If the inhale comes in through the nose then the exhale also goes out through the nose, or, if the inhale comes in through the mouth then the exhale also goes out through the mouth.

The First *Element of Rebirthing.*

CLEAR: A.) Corresponding to what is so in every *practical* way.

B.) Devoid of *make-wrong.*

COLD WATER REBIRTHING: Wet Rebirthing using water that

feels cool or cold to the touch.

COMMUNICATION: A.) Interaction between *individuals* that facilitates creation or *refinement* of *models* of each other's models.

B.) Any interaction between sentient beings.

COMPASSION:

The *pattern of energy* that occurs in one's body when one simultaneously *contemplates* the *ecstasy* and the suffering of a sentient being.

COMPLETE RELAXATION: Contracting no muscles other than to inhale, or, during *ambulatory Rebirthing,* contracting no muscles other than those that one needs to use for what one is doing. The Second *Element of Rebirthing.*

COMPLETION: A.) The moment in a *Rebirthing session* when all of the following three criteria have been met:

1. A satisfactory amount of the *Rebirthee's material* has been *activated* and *integrated.*
2. Everything that was activated has been integrated, i.e., the Rebirthee feels completely good.
3. Both the *Rebirther* and the Rebirthee agree that the first two criteria have been met.

B.) Full *manifestation* of an *intended result.*

COMPULSION: A strong and recurrent *urge.*

COMPULSIVE ADAPTATION: A *behavior* that is *motivated* by an *unconsciously chosen desire* to cause something that one is *making wrong* to more nearly meet one's *imaginary standard.* See *duality mechanism.*

CONDITIONING: Models that one *learned* from other people, but did not figure out on one's own.

CONFORMITY: Thoughts and *behaviors* chosen consciously or unconsciously to put oneself in submission to the *preferences* of another person regardless of one's own preferences. Compare *rebelliousness.*

CONFUSION: A.) The state of the *mind* when it is *holding* a *contradiction.*

B.) The *pattern of energy* that occurs in the body when one is *aware* of holding a contradiction.

Note that confusion often occurs immediately before *integration* of a *paradox.* See *humor.*

CONSCIOUS: A.) *Perceived* by the *Self* in a particular *moment.*

B.) Done by or created by the Self.

C.) Observably *aware* of one's physical *environment.*

CONSCIOUS MIND: The part of one's *mind* that is immediately accessible to the *Self.*

CONSCIOUSLY CHOSEN DESIRE: A *conscious* decision to increase one's *experience* of something that one *values.*

CONSCIOUSNESS: A.) The *Self.*
  B.) *Awareness.*
  C.) The state of being observably aware of one's physical *environment.*

CONTEMPLATION: A.) The ability of the *Self* to focus its *awareness* on one thing at a time, temporarily excluding other things from its awareness. Note that the Self is able to contemplate largely because it has set up the *mind* to *perceive* and *process information* and to "notify" the Self of any changes in the non-contemplated *reality* that the mind has been programmed to deem *important.*
  B.) Focused awareness.

CONTENT: Anything that one is actually *perceiving.*

CONTEXT: Classification of *content* according to how one interacts with it. Note that a context can be the content of another context. See *thought.* Also note that the *mind* almost always *holds* any particular content in many contexts simultaneously, but that the Self can only hold content in exactly one context at a time, though it can switch back and forth among contexts very rapidly.

CONTRADICTION: Within a given *context,* two *statements* which cannot both be *true.* Compare *paradox, duality.*

CONTROL PATTERN: Trying to control other people, external circumstances, one's present *moment-reality,* etc., as a *compulsive adaptation* to prevent the *activation* of one's own *self-delusion.*

CREATIVE POWER: The ability to produce *results,* i.e., the ability to alter *content.*

CROSS-CURRENT DESIRE: An *unconsciously chosen desire* that interferes with the *manifestation* of a *consciously chosen desire.*

CURING: Completely eliminating all symptoms of an illness. Compare *healing.*

DEATH: The irrevocable separation of the *spirit body* from the physical body.

DEATHIST: Of, or one who has, the thought "Because I am alive I must undergo *death.*

DEATH-URGE: Dying as a *compulsive adaptation.*

DESIRE: Any *thought* one has about any particular way that one's present *content* or the apparent trends of change of one's content could be better for oneself according to any particular criteria. Compare *consciously chosen desire, unconsciously chosen desire, compulsion, compulsive adaptation, intention, preference,* and *urge.*

DISAGREE: To refuse to shift *contexts.*

DISAPPROVAL: Withholding of *unconditional love* from a person in order to or as though to control that person's *behaviors* thereby.

DISCIPLINE: Choosing to engage only in those activities that most effectively *manifest* one's *goals.*

DO WHATEVER YOU DO BECAUSE EVERYTHING WORKS:
A.) A *context* in which nothing one does is *made wrong* by oneself.
B.) *The intentional holding* of a *context.* The fifth *element of Rebirthing.*

DOUBLE BIND: A situation which one *thinks* is presenting one with only two options both of which one is holding in *negative contexts.*

DRAMA: Acting out one's *emotions* rather than *taking responsibility* for them.

DRY REBIRTHING: Rebirthing oneself while no part of one's body is immersed in water.

DUALITY: Two *statements* that form either a *contradiction* or a *paradox* depending on whether one *chooses* to *hold* them both in one *context* or chooses to hold each of them in a different context.

DUALITY MECHANISM: Any one of the many parts of the *unconscious mind* that each continuously compares one's *reality* to an *imaginary standard* and *motivates* a specific *compulsive adaptation.* Also called a *"make-wrong* duality mechanism". See *duality scale.*

DUALITY SCALE. A way of diagramming specific *duality mechanisms* for easy analysis, thus:

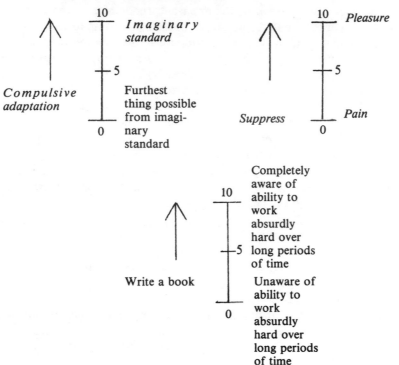

FIGURE 12: EXAMPLES OF DUALITY SCALES.

ECOLOGICAL: Acceptable to all parts of one's *mind*.

ECSTASY: A.) A *context* in which all *content* is *perfect*. Ecstasy implies not only the absence of *make-wrong* but also absolute inability to engage in make-wrong. Ecstasy is the only *context* that can ever be available to the *Experiencer*, and is one of an infinite number of contexts available to the *mind*.

B.) The state of *holding* all *experience* in the context of ecstasy.

ECSTASY PRINCIPLE: "Everybody is always in a state of *ecstasy* whether they like it or not."

ELEMENT OF REBIRTHING: Any of the five *behaviors* that one adopts in order to cause *integration* using *Rebirthing*.

EMOTION: Any of the three *kinesthetic patterns of energy* that are most often identified, i.e., *sadness, anger,* and *fear,* or any combination of them, or any of them combined with a *thought* or thoughts.

ENJOY: To *hold* in a *positive context.*

ENNUI (pronounced ''on-we''): Lack of *enthusiasm.*

ENTHUSIASM: Grateful acceptance of ALL of the following: one's *purpose,* one's present *reality,* one's *goals,* one's *plans,* one's *structures,* one's present *activity,* and oneself.

ENVIRONMENT: All of one's personal *reality* except one's own body and *mind.*

ETHICS: The *structures* that govern one's *behavior* with respect to the effects that one's behavior has on other sentient beings.

EVENTUALITY: A possible future occurrence that could affect the *manifestation* of one's *goal.*

EXISTENTIALISM: The *philosophy* centering around the *thought* that *experience* is a function of the physical body and the physical body was unintentionally created by an inexplicable and highly unlikely series of utterly random occurrences in a *Universe* that is hostile or at least indifferent to life.

EXPECTATION: What the *conscious mind thinks* is happening, will happen, ought to happen, or ought to have happened.

EXPERIENCE: A.) (transitive verb) To unite with and separate from simultaneously, *momentarily,* and indiscriminately. This is worthy of a concise explanation: Whenever something is part of your experience, you are one with it and yet different from it at the same time; you are also becoming one with it and becoming different from it at the same time. This union/separation lasts for only a moment, and in the *context* in which one moment follows another *(linear time),* the *Universe,* and therefore that which one experiences, is continuously changing; thus there is infinite variety of experience. We say that experience is indiscriminate because in any moment you are experiencing whatever you are experiencing regardless of whether your *mind* is *making* it *wrong* or is *celebrating* it, and regardless of whether the *perception* of the experience is *held* in the *conscious mind* or in the *unconscious mind.*

B.) (noun) That which one is experiencing.

C.) (intransitive verb) To have experience.

D.) (noun) The function of experiencing or the capability to experience.

E.) (loosely) Perception, or to perceive.

EXPERIENCER: The most fundamental level of one's being, at which level one only *experiences* the *environment, mind, body,* etc., but does not form *models,* and does not classify, discriminate, compare, control, *reduce,* or otherwise interact with anything. Compare *Self, mind.*

EXPRESSION: A.) *Behavior motivated* by a *kinesthetic pattern of energy.*

B.) Formulation of a *thought* into words.

EYEGAZE REBIRTHING: Two people *Rebirthing* temselves and each other while looking in each other's eyes.

FACT: A single component of a description of one's *model* of the *truth.*

FAMILY PATTERNS: Conditioning, behaviors, contexts, and *models* that one *learned* from the family one grew up in.

FEAR: The *pattern of energy* that occurs in one's body when one *makes* a conceivable future change of *reality wrong.*

FEELING: Generally, any *kinesthetic pattern of energy.* Specifically, the *kinesthetic pattern of energy* associated with an *emotion.*

FIFTH ELEMENT OF REBIRTHING: Do Whatever You Do Because Everything Works.

FIGURING OUT: The creation or *refinement* of a *model* using one's own *conscious mind* and one's own logic.

FIRST ELEMENT OF REBIRTHING: Circular Breathing.

FIRST-PERSON: The form of an *affirmation* "I (am, do, or have) _____."

FIVE BIGGIES: In Leonard Orr's *philosophy,* the five major areas of *unclarity* and *negativity* in most people's *minds,* namely:

1. *Birth Trauma*
2. *Parental Disapproval Syndrome* (PDS)
3. *Unconscious Death Urge*
4. *Specific Negatives*
5. *Other Lifetimes*

FIVE ELEMENTS OF REBIRTHING: The five *behaviors* one employs to maximize *integration* during *Rebirthing,* namely:

1. *Circular Breathing*
2. *Complete Relaxation*
3. *Awareness in Detail*
4. *Integration into Ecstasy*
5. *Do Whatever You Do Because Everything Works*

FOOLISH BEHAVIOR: Any *behavior* that delays *manifestation* of one's *goal.*

FORCED SURRENDER: The *process* by which one *acknowledges* that a particular item of *content* does not meet one's *standards* and is not going into *suppression* and that the only way that one can end one's *suffering* is therefore to *celebrate* that content whether it meets those standards or not. This is the most "painful" and "difficult" way to cause *Integration,* but it does work.

FORGIVENESS: Ceasing to *hold* someone or something in a *negative context.*

FORGIVENESS AFFIRMATION: The *affirmation format* "I forgive _____ for _____."

FORGIVENESS DIET: A term coined by Sondra Ray that means writing seventy *forgiveness affirmations* every day for seven days in a row.

FOURTH ELEMENT OF REBIRTHING: Integration into Ecstasy.

FRAME OF REFERENCE (or *REFERENCE FRAME*): A *context.*

FREEDOM: The ability of an *individual* to select among various possible courses of *action.*

FRUSTRATION: The *pattern of energy* that occurs in one's body when one *holds* the *thought* that one must do something but is unable to do it; thus frustration is a combination of *anger* and *sadness.*

GAME: A person's *consciously* or *unconsciously chosen goal* combined with the consciously or unconsciously chosen *structures* revelant to that goal.

GENEROSITY: Service for the sake of service itself rather than for any other reward.

GOAL: Anything specific that one *intends* to become, accomplish, create, or take possession of in the future.

GOD: That which cannot be differentiated from anything else.

GOOD: In alignment with one's *preferences.* Thus, when *content* is *held* in a *positive context* it is considered good; when content is held in a *negative context,* the opposite of some aspect of the content is considered good.

GRATITUDE: A.) A *context* in which the *content is acknowledged* to be a source of *pleasure* and *benefit* for oneself.

B.) The *pattern of energy* that occurs in one's body when one *contemplates* something that one is holding in a *context* of gratitude.

GRATITUDE AFFIRMATION: The *affirmation format* "I am *grateful* for _____."

GRATITUDE DIET: Writing seventy *gratitude affirmations* every day for seven days in a row.

GREED: The *thoughts* and *behaviors* that come from the *Theory of Limited Good.*

GROUP REBIRTHING: More than two people *Rebirthing* themselves at the same time and within hearing range of each other.

GUILT: A *pattern of energy* that occurs in one's body when one *holds* one's past, present or imagined future *behaviors* in a *negative context.*

HABIT: Compulsive and repeated *behavior.*

HAPPINESS: A.) *Celebration* of everything that one is *aware* of in a particular *moment.*

B.) The *pattern of energy* that occurs in one's body when one is celebrating everything that one is aware of in a particular moment.

HEALING: Eliminating an illness and its cause. Compare *curing.*

HEAVEN ON EARTH: Acknowlededgement by everyone living on Earth that everyone *experiences* everything that exists as *perfect* and that everyone has the *power* to produce any *result* that they *consciously intend.*

HELPLESSNESS: The *thought* that one is not *powerful.*

HIGH SELF-ESTEEM: Detailed *knowledge* of one's own *mind,* body and nature, combined with *celebration* of oneself.

HOLD (as in to "hold" a *thought, model,* or *context*): A.) Once one creates a thought, one "holds" that thought for as long as one *thinks* that thought is *true.* A thought can be held in the *conscious mind* or in the *unconscious mind.*

B.) Once one creates a model, one "holds" that model until one *learns* a *clearer* model.

C.) Once one classifies *content* into a context, one "holds" that content in that context until one reclassifies that content into another context, which is tantamount to inter-acting with that content in a different way.

HUMILITY: Acceptance of one's present-*moment limitations.*

HUMOR: A *context* in which seeming *contradictions* are *held* as *paradox.* See also *joke, laughter.*

HYPERVENTILATION: An abnormally high ratio of oxygen to carbon dioxide in the blood.

IDEAL: A.) In *momentary time,* an *imaginary standard* against which to judge something in one's *reality.*
B.) In *linear time,* an *ethic.*

IDENTITY: What one *thinks* one is. Identity is a *model.* Different people have different models of identity and any one person uses different models of identity at different times. For our purposes in this book, we usually use either a model of the *Experiencer* or a model of the *Self* as the model of identity, depending on the topic that is being discussed; thus, when we use the word "you", we usually mean either your Experiencer or your Self.

IMAGINARY: Part of one's *reality* but not part of one's physical *environment.*

IMAGINARY STANDARD: The way a person *thinks* something ought to be instead of the way it actually is.

IMMORTAL RELATIONSHIPS: Relationships between *Immortalists* regarded as being eternally *valuable.*

IMMORTALIST: Of, or one who has, the following two *thoughts:*
1.) It is possible for me to achieve a degree of mastery over my own *mind,* body, and *environment* that ensures that I can stay physically alive, and in perfect health, forever; and 2.) I *intend* to stay physically alive and perfectly healthy forever.

IMPORTANT: Worthy of *contemplation.*

INDIVIDUAL: A human being. This comprises the individual's physical body, *spirit body,* and the linkage between the spirit body and the physical body.

INFANCY: The period of human life between the development of the ability to survive normally outside the womb and the development of the ability to *express* one's *thoughts* verbally.

INFANCY PATTERNS: Any *negative thoughts* that one has that were first *adopted* during *infancy.*

INFANT GUILT SYNDROME: A *context* formed at birth in which one's aliveness is considered a source of *pain* or *suffering* for others and is therefore *made wrong.*

INFORMATION: Aspects of *reality.* Examples of information are color, texture, flavor, loudness, etc. Information facilitates the *mind* and *Self* in differentiating between that which is a particular thing or aspect of a thing and that which is not that particular thing or aspect of a thing.

INGRATITUDE: A *context* in which one denies that one is getting infinite *benefit* and infinite *pleasure* from the *content.*

INTEGRATION: The switching of *content* from the *unconscious mind* to the *conscious mind* while simultaneously switching it from a *negative context* to a *positive context.*

INTEGRATION INTO ECSTASY: Expanding *ecstasy* in the *conscious mind* to include all *content.* The Fourth *Element of Rebirthing.*

INTEGRATIVE PHILOSOPHY: The *philosophy* presented in this book, which centers around two main ideas: 1.) In every case one is both *happier* and more *powerful* when one takes *responsibility* for improving something than when one *makes it wrong;* and 2.) It is always possible to *hold* anything in a *positive context.*

INTEGRATIVE REBIRTHING: Rebirthing when both the *Rebirther* and the *Rebirthee* have a thorough grasp of the concept of *integration* and the use of the *Five Elements of Rebirthing.*

INTEGRITY: Engaging only in those *activities* that are congruent with one's *models* of what is *beneficial* for everyone affected by those activities.

INTENSE: Much more *prominent* than the rest of one's *reality.*

INTENTION: Absolute dedication to doing whatever is necessary to *manifest* a particular *consciously chosen desire.*

INTERPRETIVE POWER: The ability to decide what anything is, what anything is doing, or what anything means, i.e., the ability to put *content* into *context.*

INVERSION: A method of creating an *affirmation* that involves writing down a *negative thought* and then changing the fewest words possible to make the resulting sentence a *statement* of the *positive* opposite of the original negative statement.

JEALOUSY: A *pattern of energy* that occurs in one's body when one has a type of *control pattern* that comprises at least the following: *anger, fear,* and the *thought* that someone else is getting what one *values*. See also *greed, sibling rivalry, Theory of Limited Good.*

JOKE: A *communication intended* to cause *integration* by causing one to *perceive* that an apparent *contradiction* is actually a *paradox.* See also *humor, laughter.*

JUDGMENTAL: Having a tendency to *make* people *wrong.*

KINESTHETIC: Perceived by feeling without touching.

KITCHEN SINK: A basin, usually made of either porcelain or stainless steel, that is conveniently built in to the room of the house in which one prepares food, and in modern homes, has a faucet that conveys hot and cold water into the basin, and a drain that conducts water from the basin to a septic tank or sewer.

KNOW: To possess a *clear model* of. Compare *acknowledge.*

KNOWLEDGE: A.) *Clear models.*

B.) Possession of clear models.

LAUGHTER: The *expression* of the *pattern of energy* that occurs in the body when one *holds* something in the *context* of *humor.* Laughter is one of the surest signs that someone has *integrated* something. See also *joke.*

LEARN: To create, *refine* or *adopt* a *model* of.

LIE: An *intentionally* misleading *statement, acknowledged* or told as *fact,* that is not *true* within the *context* that is given or implied.

LIMITATION: The point beyond which a given *model* ceases to be practical. One *perceives* oneself as having a limitation to the extent that one is *holding* a model that does not facilitate one in doing what one *desires* to do.

LIMITED THINKING: Thinking that there is a limited supply of what one *values.* See also *Limitation, Theory of Limited Good.*

LINEAR TIME: A *context* in which past and future are real and one's *experience* flows more or less steadily from future speculation through present experience and into past *memory.* Compare *Momentary time.*

LONELINESS: A *pattern of energy* that occurs in one's body when one *makes* the physical absence of another person *wrong.*

LOSS: Change of *reality, held* in a *negative context.*

LOVE: See *Unconditional Love.*

LOW SELF-ESTEEM: Habitual make-wrong of oneself.

MAKE-WRONG: A.) (adjective) Pertaining to any *context* in which anything that actually exists is compared to an *imaginary standard.*

B.) (noun) *A negative context.*

C.) (transitive verb, no hyphen used. Often used with *content* placed between "make" and "wrong", for example, "to make poverty wrong") to *hold* in a *negative context.*

MANIFESTATION: Completion of the change of *reality* that one has *desired.*

MATERIAL: A.) Denoting that which is composed of physical matter.

B.) *Suppressed negativity.*

MATERIALISM: The *belief* that *material* things have the greatest *value.*

MEMORY: A *model* of some part of the *reality* that one originally *perceived* in the past.

METAPHYSICS: Systematic *thoughts* about the nature of *truth* and being.

MIND: The repository of *contexts* of an *individual.* The mind *perceives* and *processes information,* generates *thoughts* and *models,* and generally does exactly whatever the *Self* instructs it to do, in much the same way that a computer does exactly what the computer programmer instructs it to do. (The mind can be called "The most 'user-friendly' computer there could ever be.") The mind is created by the Self, controlled by the Self, exists to serve the Self and can be considered a plenary expansion of the Self. See *conscious mind, unconscious mind.*

MODEL: An analogous representation of something. Models exist to facilitate the *mind's understanding* of what something is or what something does. A mental model is a complex construction of *thoughts.*

MOMENT: An infinitesimal duration of time, commonly represented in physics and calculus as "d/dt" where "t" stands for "time".

MOMENTARY TIME: A *context* in which only the present *moment* is real and in which future and past are parts of one's present-time, *imaginary reality.*

MORTALIST: Deathist.

MOST PROMINENT PATTERN OF ENERGY: Whatever component of a person's *reality* is captivating the person's *awareness* most in a given *moment*.

MOTIVATION: A *thought* that causes a person to engage in a particular *behavior*.

NADI: One of the subtle, quasi-physical, channels that conduct *prana* and *apana* through the body. The well-known acupuncture meridians are the main nadis, which branch out to conduct prana to all the living cells. The flow of prana and apana through the nadis is a result of a complex interaction between the *spirit body* and the physical body, and is largely governed by the *mind*

NEED-OBLIGATION: The *thought* that one person's *sacrifice* is necessary for the well-being of another person.

NEGATIVE: Interfering with one's *happiness* or *power*.

NEGATIVE CONTEXT: A *context* in which the *content* is considered inferior to an *imaginary standard*. Compare *positive context*.

NEGATIVE MENTAL MASS: All of one's *negative thoughts* and *negative contexts*.

NEGATIVE PATTERN: A *negative context*, a *negative thought*, an *unpleasant feeling*, a *compulsive adaptation*, an *urge*, a *foolish behvior*, and *guilt*, that are all directly related to one another and to a particular matter, when they are all considered one unit.

NEGATIVE THOUGHT: A *thought* that results in *holding* something in a *negative context*.

NEGATIVITY: Ingratitude for aspects of one's *unique experience*.

NEGOTIATION: Communication engaged in to establish mutually *acknowledged structures* appropriate to the *manifestation* of a *goal*.

OFF-PURPOSE: Engaged in an *activity* that is inappropriate to *manifesting* one's *goal*.

ON-PURPOSE: Engaged in an *activity* that is appropriate to manifesting one's *goal*.

OTHER LIFETIMES: As one of the *Five Biggies*, *trauma* which was formed in a past life and which stayed with one in spite of one's dying and being reincarnated.

OVERWHELM: Lack of a *plan*.

PAIN: Any *pattern of energy* in one's body that one is *making wrong*.

PARADOX: Two *statements* which are both *true,* each in its own *context,* but either or both of which would be false if both were put into the same context. Compare *contradiction, duality.*

PARENTAL DISAPPROVAL SYNDROME: Negative thoughts formed as a result of one's parents or other parental figures attempting to control one with *disapproval* when one was a youngster.

PATTERN OF ENERGY: A.) Generally, any discrete part of an *individual's* present-*moment reality.*

B.) Specifically, a system of *kinesthetic* or physical sensation.

C.) A *thought perceived* kinesthetically.

PERCEIVE: To receive *information* from or about. Note that the *mind* and *Self* perceive and the *Experiencer experiences.*

PERCEPTION: A.) The means by which the *mind* and *Self* receive *information* about *reality.* Note that perception includes the "five senses" but includes much more also.

B.) *Awareness*

C.) That which is *perceived.*

PERFECT: A.) Complete unto itself.

B.) *Unique* and therefore incomparable to anything.

PHILOSOPHY: A system of *models, thoughts,* and *contexts* regarding the nature of human beings, the nature of the *Universe,* and the nature of their relationship to each other.

PLAN: A list of *activities* that one *intends* to engage in, that have a high probability of *manifesting* one's *goal,* that are listed in chronological order beginning at the present *moment,* and that adequately ensure that every foreseeable *eventuality* will either speed the manifestation of one's goal or at least not delay it.

PLEASURABLE: Enjoyed by at least some part of oneself.

PLEASURE: The *holding* of *content* in a *positive context.*

PLUGGED IN: In a state of *activation triggered* by something in one's *reality.*

POSITIVE: Supporting one's *happiness* and *power.*

POSITIVE CONTEXT: Any *context* in which the *content* is not considered inferior to an *imaginary standard.* Compare *negative context.* Note that a *context* may contain other contexts and a positive context may contain one or more negative contexts; thus one sometimes *enjoys* not enjoying something.

POSITIVE LANGUAGE: Words, phrases and sentences that denote and connote the inclusion of all mentioned *content* in *positive contexts.*

POSITIVE THOUGHT: A *thought* that makes one feel good.

POWER: Ability to create a *consciously chosen result* in the future.

PRACTICAL: Facilitating power.

PRANA: The life force energy of the body, derived from sunlight, food, water, air, etc., channelled through the *nadis* to all the cells of the body, which use it in the maintenance of cellular metabolism and thus convert it into *apana.*

PREFERENCE: A *model* of one's future *reality* which is *held* in a *positive context.* Preference is a function of *context* and every context generates a preference. A positive context generates a preference for the *content* to continue being as it is doing what it is doing. A *negative context* generates a preference for the content to change in some particular way and possibly for it to cease to exist altogether.

PRIVATE REBIRTHING SESSION: A *Rebirthing session* in which the *Rebirthee* pays one or more *professional Rebirthers* to assist the Rebirthee with *Rebirthing* without anyone else present.

PROCESS: A.) A means by which *content* can be shifted form one *context* to another.

B.) To compare to *models.*

PROFESSIONAL REBIRTHER: In the broad sense, anyone who receives money in exchange for assisting people with *Rebirthing* themselves. In our preferred sense, a *Rebirther* who is paid and is additionally highly competent, is motivated by *service* rather than by money, and who conducts *Rebirthing sessions* and the Rebirthing business in a professional way, and with utter *integrity.*

PROJECTION: The *perception,* however temporary, that one's *reality* is congruent with one's *model.*

PROMINENT: Captivating more of one's *awareness* than other parts of one's *reality.*

PROOF: A.) Selection or creation of a *context* in which a *statement* is *true.*

B.) Scientific proof: irrefutable logical inference that a statement is true within a given context based on irrefutable data that are also true with that same context.

PSYCHOPLASM: The "substance" that makes up one's *spirit body,* everything that one *imagines, perceives* in dreams, etc.

PURPOSE: A.) The *consciously chosen motivation* of a person's *activities.* That which one chooses to make one's life be about.

B.) A broadly worded *statement* of what one chooses to make one's life be about.

C.) The *activity* a person is engaged in at the present *moment.*

D.) The reason for engaging in a particular *activity.*

RAPPORT: Verbal and nonverbal *communication* between *individuals, conscious* and *unconscious knowledge* of each other's similarities, and inclusion of each other in *positive contexts.*

REALITY: All that the *mind perceives,* including *models, environment, thoughts,* etc.

REBELLIOUSNESS: *Thoughts* and *behaviors* chosen *consciously* or unconsciously to oppose the *preferences* of another person, regardless of one's own preferences. Compare *conformity.*

REBIRTH: A.) (intransitive verb) To engage oneself in *Rebirthing.*

B.) (transitive verb) To assist another person in learning and using Rebirthing.

C.) (noun) A *Rebirthing session.*

REBIRTHEE: A.) A person who is engaging in *Rebirthing.*

B.) The client of a *professional Rebirther.*

REBIRTHER: A person who assists people with *learning* and practicing *Rebirthing.*

REBIRTHING: A *self-directed process* the *purpose* of which is to maximize one's *happiness* and *power,* the *result* of which is *integration,* and the method of which is engaging in all *Five Elements of Rebirthing* simultaneously.

REBIRTHING BUDDY: A person who alternately *Rebirths* one and is *Rebirthed* by one.

REBIRTHING SESSION: A period of time that is devoted entirely to *Rebirthing* and related *self-improvement processes.*

REDUCTIVE: Conceptually using a component or characteristic of something as a symbol of the whole.

REFERENCE FRAME (or *FRAME OF REFERENCE*): A *context.*

REFINE: To make *clearer.*

RELEASE: (archaic) *Integration.*

REMINDER: An *affirmation* created and used in the *State-Your-Complaint Process* that states that one's *reality* always meets one's *standard,* even though one had previously not *thought* so. *Proof* of the reminder causes *integration.*

RESPONSE (to an *affirmation*): Anything the *mind thinks* about a particular affirmation.

RESPONSE INVENTORY: A list of all of the *thoughts* that one holds in *contradiction* to a particular *affirmation.*

RESPONSIBILITY: A *context* in which one both *acknowledges* oneself as the source of the *content* and acknowledges the *perfection* of the content.

RESULT: The change of one's *reality* created by one's *thoughts* and *activities.*

RIGHT: Acknowledging the *truth* within exactly one *context.* See also *disagree.*

SACRIFICE: Engaging in an *activity* that one does not *value,* or giving up an *activity* or possession that one does value, in the *belief* that doing so is necessary to produce a particular *result* that one *desires* or that one *thinks* someone else desires.

SADNESS: The *pattern of energy* that occurs in one's body when one *holds* a *context, thought* or *model* that gives one a *limitation* and one then *makes* that limitation *wrong.*

SATISFACTION: Manifestation of the *result* that one had *consciously* or *unconsciously desired.*

SCALE: A *duality scale.*

SECOND ELEMENT OF REBIRTHING: Complete Relaxation.

SECOND-PERSON: The form of an <u>affirmation</u> '(your name), you (are, do, or have) _____.''

SELF: The part of an *individual* that *perceives* and *contemplates reality,* classifies reality into *contexts,* creates and *refines models* of reality, creates and either *adopts* or rejects new contexts, discovers existing contexts and either continues to use them, rejects them, or restructures them, and either *holds content* in a given context or else reclassifies content from one context to another. Compare *mind, identity,*

Experiencer, spirit body. Note that when we use "self-" as a combining form, as in "self-Rebirthing," "self-blame," etc., this is a grammatical convenience and has nothing to do with the Self as defined here.

SELF-BLAME: Acknowledging oneself as the source of something one is *making wrong.*

SELF-DECEPTION: Self-delusion.

SELF-DELUSION: Unwillingness to *acknowledge* that one's own *negativity* is producing *results* that are in opposition to one's *purpose.*

SELF-DIRECTED: That which only oneself can choose, control and do for oneself. *Rebirthing* is an entirely self-directed *process* because no one but you can cause you to *Rebirth,* no one but you can control your Rebirthing, and no one can do it for you or produce any of its *results* for you, even if you wanted someone to do so.

SELF-ESTEEM: The *contexts* in which one *holds* oneself. See *high self-esteem, low self-esteem.*

SELF-IMPROVEMENT: Anything one does to increase one's own *happiness* or *power.*

SELF-REBIRTHING: Rebirthing oneself without the aid or presence of a *Rebirther.* Note that whenever one is engaging in Rebirthing, one is said to be "Rebirthing oneself" even if a Rebirther is assisting, but the term "self-Rebirthing" specifically implies the absence of an assisting Rebirther.

SELF-RELIANCE: Ability to produce one's own *consciously preferred results* rather than depending on other people to produce them.

SERVICE: Activity that supports everyone's *purpose* including one's own. Activity that is *motivated* and rewarded in the same *moment.*

SERVICE MENTALITY: The system of *thoughts* that *motivate service.*

SIBLING RIVALRY: Any *thoughts* or *behaviors* that one has that originated in the following two *negative thoughts:* 1) There is a limited amount of what I want; and 2) I must compete with someone in order to get what I want.

SNOB MENTALITY: The *thought* that one is a better person if one *makes* more things *wrong.*

SOCIOBIOLOGY: The theory that human *behavior* is *motivated* largely by the genetically induced impulse to propagate one's own genetic characteristics.

SPECIFIC NEGATIVES: *Thoughts* which create specific *limitations.*

SPIRIT BODY: The *"body"* that one *perceives* oneself having during dreaming, comprising *psychoplasm,* one's *Experiencer, Self, awareness, mind, creative power,* and *interpretive power.* In any given *moment* of wakefulness, one's spirit body is connected with one's physical body to the extent that one is willing to feel one's physical body in that moment. The physical body is regarded (in this model) as a *manifestation* of the spirit body's *desire* to interact with the physical world. The physical body is thus created by, controlled by, and changed by the mind, with various *thoughts* affecting various specific parts of the body. *Positive thoughts* produce *pleasant feelings* in the body and organization of the body's molecules, producing health. *Negative thoughts* produce *unpleasant* feelings in the body and disorganization of the body's molecules, producing unhealthiness. The spirit body's *preference* to *perceive pleasure* instead of *pain* results in its withdrawal from those parts of the physical body affected by negative thoughts, which withdrawal is known as *suppression.* If the spirit body's desires not to be in the physical body exceed its desires to interact with the physical world, it completely separates itself from the physical body, which separation is known as *death.*

STATEMENT: A.) A *thought* formulated into words.

B.) Any declarative sentence. By this definition, the same statement could represent many different *thoughts* depending on the *context* in which the statement is *held.*

STATE-YOUR-COMPLAINT PROCESS: A *process* that causes *integration* of a *suppressed make-wrong duality mechanism* by acquainting the *conscious mind* with the mechanism and then creating a *reminder* and *proving* that the reminder is *true.*

STRUCTURE: Anything that is created to control present and future *activities* so as to ensure a particular *desired result.*

STUCKNESS: Any item of *content that one is holding* in a *negative context* and which one feels *helpless* to change in the near future.

STUFF: *Suppressed negativity.*

SUBCONSCIOUS: Unconscious.

SUBTLE: Only slightly more *prominent* than the rest of one's *reality.* Compare *intense.*

SUPERSTITION: An *unclear model.*

SUPPRESSION: A) *Intentional unawareness* of something that is in one's *reality.*

B.) The act of making oneself unaware of a *trauma.*

SUPPRESSIVE: Considered to reduce contact between the *conscious mind* or *Self* and any *pattern of energy.*

SURRENDER: Not trying to control the present *moment. Acknowledgment* of the *perfection* of what one is perceiving. *Gratitude* for one's existence independent of the *content* of what one is perceiving.

SUSPENDED BREATH: An *unconsciously chosen integrative* method that sometimes occurs spontaneously during *Rebirthing* and involves abrupt and temporary loss of *consciousness* on the part of the *Rebirthee* so that conditions appropriate to integration can be set up without the Rebirthee having to confront *consciously* that which is feared until the *moment* of integration.

TASK AT HAND: Whatever one is doing at the present *moment* or feels impelled to do next.

TEACH: To aid in *learning.*

TETANY: The temporary and involuntary tightening of muscles that sometimes occurs during *Rebirthing.*

THEORY OF LIMITED GOOD: A *limiting model* in which that which one *values* is limited and one must compete with others in order to obtain a *satisfactory* supply of what one values.

THERAPY: The treatment of mental or physical illness.

THINK: To classify *content* into *context.*

THIRD ELEMENT OF REBIRTHING: Awareness in Detail.

THIRD-PERSON: The form of an   affirmation   " (your name (is, does, or has) _____ ."

THOUGHT: A.) The interaction between the *mind* and *content* that results in the placement of the content into a *context.*

B.) A thought as itself content. All thoughts are *perceived* and classified into contexts, thus thoughts generate more thoughts.

C.) Any *model* of a thought, such as words or *images.*

TRAINING: Any *teaching* given by a *professional Rebirther* to develop people's facility at *Rebirthing* themselves or others.

TRAUMA: *Limitation* and discomfort resulting from *making* something *wrong.*

TRIGGER: A.) To *activate* a *pattern of energy.*
    B.) To cause a *compulsive adaptation* to become operative.

TRUE LIFE: Consistent *integrity.*

TRUTH: A.) A *clear statement* of *content* in a given *context.*
    B.) A clear *model.*
    C.) *True life.*

UNCLEAR: A.) Obscured by *lies* and *suppression.*
    B.) Not *practical* is some way.

UNCONDITIONAL LOVE: Inclusion of all characteristics of someone or something in a *positive context* including all imaginable future changes that might occur in that person or thing, regardless of whether that person or thing meets one's *standards* or is likely to meet one's *preferences.*

UNCONSCIOUS (or SUBCONSCIOUS) MIND: The part of one's *mind* of which one has chosen to be *unaware.*

UNCONSCIOUSLY CHOSEN DESIRE: A decision to change something that one is *making wrong,* in an effort to gain *relief* from the discomfort that is actually caused by the make-wrong rather than the thing itself.

UNCONSCIOUSNESS: In *Rebirthing,* anything that tends to decrease the *Rebirthee's awareness* of *kinesthetic patterns of energy.*

UNDERSTAND: To possess a *clear model* of.

UNIQUE: At least somewhat different from anything else that exists.

UNIQUE EXPERIENCE: The entire *experience* of a particular *individual,* either in *linear time* or in *momentary time.*

UNIVERSE: All that is, when thought of in its entirety as being a single entity.

UNPLEASANT: Not *enjoyed* by the *conscious mind.*

URGE: *Awareness* of an *unconsciously chosen desire.* A *pattern of energy* in conjunction with a *thought* about what it would take to *suppress* that pattern of energy.

VALUES: *Thoughts* determining which things one considers *good* and *important.*

VICTIM-CONSCIOUSNESS: The *thought* that one is not the source of one's *reality.*

VIRTUES: Thoughts and *behaviors* that facilitate a person's *happiness* and *power.*

WARM WATER REBIRTHING: Wet Rebirthing in water that is over 98° F.

WEALTH: Money, goods and *services.*

WET REBIRTHING: Rebirthing oneself while any part of one's body is immersed in water.

WILL: A.) The ability of the *Self* to shift *content* from one *context* to another and to *hold* content in any context the Self *chooses.*

B.) *Intention.*

WIN: To achieve one's *goal.*

WISDOM: Ecological thoughts that facilitate one in fulfilling a *consciously chosen desire.*

WRONG: Compared to an *ideal* and found inferior to it.

YOUTHING: Replacing the cells of one's body with healthier cells that interact with one another to create a healthier body. Compare *aging.*

APPENDIX 2

Overview of Processes and Techniques Described in This Book

The purpose of this section is to make it easy for you to use this book year after year after year.

Although there is a great deal of information in this book, we really wrote it not so much to give you theory as to give you practical self-improvement methods. For this reason we have included many processes for you to use in actually transforming your mind and your life. This overview gives you speedy access to those processes.

As we have stated before, we recommend that you read this book sequentially. The processes in this book are situated following the material that will help you understand them. Reading all the material in the book that comes before each process is, in many cases, a necessity; in other cases it is not. Additionally, most of the processes in the book are things that you can do by yourself immediately; a few require the assistance of another person and with some processes the assistance of another person is helpful, but not necessary. With the Rebirthing process itself, we again emphasize that you will initially *require* the assistance of a trained and competent Rebirther to teach you to do it by yourself—an

271

ability that you can use ever after.

We use the following abbreviations to indicate the prerequisites of each process:

RA — Read All the material in the book that comes before the process.

RP — Read the Part (as in "Part I," "Part IV," etc.) that comes before the process.

RC — Read the Chapter that contains the process.

PN — another Person is Necessary for doing the process.

PH — another Person is Helpful, but not necessary, for the process.

TF — a Trained Facilitator is necessary initially.

APPENDIX 3

How We Wrote This Book

This is a truly co-authored book. First we each wrote about the things we knew best. Then we carefully and reverently read through each other's material, fleshed it out in some places, pared it down in some places, and made stylistic improvements throughout.

Part I is almost entirely by Jim; Part IV is almost entirely by Phil. Part II is mostly by Jim and Part V is mostly by Phil. Jim wrote, "Why We Call it Rebirthing," the Introduction and the Glossary. The rest of the book is virtually a half-and-half mix.

Writing this book together has been one of the most joyful experiences of partnership and synergy that either of us has ever had.

APPENDIX 4

About The Authors

PHIL LAUT

Phil Laut is Director of Associated Integrative Rebirthers. He conducts seminars and trainings about Rebirthing and related topics in all parts of the World. In 1979, he wrote and published *Money Is My Friend,* a practical prosperity guide with over 25,000 copies sold. He is the owner of Trinity Publications, the publisher of this book. He is a TV and radio personality.

Phil is a graduate of Harvard Business School, where he received an MBA degree, and before involving himself in the self-improvement field, he was a financial controller at a large computer company.

A graduate of the U.S. Coast Guard Academy, he served as Commanding Officer of a Coast Guard patrol boat in Cape Cod at age 23. He also served as Commanding Officer of a Coast Guard patrol boat in Vietnam during the height of the war there and received several decorations for this service.

Phil's seminars and trainings are characterized by gentleness, humor, practical wisdom and intuitive insight. If you are interested in his current schedule of events or are interested in scheduling a personal appearance for your group, or TV or radio show, please contact him at 213-876-6226 during normal business hours Pacific Time.

AREAS OF EXPERTISE:

Private Rebirthing Sessions and Consultations
Professional Rebirther Trainings
Money and Prosperity
Physical Immortality
Relationships

JIM LEONARD

Jim Leonard has been a professional Rebirther since 1978. He and his wife, Anne Jill, live in San Francisco where they operate the Leonard School of Integrative Rebirthing. At the School, they maintain a very active private Rebirthing practice and lead classes, seminars, and trainings, for every level of student, on the subjects of Rebirthing, Affirmations, Immortalist Philosophy, Prosperity, and Goals and Planning.

Jim is known for his quick, creative mind, his compassion, his outrageous sense of humor, the thoroughness of his presentations, and his emphasis on facilitating people in making discoveries on their own.

In 1979, he invented the technique known as Integrative Rebirthing, which is the technique of Rebirthing described in this book.

In addition to writing half of this book, Jim's first, Jim also contributed a chapter on Rebirthing Integration to Sondra Ray's book, *Celebration of Breath,* from Celestial Arts Publishing.

Jim is available for leading seminars and trainings, to be on television and radio shows, and to do anything else that maximizes his service, anywhere in the world. His address is:

2224 17th Avenue,
San Francisco, CA 94116 USA
Phone: (415) 753-0370

How I Invented Integrative Rebirthing

by Jim Leonard

In November 1972, while I was a freshman at the University of California Riverside, I had a "religious" or "peak" experience while hiking in the mountains early in the morning. During this experience, which lasted approximately 1½ hours, I had direct insight into the nature of existence. Because the experience was entirely non-verbal I was transformed but left with no means of "reducing" the experience into terms my mind could deal with.

Almost exactly one year later I had the realization that I had incorporated the insight of that experience into my mind and I was able to express it verbally. I made cautious attempts at "teaching" it to people I knew. One of these people had recall of his birth during such a session with me, although at that time I had no idea why he got that result.

During the next five years I involved myself in other pursuits and did nothing further with what I had gained on that autumn morning in the mountains.

In 1978, I started getting Rebirthed in Santa Cruz, California, by Theano Storm and Jack Szumel (both of whom are still successful Rebirthers). They also trained me to be a Rebirther and I made Rebirthing my profession. At that time I made no connections between Rebirthing and my earlier peak experience.

In the course of being a professional Rebirther two important questions came up in my mind over and over: Why does this process work, and why is it necessary to go through so much pain to get to the pleasant result?

I visited Herakhan Baba in India, in May 1979, and although he and I never once discussed Rebirthing, it was when I returned from India that I realized I knew the answers to my questions.

The first month following my return from India was a time of great joy, inspiration and creativity for me. During this time I met a man named Tai Baba (his original name was Bill French and he now goes by the name of Shiva Shiva) who had also recently had a transformational experience with Herakhan Baba. The two of us would often stay up all night telling "zen jokes" and rolling on the floor in fits of convulsive laughter.

It was in that milieu that I first brought my insight from the earlier peak experience together with my knowledge of Rebirthing. This synthesis resulted in the concept of integration and in the Five Elements of Rebirthing. I quickly found that anybody could achieve the results of Rebirthing very much faster, very much more comfortably, and very much more reliably using this method.

Since then, I have taught the technique to hundreds of people and have honed the methodology to an ever sharper edge. Today that honing process continues apace and it seems that I learn more about it every day.

Books and Tapes

by Phil Laut

BOOK

Money Is My Friend—A practical prosperity guide that takes you from prosperity thinking to every day practical application. Simple, proven techniques that are useful for everyone. Paperback, 84 pages. Over 25,000 copies sold. Single copy price $6.00 postpaid.

CASSETTE TAPES

Reclaiming Your Personal Power (Unravelling Infancy Patterns)—
A one hour cassette tape with affirmations to unravel infancy patterns of helplessness, dependency and guilt. $11.00 postpaid.

MONEY IS AN INTENTIONAL CREATION OF THE MIND—
Practical thinking applied to your financial life. Forgiveness, service, certainty, self-analysis, goals, affirmations, careers and selling. 2 tape set. 2 hours. $21.00 postpaid.

PRINCIPLES OF PERSONAL FINANCIAL SUCCESS—Effective use of your mind, your time and your money to achieve financial independence. Includes guided meditation, affirmations, time management, purpose, motivation, goals. 2 tape set. 2 hours. $21.00 postpaid.

REBIRTHER TRAINING SERIES with Sondra Ray and Phil Laut.

#1 *REBIRTHING AS A BUSINESS*—Applications of prosperity principles from two of the most experienced Rebirthers there are. Allow yourself to be a success in a career that you love. One hour. $13.00 postpaid.

#2 *WET REBIRTHING*—Methods and practices of hot and cold water Rebirthing. One hour. $13.00 postpaid.

AVAILABLE FROM:
TRINITY PUBLICATIONS
1636 N. Curson Ave.
Hollywood, CA 90046 USA
213-876-6226

WHOLESALE DISCOUNTS ARE AVAILABLE

FOR AIR MAIL DELIVERY OUTSIDE NORTH AMERICA
PLEASE ADD 75%

Suggested Reading

REBIRTHING

Rebirthing for Health Professionals by Eve Jones, Ph.D., (self-published). A detailed descripiton of the physiological processes that occur during a Rebirthing session.

Celebration of Breath by Sondra Ray. Rebirthing described by one of the world's foremost Rebirthers, with a chapter on Rebirthing integration by Jim Leonard.

Handbook of Innovative Psychotherapy edited by Ray Corsini (John Wiley & Sons). Contains an article about Rebirthing written by Eve Jones, Ph.D.

Encyclopedia of Psychology edited by Ray Corsini (John Wiley & Sons). The entry on Rebirthing is by Eve Jones, Ph.D.

GENTLE BIRTH AND INTRAUTERINE EXPERIENCE

Birth Without Violence by Frederick LeBoyer, M.D. (Alfred A. Knopf). A pioneering book about the implications and techniques of gentle birth. Contains an excellent section on the traumas of traditional hospital birth.

The Secret Life of the Unborn Child by Thomas Verny, M.D. (Delta Delacorte). Prenatal psychology and the adult implications of the intrauterine experience.

CREATIVE POWER OF THE MIND

From Here to Greater Happiness by Joel and Champion Teutsch (Price/Stern/Sloan). A clear and simple explanation of how the mind creates reality.

The Creative Process in the Individual by Thomas Troward (Dodd, Mead & Co.). One of our favorite books about metaphysics.

Spiritual Psychology by Jim Morningstar, Ph.D. (self-published). A practical, effective workbook for increasing your aliveness.

I Deserve Love by Sondra Ray (Celestial Arts). The use of affirmations as applied to relationships.

Loving Relationships by Sondra Ray (Celestial Arts). A thorough description of techniques that can be applied to intimate relationships.

The Only Diet There Is by Sondra Ray (Celestial Arts). Practical applications of forgiveness.

Creative Visualization by Shakti Gawain (Whatever Publishing). A simple and thorough description of visualizing to produce results.

A Course in Miracles (published by Foundation for Inner Peace). A highly transformative treatise on one's relationship with God.

Money Is My Friend by Phil Laut, M.B.A. (Trinity Publications). A concise, practical and complete guide to creating wealth through application of the creative power of the mind.

IMMORTALIST PHILOSOPHY

Physical Immortality—The Science of Everlasting Life by Leonard Orr (Celestial Arts). Historical origins of Immortalist Philosophy. A practical treatise on body mastery.

The Door of Everything by Ruby Nelson (DeVorss & Co.). Spiritual point of view on Immortalist Philosophy.

Life and Teaching of the Masters of the Far East by Baird T. Spalding (Five volumes published by DeVorss & Co.). Narrative account of a visit by Western scientists to immortal masters of India.

Ye are Gods by Annalee Skarin (DeVorss & Co.). An Excellent guide to personal transformation.

RECOMMENDED PERIODICAL
The Immortal News, 2402 Calle Zaguan, Santa Fe, NM 87505 Annual subscription $15.

Most of these books are available from:

The Creative Source	Heaven on Earth Books
955 W. 19th St. #E233	126 Elms Crescent
Costa Mesa, CA 92627	London SW4 8QR
714-642-3919	England
	01-673-0962

Catalogs are available on request.

A World-Wide Listing of Excellent Rebirthers Who Supported The Publication of This Book

A World Wide Listing of Excellent Rebirthers who Supported the Publication of This Book by Purchasing Advance Copies.

UNITED STATES

ARIZONA
Alan Brinson
1110 W. Myrtle
Phoenix, AZ 85021
602-870-1113

CALIFORNIA (Northern)
Otto Altorfer
234 Alta Loma
South San Francisco, CA 94080
415-589-5263

Regenesis: The South Bay
Rebirthing Center
Al and Sue Capeloto
1182 Sesame Dr.
Sunnyvale, CA 94078
408-733-1529

Elaine & Tom Driscoll
522 Robins Dr.
Corte Madera, CA 94925
415-927-1434

CALIFORNIA (Northern) (continued)
Jim & Anne Jill Leonard
2224 17th Avenue
San Francisco, CA 94116
415-753-0370

Dennis Miller
P.O. Box 865
Laytonville (Mendocino County)
CA 95454
707-984-6512

Joy Anne Pilliard, M.A.
8012 Sierra St.
Fair Oaks, CA 95628
916-967-8442
Prosperity Seminars

James Platts
1377 9th Ave.
San Francisco, CA 94122
415-661-4600

Tim Torian
Life Unlimited Books and Tapes
8125 Sunset, Suite 204
Fair Oaks, CA 95628
916-967-8442
Prosperity Seminars

CALIFORNIA (Southern)
John Fankhauser
2612 Upas St.
San Diego, CA 92104
619-296-4150

Evelyn Freedman
2905 Glenhurst Avenue
Los Angeles, CA 90039
213-665-3751

Jean Gilpin
1322 N. Harper Avenue
Hollywood, CA 90046
213-876-6638

Elaine Golden-Gealer
9765 Cashio St.
Los Angeles, CA 90035
Creator of Relationship
Discovery Weekend Seminar
213-394-1625 or
213-553-0080

Stephen J. Johnson, Ph.D.
Center for Holistic Psychology
and Education
9012 Burton Way
Beverly Hills, CA 90211
213-273-6445

Lee Kuntz
2255 30th St. #3
Santa Monica, CA 90405
213-450-8151

Phil Laut
1636 N. Curson Avenue
Hollywood, CA 90046
213-876-6226

Joe Moriarty
955 W. 19th St. #E233
Costa Mesa, CA 92627
714-642-3919

Carole Price
Holistic Body/Mind Center
7629 Herschel Avenue
La Jolla, CA 92037
619-459-6423

Sue & Flori Riggs
1041 Helix Avenue
Chula Vista, CA 92011
619-420-2161 or
619-426-6539

Manny Stamatakis
3406 Glendon Ave. #8
Los Angeles, CA 90034
213-202-0499

COLORADO
Glenda Levine
3279 S. Dayton Ct.
Denver, CO 80231
303-671-5915

FLORIDA
David DeMay
10418 NW 70th Court
Tamarac, FL 33321
305-726-4635

Yael Levitt, M.S.W.
11010 SW 139 Avenue
Miami, FL 33186
305-387-2757

Dr. Michael Ryce
World Enlightenment Center
160 S. University Dr. #A
Plantation-Fort Lauderdale,
FL 33324
A Course in Miracles Seminars
and Trainings
305 474-8884

LOUISIANA
Robert Gordon
2734 Ursulines Ave.
New Orleans, LA 70119
504-821-1623

Cathy and Ernest Lester
8237 Apricot St.
New Orleans, LA 70118
504-866-5608

MARYLAND
Mary Kent Norton
398 Ridgely Avenue
Annapolis, MD 21401
301-268-2322 or
301-261-2296

MASSACHUSETTS
Louise and Dan Brulé
P.O. Box 289
Fairhaven, MA 02719
617-999-3508

MICHIGAN
Judy Huston
18420 Donegal Ct.
Northville, MI 48167
313-349-6058

NEW MEXICO
Southwest Integrative
Rebirthing Center
Alan Hutner
P.O. Box 5391
Santa Fe, NM 87502
505-983-3059

Ken Yavit
2402 Calle Zaguan
Santa Fe, NM 87505
505-471-7993

NEW YORK
Rosetta DeGillio
525 E. 88th Street
New York, NY 10028
212-734-9060

Lori Schneiderman
250 Cabrini Blvd., #2C
New York, NY 10033
212-927-9458

OHIO
Carol Hunter
1527 Northwood Dr.
Cincinnati, OH 45237
513-761-9322
513-761-2527

Cynthia Sefton
3438 Ferncroft Dr.
Cincinnati, OH 45211
513-662-4978

OHIO (continued)
Karen Trennepohl
5074 Western Hills Avenue
Cincinnati, OH 45238
513-471-2410

Alice Woodward
6331 Silverbell Ct.
Clayton, OH 45315
513-837-8400

OKLAHOMA
Ruth Cohen & Michael Christie
139 Oakside
Moore OK 73160
450-793-8604

PENNSYLVANIA
Anthony LoMastro
2431 Brown St.
Philadelphia, PA 19130
215-765-7958

TEXAS
Loren Kyle
5440 Glenwick Lane
Dallas, TX 75209
214-956-8585

Lee Landsberg
P.O. Box 31225
Dallas, TX 75231
214-348-1926

VIRGINIA
Jimmie Worsley
1550 Moorings Drive, #22C
Reston, VA 22090
703-471-0247

WASHINGTON
Fred Lehrman
P.O. Box 21246
Seattle, WA 98111
206-643-2414 (Home)
212-799-7323 (Office)

WISCONSIN
Jim Morningstar
2728 N. Prospect
Milwaukee, WI 53211
414-962-0213

CANADA
Micheline Charron
775 Rang Pellerin
St. Celestin, QUE J0C 1G0
819-229-3347

Gayle Lang
5729 West Blvd.
Vancouver, BC V6M 3W8
604-266-3312

OUTSIDE U.S. & CANADA

GREAT BRITAIN
Ben Bartle
143 Willifield Way
London NW11 6XY
(01) 455-4063
(Rebirther and supplier
of books and tapes)

Rebirthing Association of
Great Britain
2 Jane Austen House
Churchill Gardens
London SW1
(01) 828-1793

Kali Victoire
6 Quarry Rock Gardens
Bath BA2 6EF
Avon
Phone 60717

AUSTRALIA
Euroa House
Personal Growth Centre
Michael Adamedes and
Quentin Watts
236 Darling St.
Balmain, NSW 2041
(02) 810-6100

Jan and John Usher
Birth and Development Center
144 Barkers Road
Hawthorn, VIC 3122
(03) 819-2088

NEW ZEALAND
Margaret and Darag Rennie
132 Aberdeen Road
Castor Bay, Auckland 9
(09) 469-436

ASSOCIATED INTEGRATIVE REBIRTHERS
1636 N. Curson Ave.
Hollywood, CA 90046 USA
Professional referral service of
Rebirthers
in the United States and Canada.
To locate an Integrative Rebirther near
you phone:
TOLL FREE 800-641-4645 ext. 232
Operators are standing by 24 hours a
day, 365 days of the year.